DENOMINATIONAL EDUCATION AND
IRELAND IN A EUROPEAN CONT

David Tuohy is a Jesuit priest and the former project director of Le Chelle, a trust set up by twelve religious congregations for their schools. He was also the academic advisor to the School Development Planning Initiative. He has worked in the US, Australia and East Africa, and has taught in both UCD and NUI, Galway. He has published widely in the area of teacher and leader development.

DENOMINATIONAL EDUCATION AND POLITICS

Ireland in a European Context

DAVID TUOHY SJ

VERITAS

Published 2013
by Veritas Publications
7–8 Lower Abbey Street
Dublin 1
Ireland

publications@veritas.ie
www.veritas.ie

ISBN 978-1-84730-432-2

10 9 8 7 6 5 4 3 2 1

A catalogue record for this book is available from the British
Library.

Cover designed by Heather Costello, Veritas
Printed in Ireland by Hudson Killeen Limited, Dublin

*Veritas books are printed on paper made from the wood pulp of managed
forests. For every tree felled, at least one tree is planted, thereby renewing
natural resources.*

ACKNOWLEDGEMENTS

The perspectives in this book have been developed over a number of years as a teacher. Firstly, my thanks to all those students who engaged in debates in class and who researched essays and theses that explored different aspects of education policy. My hope is that the process has been mutually enriching. I have certainly gained from their work.

In more recent years, I have been working as a consultant with different religious congregations as they looked to the future of their schools. The particular outcome of that consultation was the Le Chéile Schools Trust. My journey with these congregations has been very rewarding. It has helped clarify perspectives on national education policy, the nature of Catholic education and the relationship that exists between the two. My thanks to all involved in that process.

Since the setting up of the Le Chéile Schools Trust, I have worked with the Boards of Directors and with the executive team of the Trust. I have had the opportunity to discuss many areas of emerging education policy, and the rich experience and perspectives these dedicated professionals have brought to the discussions has broadened my perspectives. My interaction with them has given me a much deeper appreciation of the common goods we share and promote for others.

I am particularly grateful to some good friends who read early drafts of this book and gave valuable feedback to me. To Marie-Celine Clegg, Sean Goan, Anne Lodge, Michael McKeown, Anne Murray and Pat Riordan, my sincere thanks. Your support was above and beyond the call of normal friendship. Your feedback helped clarify – at least in my own mind – what I wanted to say and helped me be less obscure in how I said it.

A special word of thanks to the staff at Veritas for their encouragement, their patient work with the manuscript and the cover design.

My thanks to family and friends who tolerated my preoccupation over the past months.

CONTENTS

INTRODUCTION

As part of my work, I meet regularly with a group of business people. The group discusses all sorts of issues of professional concern to its members – topics range from ethical concerns in the workplace to the practical implications of budgets and other government initiatives. Occasionally the conversation moves to more general and personal topics; as most of the members of the group still have children in the system, it does not surprise me when they want to discuss education. They were particularly interested in the reforms of the patronage system proposed by the Minister for Education, Ruairí Quinn, in the summer of 2011. From a Church perspective, the group is quite mixed and the opinions on how denominational education should be supported differ widely. A number of the group were particularly exercised by the proposal of 'divestment at no cost to the State'; the idea that Church would voluntarily divest itself of its assets in favour of a competitor, with no gain for itself, contrasted with their experience in the business world, where similar changes are managed by takeover bids and mergers. What was particularly surprising to the group was the general public acceptance of the very different standards being applied in the organisation of education and in dealing with the Church as an organisation.

One member of the group, who is very involved in marketing, developed an analogy that focused the discussion. She proposed the scenario of people living in a rural area, where the only shopping facility was a large Tesco store. She then went on to describe five possible groups of people with different perspectives on shopping provision in the area.

The first objected to *any* large chain doing business in the community; the argument being that big chains drive local shopkeepers out of business and that they have no loyalty to the area. The problem for this group was the inconvenience and expense of living by their principles and not shopping in the store.

The second objected specifically to Tesco as the store owner, it being an English company. Their preference was for Dunnes, an Irish-owned store. As a general position, they felt that no store should have a monopoly in the area and that a choice of stores should be provided.

The third objected to specific Tesco-brand products, believing that Tesco simply rebrand products developed by others and in doing so unfairly undercut the original producers. This would be true for any owner with own-brand products. Their proposal was to insist that all stores sell the same range of products and to make no distinction between them. This solution would also cut down on in-store announcements promoting home brands, making for a more tolerable shopping experience.

The fourth group was neutral about where they shopped. They simply looked for a good deal and appreciated the convenience of the store, choosing what they wanted from the shelves and ignoring other offers; store announcements did not bother them.

The fifth group was a clear supporter of the store and the brand. The members enjoyed shopping there, believing that they were getting the best deal available and enjoying the loyalty programme and benefits associated with it.

Having outlined this scenario, she challenged the group to explore parallels with the education debate. She then went on to challenge the participants to reflect on what their reactions would be if the government decided to intervene in this situation with any of three initiatives:

- to limit the number of stores a particular chain could operate;
- to curtail stores offering their own-brand products;
- to seek an equalisation of market share by insisting that stores hand over their assets to competitors.

The group accepted the challenge and the discussion developed from three perspectives. In business, there are tensions between free market approaches and intervention strategies that promote and protect players in the market. At one extreme, there are groups who advocate totally free competition, and at another extreme there are those who advocate a strong level of State regulation. In the in-between positions, there is support for interventions to protect well-defined interests of producers and consumers. Three government strategies were named by the group in an effort to balance the need for competition and that of regulation in business:

- Stimulating certain types of businesses by offering incentives and tax-benefits: this directs business in a particular direction but it promotes competition among providers that wish to avail of the stimulus.
- Licensing some businesses, such as radio, mobile phones and taxis: this process recognises the benefits of competition, but also limits the amount of competition.
- Legal regulation of the means of competition: this is seen in anti-monopoly laws and pricing regulations.

Although there are some parallels, education does not fit into this model easily. Government involvement in regulating education is more like its management of the social welfare service, in that it seeks to ensure that all citizens can avail of the benefits they are entitled to. The curriculum on offer is made up of a mandated core and electives and providers are 'licensed' on the basis of their ability to supply that curriculum. There is limited freedom for providers to develop 'own brand' offerings. Nonetheless, there is room for difference in the way that educational services are offered, and the system provides parents with choices as to whom they may turn. Social welfare provision is mostly seen as a State function, thus it would be considered unusual for the government to promote competition in other areas of social welfare provision; yet an unusual aspect of Irish education is its 'outsourcing' to private patrons. However, the government is involved in stimulating development in education and it limits competition in the way that it determines the number and location of schools. There is a clear indication that a monopoly position exists in terms of provision, particularly at primary level. The interesting thing here is that while this monopoly situation suited the State historically, it now finds the status quo challenged. The government needs to provide for greater variety within the system, and some providers are seeking ways of rebranding their service. What was surprising for members of the group when we discussed this issue was not that this would be on the agenda but the assumption that the present patrons would cede their interests to the government, and the lack of any specific statement as to what might happen to the divested schools.

The second perspective of the group explored the parallels between the Tesco analogy and the current debate in education. In many ways, the debate is about educational ideologies. Participants focus on the type of country we aspire to, the new republic. They look at the values of education and debate how they can contribute to the bigger vision. The topics are philosophical and historical. There is a process of re-evaluating history, often with a revisionist approach to its origins in 1831, as if the intervening 180 years are something that can be written off as an aberration with no basis in a democratic process. The debate also explores the separation of Church and State in the political context of Europe, espousing different and sometimes contradictory brands of secularism. This strand of the debate proposes solutions that reflect different political ideologies about the role of the State in the provision of education and a particular ideological objection to denominational schools – the objection being that the role of religion in the governance, management and delivery of education impinges on the civil, communal and human rights of those who do not believe in it.[1] To apply the Tesco analogy, this is an objection to large multi-national organisations doing business in a local community, with particular distaste for the promotion of their own brands. The proposed solution is to offer instead a selection of small local stores, or the State provision of a single store offering the same products and service to all.

A second strand in the debate centres on the practicalities of how different needs can be met in local situations. The focus here is on the particular patron and the internal running of the school; on the social effects of education provision, particularly with regard to inclusion and diversity. There is a strong emphasis on pluralism and providing for choice within the system, and this is supported by the language of rights. Some parents object to the monopoly position of the Catholic Church. They want a different type of school whose ethos is not determined by religion or, more specifically, by a Catholic ethos. The objection here is not so much to denominational schools, but to the lack of choice available to them.

For those who find they have to 'shop' at a Catholic school (because it is the only realistic option), the problem is the way the school promotes its 'own brand' products. There are two aspects to this. The first focuses on religious education and the dominant position of the 'home' brand, the inadequate provision for other 'brands' making it difficult for children of other denominations to learn about their particular faith tradition. The second develops from this and focuses on how the school promotes its ethos. Examples of this included the pervasiveness of a religious culture, the sacramental preparation of Catholic children, the 'integrated curriculum' operating in primary schools, and also the inability of the school to operate an exemption system in a satisfactory way.[2] These contributed to the 'noise factor' in the school, like promotional announcements in a store. Proposals include the assertions that religion should be taught in an 'objective, critical and pluralist manner' so that no denomination would have a dominant position, and that schools should be limited in how they promote their own ethos.

A third strand of the debate depicts denominational education in more neutral terms. For most parents, the patronage of the school is not a major concern; they simply want good schools for their children. They believe there is little difference in the quality of care between schools and are generally happy with what is currently provided. They do not find the ethos particularly overbearing or invasive of their values, and they are confident that they can negotiate situations with their children when they are exposed to views they themselves do not agree with.

The fourth strand of the debate reflects the experience of supporters of denominational schools and their ethos. They appreciate the benefits of the school and the help they get in passing on cultural and religious values to their children. They defend their right to this service.

The complexity of different responses to school choice was brought home to me when, in preparation for the Forum on Patronage and Pluralism, I was commissioned by Church of Ireland groups to conduct a survey of parents in their schools. We explored three main questions: why they chose the school, what they expected of the school, and how satisfied were they with the school. The schools in question cater for a diverse population, with only 38 per cent of the parents coming from the four main Protestant churches. The responses indicated a high level of variation in the ideological preferences of parents in their choice of school and in their expectations of what the schools provide, especially in the area of faith. However, there was almost universal satisfaction with the experience of the schools themselves. The main focus of parents' evaluation was on the academic and social development of their children. They saw the school as a 'school' first, and then as a 'faith school'. Faith issues were largely viewed in a holistic way and judged in the context of the excellence of the academic and pastoral service offered by the school. This was especially true for those parents who are not enthusiastic about, but not antagonistic to, faith issues in school.[3] Similar patterns exist in relation to Catholic primary schools, although the level of satisfaction is not as high. This is unsurprising, given that many of those enrolling their children in Catholic schools are not exercising the same choice that parents of the Church of Ireland schools are making – they are sending their children to the only school available to them.

I return now to the original group and their third perspective – the way the debate is conducted. One comment was the tendency to see the debate on education in terms of one issue only. The group was aware of other issues in education, especially the influence of external forces such as the OECD. They were aware of the policy focus on future economic development, the concept of a learning society where, as one of the group cited the rhetoric, 'students are prepared for jobs that have not yet been created and technologies that have not yet been invented'. They were also aware of the tension that exists between producing basic outcomes of literacy and numeracy, and at the same time of fostering high levels of creativity and entrepreneurship to enhance economic growth. They were also aware of the proposed curricular reforms for the post-primary schools aimed at changing the culture of teaching, learning and assessment. Some had been affected by issues in the reorganisation of third-level courses and infrastructure, and its link with the social issues of inclusion, equity, diversity and pluralism. What surprised the group was the tendency to reduce the debate to a single issue at a time, without addressing the complexity of issues involved in educational provision or understanding how people navigate their way through the system.

On the specific issue of patronage, they noted two different approaches to the debate. The first might be classified as a dispassionate academic one, its focus on philosophical and ideological issues. Statistics are quoted outlining the changing demographics of Ireland and exploring the political consequences of that change. There is a particular stress on ethical issues related to the integration of minority groups into society. In the second approach, the debate is informed by personal stories of pain, rejection and abuse in some schools, and occasionally this is countered by positive experiences of growth and development. There is a proliferation of stories to support different viewpoints. Experiences are so diverse that it is sometimes difficult to believe that participants are talking about the same system. On one hand, there is a constructive energy seeking to respond to a new situation in Ireland. On the other, there is an opposing energy that focuses almost entirely on divesting the Church of control of schools. One is future-oriented, seeking a new vision of an integrated, multi-cultural society; the other looks to redress issues of the past, and move away from that past. At times, the rhetoric suggests that anything other than what we have would suffice. The question then becomes the appropriate way to respond to these diverse experiences and the legitimate expectations that arise from them.

My experience with this group of professionals helped focus some of the issues I explore in this book. However, the exploration is also informed by other experiences of the debate. In another area of my work, I meet with people involved in Catholic education. Reaction to the national education debate has been a lively topic in these groups as well. Their discussions have a distinct 'outsider' and 'insider' dimension. From an 'outsider' perspective, denominational education is often seen as a closed, unimaginative and ultimately destructive force. It is portrayed as an environment of indoctrination, as dangerous and damaging in its cultivation of a non-critical mindset, a disadvantage in modern society. 'Insiders' are often shocked by these accusations. Those involved in denominational schools see themselves as open, welcoming and quite diverse, citing examples of innovative practices. They point to major changes in the ethos of the schools compared with those of the mid-twentieth century. They see the schools working from the basis of very human values that can be widely shared, and present religious values as an invitation to students to reflect, not as an opportunity to force their opinions on others. Indeed, many denominational schools ask why their positive approach to life is not reflected in a greater appreciation of the religious source and inspiration that underpins their approach to education. And if the product of denominational education is to be judged by the institutional practices of young people graduating from those schools, then it would seem there is little evidence of indoctrination.

Underlying much of the discussion on education is the relationship individuals have with the political system. Ireland experienced a new energy in the political arena with the change of government in 2011. There was hope for a solution to and healing of the traumatic outcomes of economic collapse, and the need to bail out the banking system. The coalition's *Programme for Government 2011–2016* situated the inclusion and engagement of citizens as a core value:

> The Government for National Recovery will strive to ensure that every one of our citizens has an effective right, free from discrimination, to contribute to the economic, cultural and social life of the nation. Our aim, when our legislative and constitutional changes are implemented, is that Ireland will be a transformed country. By the end of our term in government, Ireland will be recognised as a modern, fair, socially inclusive and equal society supported by a productive and prosperous economy ...

> We will promote policies which will integrate minority ethnic groups in Ireland and which promote social inclusion, equality, diversity and the participation of immigrants in the economic, social, political and cultural life of their communities.[4]

Political rhetoric developed a resonance with the electorate in both the criticism of past performance that led to the current crisis and also in the proposed vision for the future. However, it also had to deal with a cynicism about the political process itself, as it was this same process that had contributed in no small way to the crisis. This lack of confidence in politics can be seen in the work of different writers representing the right and the left of political opinion.

For instance, John Waters wrote in his new book, *Was It For This? Why Ireland Lost the Plot*, of a liberal consensus that he sees as dominating Irish media and public discourse. He believes this is built on a flawed model of progress and freedom, which is, in turn, based on a secular individualism that places personal rights and self-interest at the centre of the public good. Waters reflects on the 'exclusively materialistic' principles that caused the downfall of the Celtic Tiger. In particular, he challenges the quality of public debate in Ireland, which he considers as being ruled by the sound-byte, an explosion of unchallenged and uncritical opinions, 'a two-minute hate facility' that passes as democracy. He laments that 'politics today is not politics at all, but something more like management of a minor company with an uninteresting product'.[5]

Fintan O'Toole focuses his disillusion on the quality of the politicians, as well as providing a critique of particular policy areas:

> It was public consent that made abuse of power the norm. When, in a free society, there is nothing deviant about roguery, it can only be because it accords with the values – or lack of values – of a large mass of people. This is what we have to confront ... So what does account for the amorality? Powerlessness, surely. Power corrupts, but so does a sense of powerlessness. Civic virtue comes from a belief in both rights and responsibilities, but too many Irish people don't really believe they have either the rights or the duties of citizens ... Systemic corruption demands systemic change. And the purpose of that change has to be the wholesale reinvention of Irish democracy. Irish people won't stop wheedling and nodding and winking until they believe they really have the power to shape the public realm in which they live.[6]

O'Toole has also argued that one of the main causes of this cultural failing has been the 'outsourcing' of education to the narrow morality of Churches. Despite his disillusion with the politicians and the present system, he promotes a democratic, publicly run system of education, insisting that the way forward is to create a set of institutions the public have control over.[7]

Wherever one positions oneself in regard to politics, the political arena is where the education debate is taking place. Confidence (or the lack of it) in the political process informs engagement in this debate. If there is a distrust of the politicians, then there is suspicion of the analysis of issues and the proposed solutions. This gives rise to two reactions – the framing of issues in a biased way to gain attention, and a suspicion of conspiracy and self-interest in opponents. Any commentary on the political debate on education must then pay attention to this context.

My approach to writing this book has been influenced by my own academic work. For the past twenty years, I have been involved in teaching about educational policy at an academic level. My approach has been to engage with students on three issues:

- The sources of policy development in education: where do the questions come from? Who raises them and how are they dealt with? How are decisions made? Who has voice and how do they claim it?
- The values behind the policy: this approach examines particular policies and seeks to identify the values being promoted and how the provisions of a policy enshrine these values. A particular concern is to understand the choice of provisions by examining what alternatives are available. In seeking to present an objective, critical and comprehensive analysis of the alternatives, my own 'insider' Catholic perspective as a Jesuit priest have regularly been challenged.
- The implementation of policy: this area of my teaching analyses how the provisions of a policy engage with the status quo in the education system and how they promote a successful process of change. In particular, it considers how individuals negotiate mandated policy changes in the context of their own school and established practice.

This approach to teaching was an important influence on how the book developed. The hope was to contribute to the debate in a number of ways and I saw this book as a journey of exploration. This is reflected in the way the book is organised into three parts. My first aim was to promote a greater awareness of the complexity of the debate, by naming and exploring different sources of policy. These sources reflect political, educational, practical and personal preferences. These preferences reflect different philosophical worldviews. They use language in a different way. Part I of the book explores approaches to denominational education, to the politics of diversity and pluralism and to the use of the terms 'the common good' and 'rights'. I recognise that this aim is ambitious, involving an understanding of political philosophy and of legal, educational and religious issues. Some will no doubt find the treatment of some of these issues superficial and unsatisfactory; my defence is my desire to promote is a better quality of debate rather to promote a particular solution.

A second aim in writing the book was to provide resources and my hope is that it will bring the key areas related to the question of denominational education together in one place. Part II documents how religious freedom and education – particularly denominational education – are understood in the context of other European countries. It is hoped that this information will serve to both inform and ground the debate. It may contribute to the sense that we are not the only country that struggles with these issues and the responses of different countries provide a rich tapestry. We have an opportunity to both learn from others and to contribute our experience in the international debate.

Part III returns to the Irish scene to explore the debate in more detail. My specific interest here is in taking some of the more theoretical concepts explored in Part I and the practical solutions seen in the European context in Part II and applying them to the Irish debate. Here I seek to unpick the way some of these concepts have evolved in Irish education, and in doing so have constituted the framework in which current challenges to education are positioned. In particular, I hope to explore the conceptual coherence of proposals and practices in handling these challenges.

The focus on denominational education is, of course, a limited view of the education debate as a whole. This debate in Ireland, even when dealing with the idea of pluralism, is much wider than faith schools alone. A further limitation is the focus on primary and post-primary education. Much of the energy, and finances, in education is focused on third-level, with a major reorganisation of the universities proposed for the near future. This reorganisation has major implications for denominational education as well, as the main teacher training institutions are denominational. My hope is that others will add to the debate, both in terms of the policy areas to be explored and the different perspectives they bring to some of the issues I raise. In that context, we will have a deeper appreciation of the common good, in which the rights of all are protected and enhanced.

NOTES

1. Irish Human Rights Commission, *Religion and Education: A Human Rights Perspective* (2011), #120–2.
2. Ibid., #136–7.
3. David Tuohy, *Our Faith Community*. Research Sponsored by Church of Ireland College of Education and the Board of Education and Church of Ireland Primary Schools Management Association (2011).
4. *Programme for Government 2011–2016*, p. 3, p. 54.
5. John Waters, *Was It For This? Why Ireland Lost the Plot* (Dublin: Transworld Ireland, 2012), p. 276.
6. Fintan O'Toole, *Irish Times* (27 March 2012).
7. Fintan O'Toole, *Enough is Enough: How to Build a New Republic* (London: Faber and Faber, 2010), passim.

PART I

EXPLORING CONCEPTS

I
CATHOLIC EDUCATION: A PERSPECTIVE ON DENOMINATIONAL EDUCATION

The public debate on denominational education in Ireland is almost exclusively concerned with Catholic schools. This debate has two main concerns. The first involves the Church's role in the provision and governance of schools. What is debated is the dependence of the State on private patrons, and in particular the Catholic Church, for school provision and where the position of the Church in primary school provision is recognised by all participants as disproportionate. The second is on the religious ethos of schools. Here the point of criticism is the teaching of religion and the impact of a religious worldview on students. Some commentators object to religion itself, often giving rise to strong anti-Catholic sentiments in which the Church's involvement in education is characterised as indoctrination and a quest for power and control. Others criticise the approach to religious education and focus on the inability or the failure of the Catholic school to provide for an increasing ethnic and religious diversity within schools.

The introduction outlined some stark differences between 'insider' and 'outsider' approaches to the debate. In particular, a number of critics of denominational education portray faith schools as destructive forces, both in terms of the selection of students and in the teaching of 'secular' subjects. Evidence is often drawn from historical instances rather than from current practice. Catholic schools today see themselves as very different from their counterparts in the nineteenth and mid-twentieth century; they point to major changes in the Church's understanding of itself and its approach to education. They provide examples of excellence in academic results, the diversity of intake in many of their schools and the satisfaction of most parents with their experience of the schools.

This chapter will explore what these changes look like by delineating the Catholic approach to education in official Church documents. (Although the focus here is on Catholic schools, a similar discourse on education will exist in other Christian and faith schools.) This is an insider perspective and, as such, seeks to clarify what the Church expects of itself in education. It places the approach to Catholic education in Ireland in a wider international Church perspective. The aim is not to propose denominational schools as the only answer to the issue of provision. While there are changes proposed for the patronage structure of schools, it is likely that the Catholic Church will be a provider of schools in many areas in Ireland for some time to come. Catholic schools will always be open to criticism, from outsiders and insiders alike. Outsiders will disagree with the philosophy and goals of the Catholic school and want a different approach to education; insiders may criticise the schools for their interpretation of Church documents, arguing that they are too liberal or too conservative. Both groups may criticise schools for not living up to their stated ideals. Like every organisation, there will always be grounds for improvement.

In evaluating these debates, it is important to distinguish personal preferences from critical appraisals. At times, these two processes can be confused. It is one thing to say that an organisation does not do what *I want it* to do; it is another thing to take into account something that *it should* do. We must develop a fair basis for any criticism, where the criteria for judgment are clear and the information for making the judgment is accurate.

By describing how Catholic schools see themselves, and situating their goals in the general political debate on educational provision, this chapter seeks to provide the information necessary in assessing the capacity of these schools to be of service to people with a different agenda in education, thereby providing for diversity within the system. In clarifying the values underpinning the school, this chapter may also be of help to parents in seeing the common ground and the points of divergence with their own philosophical position, and in planning for the involvement of their child in the school.

The chapter develops four main themes. The first looks at the context of change, giving some of the characteristics of the Church before and after the Second Vatican Council. This is followed by sections which seek to develop the positive position of the Church in three areas:

- Christian anthropology: the Church's understanding of the purpose of world, humanity and society, and how it interprets the needs of modern culture.
- The role of education: how the Church looks at education and its benefits for the individual and for society.
- The Catholic school: this section looks at the marks of the specifically Catholic school.

The chapter concludes by looking at the provision of Catholic schools and the issues that arise in the political arena, with an emphasis on the Irish context.

1. THE CONTEXT OF CHANGE

In the period immediately prior to the Second Vatican Council, the Catholic Church identified itself as both a spiritual reality (linked with the kingdom of God) and a human organisation. It considered itself the perfect society, which had been established by Jesus and entrusted with his message, and defined itself in terms of four essential marks: one, holy, catholic and apostolic. This gave rise to an unshakeable confidence in its own message, and it deemed that outside the Church there was no salvation. Other Christian Churches were seen as lacking the marks of the one, true, Catholic and apostolic Church; other religions were deemed to lack any power of salvation because they did not focus on Jesus. Secular society was also regarded with suspicion and, in general, was seen as a threat to spiritual development. Church statements were often critical and condemnatory of non-Church culture, and uncritical of its own culture.

The Church was organised in a hierarchical way, its structure highly centralised around the Pope and Rome. Its teaching was paternalistic, authoritarian and legalistic. Uniformity in belief, discipline and worship was important – Mass was said in Latin in every culture. There were universal rules and regulations which placed concrete demands on membership, e.g. regular attendance and reception of sacraments. There was a strong emphasis on piety and devotions, and lay people were generally passive with regard to participation (pray, pay, obey). Religious education focused on the catechism rather than on scripture, and there was a focus on guilt and sin rather than love and redemption.

The Second Vatican Council took place between 1962 and 1965. In calling the Council, Pope John XXIII spoke of the need to update the Church and promote Christian unity. In his opening address to the Council, he insisted that the modern world needed to see that the Church had been updated and intellectually reinvigorated. He felt that the world at the time was marked by a spiritual poverty and required the vitality of a renewed Church. However, he wanted the Church to offer the 'medicine of mercy' and encouragement, rather than severe condemnations. Perhaps the most telling achievement of the Council was the new understanding of the Church that emerged: it was defined as the 'people of God' and not simply a hierarchical structure; as a 'sacrament' to the world with an active mission in all sectors of human society.

Although it defined no new dogma, the Council set in motion a 'Copernican revolution' in terms of Church practice. There was a new focus on scripture rather than apologetics. Altars were turned around so that priests faced the people. Latin gave way to the vernacular in liturgical celebrations. New approaches emerged to theology and the teaching of religion. The Council stressed the Church's solidarity with humanity instead of its separation from the secular world. This gave rise to a new focus on social and charitable activities, especially related to justice for marginalised groups. There was a new involvement of lay people in ministries and the lifestyle and apostolate of religious congregations changed dramatically. In general, there was a greater emphasis on dialogue with culture. Catholics were encouraged to see the world as a new opportunity to see God at work in 'the signs of the times' rather than as a threat and a distraction.[1]

2. CHRISTIAN ANTHROPOLOGY

The Church sees its mission as deeply rooted in a particular understanding of the world and the position of humankind in that world. Its doctrine is basically a metaphorical narrative describing

God's relationship with the world and with humankind. Andrew Greeley describes the Catholic imagination as fired by a sense that creation is 'God in disguise'.[2] God is present in the world, revealing himself in and through creation. He can be known in the physical reality of creation, in the inner workings of human desires, in the pattern of history and also in the special revelation of Jesus Christ.

The wonder of creation leads to a sense of God's power and glory. This has been echoed in the psalms of the Old Testament: 'The heavens declare the glory of God; the skies proclaim the work of his hands. Day after day they pour forth speech; night after night they display knowledge' (Psalm 19).

In the New Testament, Paul was clear that all people can come to know God through reason and live faithfully according to his law. In the Letter to the Romans (1:20-23), he was clear that any failure to recognise God was due to defects in human thinking – particularly the regular failure involved in confusing the elements of creation with the Creator himself.

The human person is made in the image of God. As a work of God, each person has both a divine origin and an eternal destiny that transcends the physical world.[3] It is from this reality that the dignity of the human person derives, making each person equal in the sight of God. Therefore, reflection on human experience also brings knowledge of God. This is especially true of the search for truth and beauty; the desire to find the good and live a moral life; the experience of freedom and conscience; the longings and hope for happiness and for the infinite. St Paul wrote that the love of God was written on the hearts of each person, and St Augustine expressed this in a prayer: 'You made us, and our hearts are restless until they rest in Thee.'[4]

The search for meaning is not an individual pursuit. In Christian thought, human nature is essentially relational: God created humankind to live socially, not in isolation. We become more fully human through social relationships, through interaction and community. We develop through the experience of family, friendship, companionship and cooperation in work and leisure; through shared commitments and meanings which support our own development and contribute to the development of others. However, we live in an imperfect world – not just in the sense that the world is still evolving to something better, but because of the experience of evil. This gives rise to a sense of the 'world as it is' and the 'world as it ought to be'. Usually, this refers to the moral rather than the physical world, but it is true for both. Evil is seen as the rebellious idolatry by which humans worship elements of creation rather than the God who made them, which gives rise to alienation and exile from God. This is seen in the Adam and Eve story. They were told that, if they ate the forbidden fruit, they would experience death. What happened to them was that they were exiled from the garden. The natural transience associated with human life, death, took on a new significance. Evil became a moral death, a turning to 'no life, an existence without God'.

The Christian position holds that not only do we search for God, but God also searches for us. God wishes to be revealed to the whole world. He wants creation to come to perfection and he wants to reconcile the moral dimension in which people experience alienation from God. God's plan to redeem the world – to free its natural goodness from the shackles of enslavement – is told in the choice of the Chosen People. The story of the scriptures is a story of God's relationship with humanity and the response of a community to that revelation over time, with all its examples of fidelity and infidelity. The story tells of a gradual development of human appreciation of who God is through different cultural experiences and reflection on them. This is often referred to as God's providence, his direct care for the world. From this perspective, human history is seen as a drama of God revealing himself – in the actions of individuals, in the response of groups or whole nations, and in the lessons to be learnt from the consequences of these actions. In this context, faith is openness to human existence being taken up in a cosmic story whose final meaning is promised but not yet clear.

The fullness of revelation is seen in the person of Jesus. His coming is not seen as an interruption or distortion of nature. God's providence works through human activity. The two are not in opposition to one another. There is a unity between the achievements of human talent and energy and God's power. Therefore, the life of Jesus becomes an example of what can be achieved by human nature. The destiny of humankind is seen in the life of Jesus, but particularly in his resurrection, which is both a promise of fulfilment (the Omega point of Teilhard de Chardin) and also of redemption (the reconciliation of the world). The Christian hope is that what God did for Jesus at the resurrection he will do for humankind, and for the whole cosmos.

For the Christian, creation is an unfinished project, and humankind has a vital role in its unfolding. Human achievement is also a sign of God's grace and the fulfilment of his mysterious design. In Church documents, there is a sense of excitement and opportunity in the commentary on human progress and ingenuity.[5] One example of this perspective is found in *Gaudium et Spes*:

> New ways are open, therefore, for the perfection and the further extension of culture. These ways have been prepared by the enormous growth of natural, human and social sciences, by technical progress, and advances in developing and organising means whereby men can communicate with one another … and thus little by little, there develops a more universal form of human culture, which better promotes and expresses the unity of the human race to the degree that it preserves the particular aspects of the different civilisations.[6]

The advances in culture are seen as the result of human activity in the ever-deepening search to understand the world. This is accompanied by a desire to build a better world based on truth and justice, giving rise to a new humanism in which human activity is defined first of all by a responsibility to others and to history. However, these aspirations are not always realised. The Church clearly expresses its awareness of the tension between the ideal and the reality. The documents cite hunger, poverty, illiteracy and the many bitter social, economic, racial and ideological disputes that proliferate in society.[7] The progress of each age seems to bring new tensions rather than remove all tensions from human existence.

In the analysis of the tensions that arise from human progress, the Church documents express concern at a new form of enslavement of the human spirit due to an excessive focus on the 'things' of technology and on an efficiency that depersonalises the role of human beings. Two symptoms of this culture are a secular mindset and what Benedict XVI described as the 'tyranny of relativism'. Given the nature of human reflection, the 'intimate and vital bond of man to God' can be forgotten, overlooked, or even explicitly rejected. Such attitudes can have different causes. There can be an over-confidence in the ability of humanity to explain creation through science. This also gives rise to a sense of independence that rejects any relationship with God. Some, in rejecting a distorted image of God, reject the God of the scriptures. Others reject God because of the evil that is seen in the world – and this can include the scandals perpetrated by believers in their actions and teachings. Others are affected by religious ignorance or indifference. Some are distracted by their involvement in worldly affairs and hold that a religious belief in the future distracts humankind from the task of developing the freedom that is possible. Taken together, they constitute a culture that is anti-religion and atheistic.[8]

Whereas much progress has been made in purifying our notion of God, distinguishing religion from a magical or superstitious worldview, this has often developed as presenting the rejection of God as a requirement for a modern scientific society – an attitude that also dominates a new humanism in philosophy, literature, the arts and the interpretation of history – and in some countries has become enshrined in civil laws.[9]

A by-product of such an approach to life is seen in moral relativism, which is based on confusion between 'responsible freedom' and 'liberty to do what one wants'. Moral judgments are based on passing superficial ideas that provide short-term benefits rather than the absolute values promoted by the Church. In response to this, the Church focuses on the inner spiritual dynamism of the human person, which seeks moral freedom by reflecting on the ethical implications of new discoveries for present-day living. The invitation is to reflect on the discoveries of the sciences to discern their positive benefits in the service of humankind, and to ensure that they are used for that purpose without compromising the dignity of the person. From the Christian perspective, there needs to be a balance between intellectual development and the capacity to reflect on the moral implications of these developments as informed by a comprehensive view of reality.[10]

It is within this context that the Church sees the importance of education. There is a strong focus on education empowering the human person to make free choices in order to enhance their own dignity and to contribute to the common good:

One such demand is a pressing need to ensure the presence of a Christian mentality in the society of the present day, marked, among other things, by cultural pluralism. For it is Christian thought which constitutes a sound criterion of judgment in the midst of conflicting concepts and behaviour: 'Reference to Jesus Christ teaches man to discern the values which ennoble from those which degrade him.'[11]

3. THE TASK OF EDUCATION[12]

Behind every approach to education is a philosophy of the human person. The Christian philosophy focuses on the dignity of the human person, which is based on four pillars:

- Human beings are made in God's image and from this is derived the dignity of each person.
- The divine spark exists within each of us, and we are called to allow this grace to develop within us.
- We are both blessed and broken, and we experience this tension in our relations with others and in our successes and failures.
- We have a future and destiny beyond this world, and this gives us hope in the face of adversity.

Developing the person becomes the key element of any educational system. The focus is on holistic growth, where intellectual, aesthetic, creative, emotional and moral development is integrated. The aim is to produce people who have inner freedom. This freedom allows them to discern the reality of their lives, to find core values to live by and to choose these values. From the Church's perspective, education is directed to the inner life of the person and promotes a fully integrated human person. Education opens the person up to life as it is, and helps create a definite attitude to life as it should be. This process develops dispositions of critical reflection and judgment, as well as responsible action to promote the common good.[13]

As well as the psychological development associated with the individual, education also helps integrate the individual into the community. There are three dimensions to this integration: an understanding of the culture; professional preparation for a career; and an orientation to the common good, which promotes justice and peace for all.[14] The focus of growth is on empowering students to think for themselves, to make judgments and decisions. Specifically, Church documents warn against providing any pre-packed simple answers; there is a focus on experiential learning, which engages the student and promotes a commitment to a constant search for the truth and seeks to relate education to the lives of the students:

> Culture is only educational when young people can relate their study to real-life situations with which they are familiar. The school must stimulate the pupil to exercise his intelligence through the dynamics of understanding to attain clarity and inventiveness. It must help him spell out the meaning of his experiences and their truths. Any school which neglects this duty and which offers merely pre-cast conclusions hinders the personal development of its pupils.[15]

Religious education is seen as a core element of any education, and is promoted both in terms of the rights of parents to endorse a religious outlook for their children and with respect to the benefits of such an education to the individual and to society:

> A concept of the human person being open to the transcendent necessarily includes the element of religious education in schools: it is an aspect of the right to education. Without religious education, pupils would be deprived of an essential element of their formation and personal development, which helps them attain a vital harmony between faith and culture. Moral formation and religious education also foster the development of personal and social responsibility and the other civic virtues; they represent, therefore, an important contribution to the common good of society.[16]

The core position of religious education does not interfere with the teaching of other subjects, each of which has its own methodologies. In that way, there is not a 'Catholic mathematics', 'Catholic economics', 'Catholic science' and so on. However, the Christian approach recognises that all branches of study raise key questions about the world we live in and the role of humankind. It is essential that students are taught to evaluate the issues raised in the different subjects according to sound ethical criteria:

> Individual subjects must be taught according to their own particular methods. It would be wrong to consider subjects as mere adjuncts to faith or as a useful means of teaching apologetics ... Their aim is not merely the attainment of knowledge but the acquisition of values and the discovery of truth.[17]

At different stages, the Church documents comment on the importance of particular subjects and their benefit to the individual. For instance, the study of science and technology is seen as giving a greater understanding of God's creation. As well as promoting a search for depth, it should also promote a sense of wonder at the breadth and complexity of the universe. The documents also encourage teachers to deal with the moral issues that arise in the application of many developments in science and technology, and not to shirk this responsibility.[18]

The Church has also strongly advocated the critical study of culture in the humanities. Philosophy, history, literature and art bring students in touch with their own heritage and that of others. This study develops students' aesthetic sense and develops a deeper awareness of all people as one human family. Students come to appreciate the struggles of societies, families and individuals, and they see the depth of the human heart, in its heroic and darkest expressions. This study both enlightens the religious quest of the individual, and provides criteria for judging it.[19]

In summary, the engagement of students is geared toward holistic growth, characterised by the integration of life experiences, culture and faith and leading to a commitment to service. The aim of Catholic education is:

- To assist in the total development of the individual student: aesthetic, creative, cultural, emotional, intellectual, moral, physical, political, religious, social and spiritual.
- To develop each student's ability to engage in clear thinking, discerning judgment and responsible decision-making.

- To enhance each student's capacity to think and experience creatively and intuitively.
- To educate students in their Catholic faith and to invite them to commit themselves to a life centred on Jesus and his values.
- To cultivate the skills necessary for finding personal meaning and leading a productive life as a member of a community.
- To promote a deep sense of appreciation of and responsibility for the natural environment.
- To foster the critical assimilation of culture.
- To develop a particular awareness in students of being called to be positive agents of change in society.
- To promote a commitment to justice, peace and the development of self and others.

4. THE CATHOLIC SCHOOL

The concept of the Catholic school is informed by this vision of education. The Catholic school is not simply concerned with religious formation – it involves the formation of the whole person, and offers an education in all areas of life. One of the characteristics of the Catholic school is the excellence of the general education it provides:

> To understand fully the specific mission of the Catholic school it is essential to keep in mind the basic concept of what a school is; that which does not reproduce the characteristic features of a school cannot be a Catholic school.[20]

While performing this service, the Catholic school focuses in a special way on the holistic formation of the person:

> The Catholic school sets out to be a school for the human person and of human persons. 'The person of each individual human being, in his or her material and spiritual needs, is at the heart of Christ's teaching: this is why the promotion of the human person is the goal of the Catholic school.'[21]

This formation will be seen in some core marks of the Catholic school, which echo through all the documents on Catholic education, and were part of the Irish Bishops' statement *Vision 08*.

4.1. THE FORMATION OF THE INDIVIDUAL

Parents are the first educators of their children. Thus schooling, particularly primary schooling, is seen as an extension of the home. All others involved in education – the school, the State and the Church – act in the name of parents, with their consent and authorisation. Thus, in developing the Catholic school, particular attention is paid to the relationship that exists between parents and children, how parents want their children to grow and develop, and the type of atmosphere in which they want that formation to take place.

The approach to formation is guided by the vision of the child as 'a child of God', who will grow to be an active citizen of this world, but also will be prepared for a life with God in heaven. According to Church documents, the Catholic school:

- is a privileged place which fosters the formation of the whole person and is intentionally directed to his or her growth;
- provides 'an integral education which responds to all the needs of the human person' by developing, in an age-appropriate way, the intellectual, physical, psychological, moral and religious capabilities of each student.

The inspiration for formation is always the person of Jesus, who is the foundation of the enterprise. He is the centre of the school, and the values of the gospel become the leaven that animates all activities in the school – the curriculum, the community life and the pastoral programmes. Even the physical environment of the school is meant to be conducive to personal growth and formation:

> The Catholic school is committed thus to the development of the whole man, since in Christ, the perfect man, all human values find their fulfilment and unity. Herein lies the specifically Catholic character of the school. Its duty to cultivate human values in their own legitimate right in accordance with its particular mission to serve all men has its origin in the figure of Christ. He is the one who ennobles man, gives meaning to human life, and is the model which the Catholic school offers to its pupils.[22]

Students are to be encouraged to reflect on their life experiences and to develop Christian attitudes and virtues which focus on inner freedom and service to others. This is to happen in a way that is appropriate to different stages of development. The formation also helps the students integrate their own culture and its history into their identity, to be carried through to their career and life plans:

> Human culture remains human, and must be taught with scientific objectivity. But the lessons of the teacher and the reception of those students who are believers will not divorce faith from this culture; this would be a major spiritual loss ... a believer is both human and a person of faith, the protagonist of culture and the subject of religion. Anyone who searches for the contact points will be able to find them. Helping in the search is not solely the task of religion teachers; their time is quite limited, while other teachers have many hours at their disposal every day. Everyone should work together, each one developing his or her own subject area with professional competence, but sensitive to those opportunities in which they can help students to see beyond the limited horizon of human reality.[23]

In summary, the aim of Christian formation is the integration of faith and life, characterised by a constant search for the truth, by students and by teachers.

4.2. SEARCH FOR THE TRUTH

In the opening stanza of 'Choruses from the Rock', T. S. Eliot sounds a note of despair and frustration at the endless cycle of idea, action, invention and experiment which seems so non-productive:

> Where is the Life we have lost in living?
> Where is the wisdom we have lost in knowledge?
> Where is the knowledge we have lost in information?
> The cycles of Heaven in twenty centuries
> Bring us farther from God and nearer to the Dust.

The focus of Catholic education is to help the student move beyond information to knowledge, wisdom and the fullness of life. There is a strong conviction throughout the documents that humankind searches for truth and meaning, and that this search is inspired by faith:

> Although Christian life consists in loving God and doing his will, intellectual work is intimately involved. The light of Christian faith stimulates a desire to know the universe as God's creation. It enkindles a love for the truth that will not be satisfied with superficiality in knowledge or judgment.[24]

The role of the Catholic school is to provide a structured approach to that search. It focuses the questions of the students, giving them a context for their search and the application of the answers to their own lives. As in the task of education, the autonomy of different disciplines is recognised in both the validity of their questions and their methodologies. The Church believes that all academic searching that is authentic will lead to a greater appreciation of God, who is present in the study of human history and achievements.[25]

4.3. EVANGELISATION THROUGH WITNESS

Frequently, there is confusion between the terms 'indoctrinating', 'proselytising' and 'evangelising', as applied to the work of the Church. 'Indoctrinating' refers to processes, often coercive, which cause people to act and think uncritically according to a certain ideology. 'Proselytising' offers inducements to change from one religious perspective to another. 'Evangelising' is understood as a process of teaching about one's own religion in order to make it known to others. Evangelisation may be direct (teaching) or indirect (witnessing). The Catholic school practices evangelisation, its students being invited to hear and reflect on the Christian message.

In teaching, there is a focus on the Catholic worldview outlined above: a critical dialogue between faith, science and culture. More important, however, than the content is the quality of relationships and the example of teachers. These are seen as the main identity of the Catholic school. The message in Church documents is that students learn more by example than from the formal process of pedagogy: 'Modern man listens more willingly to witnesses than to teachers, and if he does listen to teachers, it is because they are witnesses.'[26] This witness is to be seen mainly in the authenticity of the lives of teachers – in their own pursuit of the truth.

> The extent to which the Christian message is transmitted through education depends to a very great extent on the teachers. The integration of culture and faith is mediated by the integration of faith and life in the person of the teacher. The nobility of the task to which teachers are called demands that, in imitation of Christ, the only Teacher, they reveal the Christian message not only by word but also by every gesture of their behaviour. This is what makes the difference between a school whose education is permeated by the Christian spirit and one in which religion is only regarded as an academic subject like any other.[27]

4.4. A Sense of Community

A sense of community is essential to a Catholic school. This derives from the respect that is given to each individual and to the sense of collaboration between local partners in the school. In particular, its sense of community is inspired by its focus on Jesus as a model of behaviour and the values of the gospel:

> Catholic schools must be seen as a meeting places for those who wish to express Christian values in education. The Catholic school, far more than any other, must be a community whose aim is the transmission of values for living.[28]

This sense of community is worked out on three levels: a general climate of acceptance and trust; a sense of collaboration with agencies in the local community; and the connection with the local and universal Church. The aim of community is to create a family spirit, based on trust and spontaneity, especially in the primary school.[29]

The community spirit is also seen in the interpersonal relations between teachers and students. A mentor-like relationship is promoted as the most conducive to the teaching–learning dynamic. This relationship develops a productive discipline and allows for a differentiated approach to learning, geared to the needs of individual students:

Catholic schools, then, safeguard the priority of the person, both student and teacher; they foster the proper friendship between them since 'an authentic formative process can only be initiated through a personal relationship'.[30]

The social dimension of the school is also evident in the school's place in society and in how it collaborates with other institutions. This partnership is of benefit to the school and to society. The school 'contributes to building a network of relationships that helps students to develop their sense of belonging, and society itself to develop a sense of solidarity'.[31]

The school's link with the Church is developed in a number of different ways. At a school level, there is a focus on 'sacramentality'. By this is meant that students can be reminded of a religious reality through the physical – in particular works of art that decorate the school. This can also be enhanced by celebrations within the school, including specific liturgical celebrations. The Catholic school is also linked with a parish or diocese. The Church documents develop this link, not just in terms of the role of the bishop in approving the Catholic school, but also in terms of the vital role the school plays in the pastoral activity of the Church.[32] This sense of Church can be enhanced by focusing beyond the local Church community. In particular, where schools are run by religious congregations, there are often opportunities to 'twin' with schools in other cultures, broadening the horizons of the students.[33]

4.5. RELIGIOUS EDUCATION

Religious education must develop alongside the other disciplines that engage the student and must ensure a harmony between the student's appreciation of the other subjects and their religious sensibility. As well as being a discipline in its own right, religious education is seen as an opportunity to help a student integrate what they learn in other disciplines into a coherent worldview.

It is necessary, therefore, that religious instruction in schools appear as a scholastic discipline with the same systematic demands and the same rigour as other disciplines. It must present the Christian message and the Christian event with the same seriousness and the same depth with which other disciplines present their knowledge. It should not be an accessory alongside of these disciplines, but rather it should engage in a necessary inter-disciplinary dialogue.[34]

Religious education is seen as part of the formation of students. It is linked to the wider reality of their faith life in the home and in the community. In this regard, the Church documents make a distinction between 'religious education' in schools, which focuses on developing knowledge about the Christian message and event, and 'catechesis', which is the process of integrating the student into the life of the Church. Although distinct, these processes are closely linked. Religious education seeks to give knowledge about the nature of religious belief, about Christianity in particular and how Christians try to live their lives. Catechesis uses the same elements and seeks to promote spiritual, liturgical, sacramental and apostolic maturity. Catechesis supposes the hearer is a believer or searcher and has a wider spiritual support in the family and in the Church community. It also looks at integration as a life-long process. Knowledge contributes to a mature faith and helps to deepen the faith life of the student. Catechesis helps integrate that knowledge into a coherent framework. The Catholic school plays an important role in both processes.[35]

4.6. INCLUSIVE SERVICE TO THE COMMUNITY
The Catholic school is seen, first and foremost, as a service to Catholic parents in helping them to provide an education for their children. However, it is also seen as a means of evangelisation and witness, and therefore it offers itself as a service to all, non-Christians included. The Church is convinced that this is a positive benefit to all who attend. In different countries, there are major restrictions on religious activities within Catholic schools and many of the students are non-Catholics. However, they value the education that is offered, in particular the respect that is given to them and their beliefs:

The Catholic school is far from being divisive. It does not exacerbate difference but rather aids cooperation and contact with others. It is open to others and respects their way of thinking and living.[36]

The focus of religious formation in a school recognises that each student is someone on a journey of discovery, constantly seeking the truth. The freedom of religion that is everyone's right is at the core of how students are to be treated. This precludes any use of compulsion or coercion in promoting a religious viewpoint.[37] Even though the Church remains convinced of its own privileged position with regard to the truth of human existence, it insists that faith must be a free response to God:

> It is one of the major tenets of Catholic doctrine that man's response to God in faith must be free; no one therefore is to be forced to embrace the Christian faith against his own will ... the act of faith is of its very nature a free act.[38]

Whereas there is a clear understanding of the essential religious freedom, it is admitted that this understanding has not always been operative in behaviour. This refers to the Church's attitude to different groups outside the Church, as well as to restrictive and exclusive practices within the Church:

> In the life of the People of God, as it has made its pilgrim way through the vicissitudes of human history, there has at times appeared a way of acting that was hardly in accord with the spirit of the gospel or even opposed to it. Nevertheless, the doctrine of the Church that no one is to be coerced into faith has always stood firm.[39]

The care of the right to religious freedom is seen as shared between individual citizens, social groups, government and the different religious communities (the Churches). The right is seen as a freedom to search, believe and act according to one's discovered truth, balanced by a responsibility to respect and promote this for others. Coercion is seen as both an abuse of one's own right and an infringement of the rights of others. It sees this freedom as leading people to act with greater responsibility in fulfilling their duties as citizens, rather than as helping them to withdraw from public life, and it promotes the position that society will benefit from the moral qualities of justice and peace that come from a genuine religious commitment.

5. PROVISION OF CATHOLIC EDUCATION

The approach to education within the Catholic Church follows a standard discourse – a human anthropology, a vision of education and a vision of the school. The Church is aware that others have developed a similar discourse but arrived at different positions and values. The Church is also aware of the controversy that can exist at both the theoretical level and also at the level of practical politics, where there is a demand for different approaches to the provision for education within a State. In commenting on different perceptions of its own Catholic school, it recognises these tensions and asserts the rights and freedom of individuals and communities to promote a shared philosophy based on religious beliefs:

> According to others, Catholic schools have outlived their time; as institutions they were a necessary substitute in the past but have no place at a time when civil authority assumes responsibility for education. In fact, as the State increasingly takes control of education and establishes its own so-called neutral and monolithic system, the survival of those natural communities, based on a shared concept of life, is threatened. Faced with this situation, the Catholic school offers an alternative which is in conformity with the wishes of the members of the community of the Church.[40]

When the Church speaks of State provision of education, its main focus is on the right of parents to make a free choice of the type of education they want for their child. In trying to ensure that this right can be freely exercised without too much hardship for parents, the Church asks that governments provide real choice for parents, and that they support parents in the choices they make. This demand extends to all schools and is based on three key principles: (a) the right to freedom of religion; (b) the liberty to pursue objectives without State interference, also known as a principle of subsidiarity, where as much freedom as possible is located at individual and local level; and (c) distributive justice, which provides the same support for all citizens and does not penalise some for choosing a particular school in accordance with their conscience.[41]

From a Church perspective, the Catholic school is set up primarily as a service to Catholic parents. It is also a statement of the mission of the Church to share its message with others and to witness to the truths it espouses. A survey of different countries shows that Catholic schools cater for a wide variety of situations, and Catholic schools work out their existence in a local juridical and cultural context.[42] In some countries, the schools are private and elitist; they have no State support and can only be afforded by a small group of parents. Some of these schools try to provide scholarships for students who would wish to attend. In other areas, Catholic schools exist as part of the general fabric of educational provision, but because of the demographic distribution of Catholics, a high proportion of their students are non-Catholics. In these countries, Catholic schools have a good reputation and become the school of choice for parents of different faiths and denominations.

Church involvement in the provision of schooling in Ireland has arisen from a particular history, and this will be discussed in more detail in later chapters. As far back as 2007, when the Irish bishops reflected on the policy of provision into the future, they freely recognised that there was a need for fewer Catholic schools. Their focus on diversity looked at two dimensions – catering for diversity within the system, and catering for diversity within the school:

Some places are currently experiencing huge inflows of new residents, sometimes doubling or trebling the enrolment of parish schools in the space of a few years. This usually happens because there is no other educational provision in the area. It is sometimes the case that people choose the Catholic school simply because it is the only school available, and not because they wish their children to have a Catholic education. This can cause difficulties for parents who do not share the ethos of a Catholic school. It can also put an unfair financial and administrative burden on the parish. We feel that in such circumstances the Church should not be left with the task of providing for the educational needs of the whole community. As the Catholic Church accepts that there should be choice and diversity within a national education system, it believes that parents who desire schools under different patronage should, where possible, be facilitated in accessing them. In new centres of population it is incumbent upon the State to plan for the provision of school sites and to ensure, in consultation with the various patron bodies, that there is a plurality of school provision reflecting the wishes of the parents in the area.[43]

This statement points to some of the service provided by Church patrons in the governance of education. The financial and administrative services provided by patrons are often overlooked in the current debate. It also points to the *de facto* response the Church has made in accommodating urgent educational needs. In the past, the Catholic school would have been seen as being exclusively for 'the education of Catholics'. In its new understanding of itself, the focus is more on the values it promotes in a 'Catholic education for all'. This openness is part of a universal stance in Catholic education, and not simply a political response to a particular situation in Ireland. When students are accepted into the school, they are made feel welcome and their different beliefs are catered for as much as possible. The basis for this welcome is seen as the fundamental dignity of the human person:

> The Catholic school welcomes diversity and strives for inclusivity. It is open to people of other denominations and other faiths, welcomes them into its community and respects their beliefs: the religious freedom and the personal conscience of individual students and their families must be respected, and this freedom is explicitly recognised by the Church. On the other hand, a Catholic school cannot relinquish its own freedom to proclaim the gospel and to offer a formation based on the values to be found in a Christian education; this is its right and duty.[44]

This approach to diversity is seen as enrichment to the school as well as a service to the student. A central aspect of the welcome of different groups is a respect for religious freedom, which is balanced by a commitment to promoting the religious dimension of life in an invitational and non-coercive manner:

> While it maintains its own ethos and provides religious instruction and formation in the Catholic Faith, the Catholic school sees this diversity as an opportunity for dialogue and understanding with those of different faiths. It seeks to co-operate with parents of other traditions who wish to provide religious instruction for the

children in their own tradition. This welcoming ethos explains why Catholic schools are among the most inclusive schools in Ireland today.[45]

Church documents strongly protect the right of parents to give religious instruction to their children, and to have some help in doing that as part of a holistic education. Even in State-run schools, the Church insists that religious education be available that is respectful of the faith and denominational wishes of parents. The documents warn of ways in which the approach to religious education may fall short of a genuine religious education:

> The marginalisation of religious education in schools is equivalent to assuming – at least in practice – an ideological position that can lead pupils into error or do them a disservice. Moreover, if religious education is limited to a presentation of the different religions, in a comparative and 'neutral' way, it creates confusion or generates religious relativism or indifferentism. In this respect, Pope John Paul II explained: 'The question of Catholic education includes ... religious education in the more general milieu of school, whether it be Catholic or State-run. The families of believers have the right to such education; they must have the guarantee that the State school – precisely because it is open to all – not only will not put their children's faith in peril, but will rather complete their integral formation with appropriate religious education. This principle must be included within the concept of religious freedom and of the truly democratic State, which as such – that is, in obedience to its deepest and truest nature – puts itself at the service of the citizens, of all citizens, in respect for their rights and their religious convictions.'[46]

This approach to education gives rise to a number of challenges in the political arena:

• What is the operative 'anthropology' in the provision of education in the State? How does this anthropology cater for different worldviews? What is the approach to diversity that the State adopts? How much freedom does it give to different groups to develop their own identity within the State? Do they regard groups as a strength or a weakness in terms of social cohesion?

- How does the State support different groups within the education system? To what extent does it support rights to religious freedom and the freedom to set up schools? In particular, what support does it give to parents who seek to exercise this right?

- Within a State system of education, what support is given to parents with regard to specific aspects of the education of their child – especially religious education? To what extent does the State seek 'not to offend parental choice' or to 'support parental choice'?

NOTES

1. The work of the Council is developed in four main documents: *Lumen Gentium*, Dogmatic Constitution on the Church; *Gaudium et Spes*, Pastoral Constitution on the Church in the Modern World; *Gravissimus Educationis*, Declaration on Christian Education; and *Dignitatis Humanae*, Declaration on Religious Freedom.

2. Andrew Greeley, *The Catholic Imagination* (Berkeley: University of California Press, 2000). Summary from introduction, although 'God in disguise' is my own term.

3. *Religious Dimension of Education in a Catholic School*, 56.

4. Romans 5:5; Confessions, Book 1, chapter 1.

5. Leo XIII, *Rerum Novarum* (1890–91); Pius XI, *Quadragesimo Anno* (1931); Pius XI, *Divini Redemptoris* (1937), John XXIII, *Mater et Magistra* (1961): John XXIII, *Pacem in Terris* (1963); Paul VI, *Ecclesiam Suam* (1964).

6. *Gaudium et Spes*, 54.

7. Ibid., 4.

8. Ibid., 7, 19–21.

9. Ibid., 7.

10. Ibid., 8.

11. *The Catholic School*, 11.

12. The Church's position on education has been developed in a number of key documents published since the Second Vatican Council: *The Catholic School* (1977); *Lay Catholics in Schools: Witnesses to Faith* (1982); *The Religious Dimension of Education in a Catholic School* (1988); *General Directory for Catechesis* (1997); *The Catholic School on the Threshold of the Third Millennium* (1998); *Consecrated Persons* (2003); *Educating Together in Catholic Schools: A Shared Mission between Consecrated Persons and the Lay Faithful* (2007).

13. *The Catholic School*, 31.

14. *Lay Catholics in Schools: Witnesses to Faith*, 12.

15. *The Catholic School*, 27.

16. Congregation for Catholic Education, Circular Letter to the Presidents of Bishops' Conferences on Religious Education in Schools (2009), 10.
17. *The Catholic School*, 39.
18. *Religious Dimension of Education in a Catholic School*, 54.
19. Ibid., 60–1.
20. *The Catholic School*, 25.
21. *The Catholic School on the Threshold of the Third Millennium*, 9.
22. *The Catholic School*, 35.
23. *The Religious Dimension of Education in a Catholic School*, 51.
24. Ibid., 49.
25. *The Catholic School*, 46.
26. Paul VI, *Evangelii Nuntiandi* (1975), 41, quoting his own *Address to the Members of the Consilium de Laicis* (2 October 1974), AAS 66 (1974), p. 568.
27. *The Catholic School*, 43.
28. Ibid., 53.
29. *The Religious Dimension of Education in a Catholic School*, 40.
30. *Lay Catholics in Schools: Witnesses to Faith*, 33.
31. *Educating Together in Catholic Schools: A Shared Mission between Consecrated Persons and the Lay Faithful*, 47.
32. Ibid., 50.
33. Ibid., 51.
34. *General Directory for Catechesis*, 73.
35. *Religious Dimension of Education in a Catholic School*, 68–9.
36. *The Catholic School*, 57.
37. *Dignitatis Humanae*, 2.
38. Ibid., 10.
39. Ibid., 12.
40. *The Catholic School*, 20.
41. *The Catholic School on the Threshold of the Third Millennium*, 17.
42. *The Catholic School*, 2.
43. *Irish Episcopal Conference, Primary Education in the Future* (2007).
44. *The Religious Dimension of Education in a Catholic School*, 6.
45. Irish Catholic Bishops' Conference, *Catholic Primary Schools: A Policy for Provision into the Future* (Maynooth, 2007).
46. Circular Letter to the Presidents of Bishops' Conferences on Religious Education in Schools, 12.

2

DIVERSITY AND PLURALISM: THE ROLE OF POLITICS

The context of society determines the educational needs of its citizens. Stephen Covey, in *The Eighth Habit*, reflects on different phases in the history of civilisation. He named the first phases as the 'hunter-gatherer', 'settled agrarian' and 'urban industrial'. Each phase was distinguished by a level of production, by requirements of cooperation and differentiation of functions, and also by the knowledge required for success. Each phase had different learning needs and societies adapted to ensure that their members acquired these skills, making certain the survival of the group. Approaches to teaching and learning, the formal role of the teacher and the institutional role of the school changed to meet these needs. Covey claims that we have now entered an 'information age', which heralds a movement away from production (things) to information (people). The focus is on constantly learning, improving and applying new technologies. In the transition to this new age, traditional roles in society have become more transient. People no longer develop their identity around stable work functions; they define themselves in terms of core values and preferences. Covey sees the leadership challenge of this new age as adapting traditional institutions to a more flexible, person-centred approach.

What Covey describes at a personal level can also be seen in large-scale political movements: civil-rights, cultural and political movements associated with the Arab spring of 2010, ethnic and religious groups, feminism and sexual orientation. The rhetoric of these movements focuses on the theme of liberation of the person. It starts with an analysis of the oppression that resulted from stereotyping, violence, exploitation, marginalisation or domination. The antidote to such oppression is proposed as the rising above of the negative script associated with an externally imposed identity and the forging of a more positive statement of that identity, by reclaiming, reframing and transforming the underlying values. Identity has become an important issue in political discourse and brings challenges for models of self, political inclusiveness, solidarity, protest and dissent.

The development of 'identity politics' is one lens through which the exploration of educational provision is viewed. The last chapter described how the identity of Catholic education has developed over the past fifty years, situating that identity in terms of an anthropology that might be institutionalised in an education system and in Catholic schools. In the final section of the chapter, it was recognised that this perspective on the human person, on society, education and schooling is one of many such formulations. Other groups have different anthropologies. Some share a lot of common ground with the Catholic position. Others are radically different.

As different groups emerge who are confident in asserting their identities and in pursuing their own interests, there is a new challenge to society to manage these identities. Frequently, the political agenda is framed as a struggle between dominant elites and oppressed minorities. This approach has the potential for serious fragmentation between different interest groups. A major concern for politics is to ensure a level of social cohesion so that diverse groups can live in harmony.

Just as many groups turn to education as a means of supporting their identities, society also turns to education as a means of promoting attitudes of tolerance, respect and mutual understanding. The education system is seen as both a source of enhancing diversity and also of promoting social cohesion. This can create tensions. This chapter explores the dynamic through which this tension is worked out. This exploration develops around five questions:

- What do people expect of society, and how do they engage with others in society?
- If people are different, and have different ideas, what are the implications of that for society?

- Are there different types of issues that emerge, and do people expect these issues to be handled in a particular way?
- Are there different ways of handling diversity and what are the consequences of these different approaches?
- Who has responsibility in society for promoting diversity and social cohesion?

1. EXPECTATIONS IN A LIBERAL DEMOCRACY

Government in Ireland, along with most Western governments, is described as a liberal democracy. The State is the political community organised around certain values. Broadly speaking, these values focus on cohesion, prosperity and justice. For these values to flourish there must be an infrastructure in which the legitimate plans of individuals, groups and communities can be realised. A society develops different ways to promote and protect these values. For instance, the economy allows citizens to exchange goods and services and develop a particular style of living; the legislature enacts laws that embody an understanding of justice and fairness in how citizens relate to one another; the judicial system ensures that contracts are fulfilled and adjudicates between individuals and groups in matters of dispute to ensure justice.

The formal responsibility for developing this infrastructure belongs to the government. The government takes on executive, legislative, judicial and bureaucratic roles. The term 'government' is sometimes used to refer to the cabinet of ministers that oversees the executive function responsible for developing legislation, promoting order and administering a welfare system. Citizens may also enter into arrangements on a voluntary or informal basis to regulate their own cooperation.

The term 'democracy' is derived from the Greek, 'to rule by the people'. The image is of a group of citizens gathered together discussing what is best for the State, and how they should structure their lives and their cooperation. However, this image is idealistic and is based on ideas from early Greek philosophy and the politics of Athens. As a means of governance, it is only practical with a relatively small group of citizens – and the citizenship of Athens was confined and elitist. Yet the term remains, and has come to signify the involvement of people in influencing political decisions that affect their lives.

A more expansive definition of democracy is 'government of the people, by the people, for the people'. This specifies the goal of politics as a way of organising people through laws and public institutions. This is the focus of government 'of the people'. The definition also develops the complexity of relationships that can exist 'by' and 'for' the people. In general, the term 'by the people' suggests that people participate in the crucial decisions affecting their lives. Yet, in practice, the right to participate in the democratic process is not universal. For instance, voting is limited to adults who do not have an impediment (insanity, etc.). In the past, it was even more limited, when women had no vote, and only those with a certain amount of land could vote.

Direct participation in decision-making is normally infrequent. Our most immediate experience of participation in such direct democracy is when we vote in a referendum. The democratic process is normally conducted through representative democracy. Voters elect representatives who carry out the specialised work of politics on their behalf. The representative character of the elected group is an indirect government 'by the people'. It promotes a division of labour whereby 'the people' are represented by a group with specialised expert knowledge and experience, supposedly giving rise to dispassionate and fairer decisions between competing interests. When elected, those who govern do so for all the people, not just those who elected them. Voters also have regular opportunities to review the performance of politicians and, in a competitive environment, choose their representatives. Regular elections are meant to ensure an affirmation that those who govern are responsible and representative of the wishes of the people. In elections, the focus is on those who will make the decisions, not on the decisions themselves, although these may be linked through election manifestos and promises. What gives this process its democratic character is the accountability of those elected to the people. Public approval or disapproval of a particular government (in an election) takes place in the context of the electorate's beliefs about what the State should be, and how it should be governed. A judgment may be triggered by particular decisions of government, but the judgment is essentially about those who govern.

At the core of the liberal concept in politics is the promotion of individual liberties. This is based on the anthropology that individuals are free to develop their own values without interference, constrained only by the demand that others have the same liberties. It is inevitable that this will give rise to conflicting social philosophies and rival political movements representing the interests of different individuals and groups in a society. These groups articulate popular demands or interests and ensure government responsiveness. The role of the government is to regulate and facilitate these groups, with a view to promoting, protecting and enhancing the maximum amount of individual freedom and choice. The political process is reinforced by the culture of a market economy based on supply and demand, where individuals compete for rewards in buying and selling goods and services. The economy is open to different degrees of regulation – varying from a laissez-faire market with minimum regulation, to a regulated market with intervention to support growth. In a similar way, citizens compete to have their 'identity' needs institutionalised and supported by society.

The political process is dominated by a parliamentary system in which an executive (the cabinet) is responsible to the elected representatives. The powers of the different actors are determined in part by the Constitution, and may have other actors such as a monarch, a president or a second parliamentary chamber. Essential to the operation of such a constitutional parliamentary democracy is the widespread and even distribution of power among different groups, a responsiveness of these groups to their members and a neutral civil service which allows easy access to government. At the core of the process is dialogue. Interest groups present their ideas and demands, and these become part of the deliberations of government, which seeks to respond to conflicting demands. The belief is that the conflict, the dialogue and the decision-making will give rise to the best possible solution for a society. The key requirement for government in making decisions is that it be fair and just, that it not take sides with any one group or give them undue privileges, thus discriminating against another. They seek the best result 'for the people'.

The process of democracy outlined here is an ideal. We have seen many different ways in which this ideal can be frustrated:

• Ideally, the State is the context for justice. However, the State can be an instrument of oppression if its institutions do not respect the dignity of individuals. They become impersonal bureaucracies that dominate or oppress people rather than encourage their participation through subsidiarity, cooperation and solidarity. Totalitarian regimes have been a regular feature of history.

- Some groups seek to impose their will on others without engaging in any form of dialogue. They use violence, or threats of violence, to intimidate others and to impose their will on them. In effect, they deny the distribution of power within society, disenfranchising those who differ from them. This can be particularly devastating in the case of ethnic violence or civil war.

- Small groups in a society may be blocked from participation by the 'tyranny of the majority', where the number desiring a particular outcome is taken as an indication of the desired outcome, rather than seeking a 'win-win' approach that caters for and integrates smaller groups. The power-sharing structures in Northern Ireland, for example, are an attempt to focus on integration of different ideas rather than a strict majority rule.

- Groups can seek to gain advantage for their own position by hiding or distorting information. A common form of political engagement is through propaganda which promotes a particular aspect of the debate. Some groups have resources which, when used in the spread of ideas, give a distorted perspective on an issue.

- Politicians sometimes do not act for the good of all. They can be influenced by pressure groups and it is a regular feature to see such pressure groups present their case in public demonstrations. A particular ethical issue for politicians is to deal with the rewards that can be promised by some groups in a society, enticing them to make decisions that are self-serving, and which promote their chances of re-election.

The existence of distortions is not an argument against a liberal democracy. As the American author Don Marquis said, 'An idea is not responsible for those who believe in it.' This is true for those who are over-zealous in pursuing the goal of democracy and who act in a paternalistic way, deciding that they know what is good for others. It is also true for those who deliberately distort an idea for their own goals. The response to these events is not to abandon the ideal but to protect it. In a liberal democracy, there are checks and balances against activities that frustrate the democratic process. These can work at an international level, through organisations such as the United Nations, and at national level, through an independent judicial system where people have redress for particular actions. Another aspect of the process is the media, where citizens can present ideas, be informed and can also engage in the debate.

The emerging debate on education illustrates aspects of the democratic process. At one level, the debate has focused on the needs of minority groups against a large majority. They have presented their needs with an expectation that these needs will be recognised and acted on. The debate has been carried on at a number of levels – academic and popular, local and national. Individuals and groups have taken the opportunity to present their case in the media, as well as to individual politicians and political parties. In more recent months, there have been opportunities for such groups to participate in formal consultative processes, not only stating their needs but also commenting on possible new structures and proposing other creative solutions. In many ways, the process has sought to promote wide participation 'by the people' in order to discern the democratic will 'of the people' so that a suitable system can be put in place 'for the people'.

2. DIVERSITY AS A VALUE IN A DEMOCRACY

The diversity of a population can be described on any number of characteristics – age, ability, interest, wealth, ethnic origin, language and religion. At its most basic, the concept of diversity is quantitative – it gives a descriptive measure of different characteristics within a community. The granting of Irish citizenship to 2,200 individuals in January 2012 is one aspect of measuring ethnic diversity in Ireland. At that ceremony, the Taoiseach said that the government was processing 22,000 applications for citizenship. In the 2011 census, 544,357 non-Irish nationals lived in the country, an increase of approximately 30 per cent on the previous census. This indicates that Ireland is becoming a more ethnically diverse country.

Another quantitative indicator of diversity reflects religious affiliation. In the 2011 census, over 90 per cent of the population described itself as Christian. There has also been a marked increase in non-Christian religions. A particular focus of many commentators has been the increase in those who indicated that they had 'no religion' or that they were 'atheist' or 'agnostic', or that otherwise did not answer the census question. This is taken as an indication of the growth of a secular society, with this growing group being the largest 'belief group' outside the Catholic Church.

Religion	Number 2006	Number 2011	Per cent 2011
Roman Catholic	3,681,456	3,861,335	84.2
Other Christian	241,474	289,609	6.3
Non-Christian	57,832	87,157	1.9
No Religion	186,318	269,811	5.9
Atheist	929	3,905	0.1
Agnostic	1,515	3,521	0.1
Not answered	70,322	72,914	1.6
	4,239,848	4,589,252	

Table 2.1. The distribution of responses to questions on religious affiliation in the Irish census data for 2006 and 2011.

It is worth noting the difference in the type of information being interpreted in these two sets of figures. The distinctions explored here do not deny an increasing 'secularisation' in Irish society, but simply point to the cautious use of data. With regard to people applying for citizenship, there is a clear movement from non-citizenship to citizenship. The applicant has a verifiable State of origin other than Ireland. However, when individuals categorise themselves as having 'no religion' or fail to respond to the question about religious affiliation, the interpretation is more ambivalent. The category 'no religion' could mean a rejection of a belief in God. It could also mean that the individual believes in God, but has no formal affiliation to an organised faith or denomination. There is also a nuance in the use of language, where people describe themselves as 'spiritual' but not 'religious'. The 'spiritual' self may be based on theism, or may be non-theistic as in, say, Buddhism. Those who see themselves as 'spiritual' could legitimately fill in the census form as 'having no religion'. Also, the failure to answer the question could indicate 'no religion', 'no affiliation to an organised religious group' or 'I do not want to respond to this question.'

A similar ambivalence arises around those who describe themselves as belonging to a particular denomination. There is no indication of the level of their commitment. To use the analogy of golf club membership, there can be pavilion members (those who are affiliated to the club but do not participate in the main activity of playing golf); country members (those who play occasionally); and full members (those who participate fully). These shades of meaning are not available in the 'naturalised citizen' census category, although we can also note different levels of involvement in being a citizen. Some may vote in all elections. Others may vote only occasionally. Others turn out for referenda where the issue is important to them. Others may choose not to vote at all. Categorisation of 'member', 'religious affiliation' and 'citizen' allow for different levels of engagement. The labels are not 'either-or' descriptions and allow for nuances.

Self-assignment on the basis of religious belief is simply that – a description by individuals of their religious identity; it does not describe their attitude to others who profess different religious or philosophical beliefs. Commentators have to be particularly careful in extrapolating from such statements of affiliation what the political stance of people in any one group may be on subjects vaguely related to such affiliation.

The distinction points to an important qualitative dimension in diversity. Most people readily agree that all citizens should have equal access to agreed services within the State, so that any differentiation made on those characteristics that allow for easy quantitative measure – gender, State of origin, age – would be unjust. However, when responding to characteristics that allow for qualitative differences within the different measures, the dynamic becomes more complicated. The demand for different approaches to education is an example of this type of complexity. Individuals may seek help from the education system in promoting their identities, but often the identity that is to be promoted is nuanced and adaptable, worked out in response to abstract ideologies and to the practical demands of living with others.

The political interest may not be in the promotion of particular identities – that is seen as a freedom for the individual to pursue for themselves – but its agenda is more likely to be concerned with the peaceful coexistence of different beliefs, convictions and lifestyles. As a political philosophy, pluralism demands of citizens that they negotiate their legitimate interests in a spirit that acknowledges and respects the diversity of such interests. At the core of the pluralist agenda is the concept of equality of individuals and interests. At a basic level, this means that individuals should not be at any disadvantage because of some characteristic they have, and over which they have no choice

– e.g. quantitative measures such as gender and ethnic origin. More importantly, it focuses on the qualitative dimension and promotes the exercise of individual choice, where individuals have legitimate options. The pluralist system promotes liberty and freedom in making choices between options. Arising from this agenda is the possibility of the full participation of every citizen in public life. It seeks to give equal voice and power to each person to influence the public debate.

3. POLITICAL ISSUES IN A DIVERSE SOCIETY

At the beginning of this chapter, a third question asked about expectations of how different types of interests might be handled in a society. The commitment to individual liberty guarantees a wide range of interests in a society. In practice, individuals find it more effective to pursue their interests if they have the support of others. Numbers are an important factor in successful politics. Therefore, in the public arena, individual actors use resources to influence others to agree with them and help them achieve their interests. These resources may involve incentives related to benefits (money, leisure or other rewards), status (expertise or position) or morality (legitimacy, meaning and purpose). When such interests impact on the public life of society, the role of the State is to facilitate the dialogue between competing interests and to ensure that everyone adheres to the rules of negotiation. Decision-making is based on the practical working out of how diverse interests can co-exist. The focus is mainly on the practical rather than the theoretical. Political philosophers may run seminars on 'What is *the best* way to handle this situation? What is *a good* solution here?' The main concern of the government cabinet meeting is 'What *will work* here? What will satisfy most of the people involved in the dialogue?'

The realm of the theoretical and the practical can be differentiated by the types of questions asked. However, we need to be cautious about seeing them as separate areas. Theorists need to apply their categories to practical situations and show their relevance. Their task is to clarify the value–action relationship. In doing so, people see a link between their actions and a bigger picture, and this affects motivation. Practitioners make practical choices; their task is to justify their choices in terms that make sense to participants and that harness their willingness to work for the implementation of decisions.

This frequently involves linking a practical decision to a more general theoretical framework promoting personal interests within a common vision. The important thing to remember is that the theoretical and the practical are two sides of the one reality. They have a 'both-and' rather than an 'either-or' dimension.

Pluralism reflects diverse and competing centres of power in society. This creates a marketplace for ideas; and different centres of power use their resources to promote ideas linked to their interests. This process gives rise to conflict between competing interests. This section seeks to distinguish types of conflict that arise from diverse interests. There are different approaches to the resolution of these types of conflict, and it is important to recognise the level of the conflict in proposing a political solution.

3.1. CONFLICT ABOUT LEGITIMACY OF INTERESTS

At a basic level, there can be conflict about whether something is a legitimate 'good' and whether it can be pursued. An example of the legitimacy concern can be seen in debates on issues termed 'moral'. As a moral position, protagonists might claim that their position is such that it requires all citizens to live according to its standard. The focus of these protagonists is on the nature or substance of the claim. For instance, in a debate on abortion, one claim is that abortion is not a legitimate choice. The focus here is usually an 'elective' abortion rather than the termination of life in a crisis situation in order to save the life of the mother. The argument is that the undisputed right to life agreed for all citizens should be extended to the person who has not yet been born. From this perspective, abortion denies the basic right of life to a human person, and this fact denies its legitimacy. The opposing view focuses on process. The claim here is that people have different legitimate concepts of the human person and it is not appropriate for the State to make a judgment about which is correct. In this argument, priority is given to the right of each individual to choose according to their beliefs. In both cases, the protagonists who put forward these arguments work from a particular belief system and find the legitimacy and authority of their positions within that system.

Legitimacy is not always debated in terms of absolute moral principles, however. For instance, in the debate on education provision, one argument used against denominational education is that in a republic, the main aim is to educate for citizenship and therefore it is inappropriate for the State to support an organisation (e.g. religion, Church) that claims a different loyalty. The claim here is not about the legitimacy of religious belief or affiliation in itself, but the appropriateness of State support for a particular purpose. Behind this is a particular concept of what is meant by 'republic' and 'citizenship'. The counter-argument to this position affirms religious affiliation as a right of citizenship, and promotes the common ground between the goals of the republic and religion.

In debating political issues, the language used reflects different influences on people's value systems – religious, scientific, political, philosophical and social. Individuals express their views using the language that makes sense to them. However, as the purpose of political debate is to persuade and influence decisions, using 'insider' language (that is, language best understood within a particular tradition) may not be the best strategy. The role of government in such debates is to frame issues according to a public language. Values expressed in terms of personal beliefs are reframed in terms of individual rights, freedoms or duties as citizens. What gives weight to an argument in the public arena is not so much the source of the belief but the degree to which that belief finds common ground with the criteria of a public language.

In moral and ethical debates, the question is often 'Is this position right or wrong, good or bad?' If there is agreement on the answer, then there is no conflict. Disagreements, however, give rise to political problems, for often the different positions are mutually exclusive. In a liberal democracy, there can be different expectations on the role of the State in dealing with this type of issue. One expectation is that the State should not make a judgment about the morality of any position, but seek a compromise that allows different viewpoints to co-exist. A second expectation is that the State would defend a particular worldview that represents a majority or an agreed anthropology. Efforts have been made to forge this anthropology in human rights covenants. The next chapter will return to the way in which dialogue takes place in the language of the common good and human rights.

3.2. CONFLICT OVER DISTRIBUTION OF 'GOODS'

A second type of conflict arises where there is general agreement about the goods to be pursued, but there is disagreement about its distribution. This happens when the goods being pursued by individuals is limited and not everyone can benefit from it, or at least not to the extent they want. Distribution issues arise in a number of ways.

The first occurs where the goods are mutually exclusive – when two legitimate goods cannot exist together. For instance, you cannot satisfy the demand that a school provides for religious education of a particular type and the demand that there be no religious education in that same school. The compromise position that when religion is taught, those who do not want it can be exempt, only partially satisfies the desires of those who do not want religion in their child's school.

A second issue arises when there is competition for a limited number of goods, resulting in some people getting what they want and others not. This can be thought of as a 'win–lose' situation. A common example of this type of distribution is in the area of employment. If a company advertises for a position, it engages in a selection process. To do this, it sets criteria for the selection and then judges individual applicants according to these criteria. The issue at stake here is that the distribution of some goods in society is not based on equality between people, but on some other principle – achievement, merit, talent. In general, there is agreement that the goods are limited (there is only one position in the company) and that some distribution must be made (only one person can be chosen from among the applicants). The political issue in the distribution of goods is the choice of criteria on how they are to be distributed and ensuring that the criteria are fair and applied correctly.

A similar approach can be seen in the field of education in the selection of students for third-level places. This is more complex than the employment situation, in that there are many different types of courses available to students and the same student meets the criteria for a number of these courses. However, the places available in third-level institutions are limited and, in particular, the number of applications for places on prestigious courses outweighs the number of places available. The allocation of places is based on a points system, rewarding achievement in the Leaving Certificate. Disagreement can arise over the validity of the criteria used, or more frequently, on how those criteria are applied. It has been suggested that success in the subjects examined in the Leaving Certificate is not a good basis for judging suitability for particular third-level courses and careers. The argument goes that the purpose and design of the different Leaving Certificate courses is such that examination success is not predictive of success in particular career pathways. This argument questions the legitimacy of the system. A different type of argument focuses on the operation of the system. It has been suggested that for some courses, applicants who have studied certain subjects for the Leaving Certificate, for instance higher-level mathematics, should have bonus points for entry to courses in, say, engineering. The focus of this argument is on how the criteria should be applied and the fairness of that application. In both arguments, there is a general acceptance that there must be some distribution – by limiting access to the courses – and that merit or achievement should, in some way, be involved. The politics of such a situation is to find as much agreement as possible on the criteria to be used, and then to find ways that are 'transparent' in how they are applied.

A third distribution problem is when there are goods to be distributed throughout a system, and different participants in the system compete for a share in these goods. Unlike the mutually exclusive goods, or the selection process that exists in employment or the allocation of third-level places, in this situation everyone is eligible for something. One instance of this is the development of a national budget, where there are limited resources to be distributed and different services, such as education, health and social welfare, must compete for these resources. The role of politics is to make judgments between the different needs. In general, there is no disagreement that supporting these services is a good thing. The question is not 'Should these areas be supported?' but rather 'How much support should these areas be given?' Once the allocation is made at national level, there is then competition at departmental level. In education, there may be competition between primary, second-level and third-level sectors for funding; there may be competition for money to be allocated to teacher salaries, to particular programmes or to capital investment. The demands for such funds may be accompanied by requirements (criteria) of productivity, effectiveness, usefulness, etc. For instance, a particular issue in Irish education is the funding of small schools. Ireland has a high proportion of small, one-to-four teacher schools serving rural communities, and these are expensive to maintain. The competition for funding for these schools involves complex political criteria relating to economic efficiencies, educational issues and the social benefits to a local community.

3.3. CONFLICT OVER CONSEQUENCES

A third type of conflict arises where there is general agreement about the legitimacy of what is being pursued by different individuals and there is also general agreement about the process to be used in arriving at decisions, but when the decision is implemented, individuals feel aggrieved that their legitimate interests are not being met. One example of this in education can be seen in the operation of admission policies to schools which do not have sufficient places for all the applicants. This requires that some selection be made and some parents or students do not get their preferred choice of school. There are some differences between this situation and a conflict over scarce resources because, in this context, every child has the right to a school place. This right is not being denied; the issue is the availability of a place in a particular school of choice.

In seeking a place for their child, parents are pursuing a legitimate interest. In designing an Admissions Policy, schools develop criteria to adjudicate between the legitimate interests of all the parents who apply for a place for their children. In doing so, they also negotiate their own right to apply criteria that promote the characteristic spirit of the school. These rights are enshrined in legislation. The operation of such an Admissions Policy may not be contentious over a period of time, as the school may have sufficient places for all applicants. However, because of changed demographics, there are now parents who find that their individual interests are thwarted. It is recognised that there are limited places in the school and that some selection must be made. The school acts according to agreed, legitimate criteria, and it applies these in an unbiased manner. The parents, in pursuit of their legitimate goals, now seek a change in either the criteria or in the way they are applied, so as to give them a better chance to realise their goals. In effect, they see a conflict in the balance of power between the status quo of the current Admissions Policy and their ability to realise their interests.

4. RESPONDING TO DIVERSITY

A second approach to looking at the issues that arise in a liberal democracy is to use Etzioni's classification of goals.[1] Etzioni described three types of goals – order, economic and cultural – each of which has a different substantive focus and importance in the norms of a group. The three goals are normally associated with typical approaches to the use of power, and often give rise to particular modes of engagement by group members. The different dynamics that develop around the use of power and responses to that use have implications for the quality of relationship in diverse society:

- With order goals, the most common use of power is what Etzioni termed **coercive**. This involves the use of threat or penalty to ensure compliance, and typically participants adapt by a sense of alienation, seen in a 'them–us' language which can have varying levels of intensity.
- With economic goals, power is used in a **remunerative** way – power-holders reward participants according to a particular scale for performing their functions. The typical response to this type of power is calculative and utilitarian, where people measure the cost-benefits of compliance.
- With culture goals, the use of power is **symbolic**. This strives to place a moral imperative to behave in a particular way by appealing to the value inherent in the behaviour, and the desired adaptation is commitment.

Etzioni's description of organisations postulated a necessary congruence between goals, use of power and the response of participants. In the absence of congruence, the success of achieving certain goals is likely to be transitory. Organisations might try to implement cultural goals through coercive means. This might promote behaviour modification, but any change would regress when the threat of sanction was lifted because the underlying values were not internalised.

It is interesting to reflect on the impact of compulsion (coercion) and extra rewards (remuneration) on the cultural goals with regard to the Irish language in the period between 1922 and 1984. At that time, it was necessary to have a passing grade in Irish in order to be awarded a Leaving Certificate, no matter how well you did in other subjects.

There were 'remunerative' benefits in marking schemes and in financial grants to schools that taught through Irish. Study of the Irish language is still compulsory in order to be recognised as a student, and a pass in the subject is still necessary for entry into some third-level courses and the public service. The question is how successful this approach has been in promoting a commitment to a Gaelic culture. This can be contrasted with the success of changing from a Gaelic-speaking to an English-speaking culture in the nineteenth century. There were certainly some coercive practices (such as the *bata scóir*)[2] but the main determining factors were practical and symbolic, in that all official business was done through English and knowledge of English became a valuable asset in the emigration that accompanied the Famine period. A similar reflection can be applied to the changing levels of commitment to religious institutions. It can be argued that a culture of compliance in terms of practice and doctrine did not sustain a commitment to internal norms and beliefs, and that the mismatch between cultural goals and coercive methods has led to alienation of many people from organised religion. A similar mismatch can be seen in the popular analysis of the development of the current economic crisis, where the regulatory system (coercive methods) did not impact on ethical actions (cultural norms).

Etzioni's typology of cultures within organisation gives a useful template for reflecting on different approaches to diversity, as it is based on three constituent elements: the goals to be achieved; the methods used to promote it; and the impact of these methods on the participants. This section examines three possible approaches to diversity: assimilation, accommodation and integration.

4.1. ASSIMILATION: TREATING EVERYONE THE SAME AND IGNORING DIFFERENCES

One approach to diversity is a form of denial of the point of diversity. It believes that there is no basis for distinguishing between people and that everyone should be treated in the same way. The most common instances of this approach relate to order goals. For example, when visitors come to this country, they are expected to drive on the left. It would be chaotic to accommodate people who want to drive on the right as a mark of respect for the culture they came from. Similarly, people are expected to do business in an Irish currency. However, the common currency of the euro and foreign exchange agencies facilitate these visitors. Similarly, people who work in Ireland are expected to pay Irish taxes and follow Irish laws. No distinction is made between people in the application of these rules. All are expected to conform. Assimilation has also been used with social and cultural goals. Perhaps the most notable historical instance of this approach was the 'melting pot' assimilation of different ethnic groups in the United States, symbolised by the motto *e pluribus unum* (from the many, one). This was elaborated on in a letter by Theodore Roosevelt shortly before his death in January 1919, which reflected his approach to the process of Americanisation during his time as president:

> In the first place we should insist that if the immigrant who comes here in good faith becomes an American and assimilates himself to us, he shall be treated on an exact equality with everyone else, for it is an outrage to discriminate against any such man because of creed, or birthplace, or origin. But this is predicated upon the man's becoming in very fact an American, and nothing but an American ... There can be no divided allegiance here. Any man who says he is an American, but something else also, isn't an American at all. We have room for but one flag, the American flag ... We have room for but one language here, and that is the English language ... and we have room for but one sole loyalty and that is a loyalty to the American people.[3]

Three perspectives are notable in this letter. The first is the recognition of the fact of diversity based on creed, birthplace and origin and the need to be respectful of these characteristics. As discussed with regard to the census returns in Ireland, this is quantitative data about the person. The second perspective focuses on qualitative issues; the good enjoyed by the 'insiders' is seen as being better and preferable to what the 'outsiders' bring and therefore the duty of the 'outsiders' is to adapt their desires to those of the 'insiders'. A third perspective refers to the responsibility for the assimilation; at one level, the onus is placed on the 'outsider' to adapt, to learn new ways and to develop a new set of loyalties, a new language. The 'insiders' take a passive role by treating everyone the same, as they expect the 'outsiders' to live up to the norms already in place.

The realisation of 'insider' norms represents a coercive use of power. This can be aggressive or benign. The aggressive approach targets particular groups or practices, seeking conformity to the norms of the dominant group. The assumption is that (a) the dominant group will fully accept members of new minority into the group, although in practice they may always remain second-class citizens, and (b) the minority members are prepared to cede previous attitudes and practices in order to be members of the main group. In mathematical terms, the equation has been given as: $A + B + C = A$ (where A is the dominant group and B and C are minorities). Assimilation can be promoted by positive reinforcement of 'insider' norms. For Roosevelt, the artefacts of reinforcement included the flag, the language and the oath of allegiance. These artefacts were common in the public school system. Assimilation can also be promoted by negative reinforcement, where certain practices, especially the maintenance of a home language, are ridiculed or prohibited. Therefore, if one wants to participate, one has to adapt fully to the norms of the group, and there is no tolerance for other practices.

A more benign approach is to ignore differences and allow a gradual assimilation, letting people adjust over time. The process works on trade-offs. In the history of migration, integration into the new society often takes place through the children and grandchildren of the migrants, with the first generation being slower to relinquish cultural and linguistic norms. The key to this approach is the importance of belonging. Maslow recognised the essential social element of human existence, showing how belonging as a need emerges as soon as the physiological and safety needs have been guaranteed. Rather than seeing these needs being sublimated by moving higher up a hierarchy, Hersey focused on the distribution of these needs in a person's life, and concluded that belonging needs are a core element of human motivation at all times.[4]

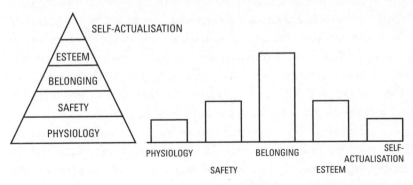

Figure 2.1. Maslow's Hierarchy of Needs (left), and Hersey's view of the distribution of these needs (right).

In practice, the process of assimilation is not always easy, with tensions arising on both sides. New groups are often seen as competitors for social rewards rather than as partners in achieving common goals; this results in a lack of acceptance of the minority group by the majority. For minority groups seeking full participation, focus is often on their participation in particular areas of life – economy (employment, social welfare, housing), politics (representation), education – but demands some element of separation in terms of family, religion and recreation.

4.2. Accommodation: Transaction and Structural Responses

The cornerstone of accommodation is a positive tolerance of differences. There is an acceptance of the existence of autonomous groups within society and a reluctance to enforce a particular 'meta-narrative' on others. This aims to protect the diverse characteristics of individuals and groups, and to ensure that they are not discriminated against. One approach is to find a middle ground between competing groups, where each party cedes some of their demands in order to ensure freedom to pursue other interests. At its most unsatisfactory level, this is characterised as finding the lowest common denominator and setting that as a standard. It results in neither party being entirely satisfied with the outcome. Another approach is a commitment to putting structures and incentives in place to ensure that all groups, especially minority groups, have a voice in decision-making. The voting system of Proportional Representation aims at ensuring that smaller groups in a society have a better opportunity to be elected. The development of power sharing structures in Northern Ireland in 1998 represents another approach to ensuring voice and representation. Quota systems have been applied in some public service recruitment policies (Police Service of Northern Ireland, focusing on Protestant and Catholic applicants, gender representation on Boards of Directors of State or semi-State bodies). Some of these initiatives are enshrined in law, reflecting a new awareness of individual rights.

One outcome of such initiatives can be seen as capacity building. This provides an infrastructure for diverse groups to participate in society and to realise their goals. The focus is on opportunity. For the most part, the initiative still rests with individuals to pursue their own goals. For various historical or social reasons, including discrimination or repression, some groups may find it difficult to use the infrastructure to their advantage. This can give rise to a process of affirmative action, a process that is often referred to as 'levelling the playing field'. This process does not give distinct and separate rights to particular groups, but develops ways of helping these groups to achieve their legitimate interests by the effective use of rights that all groups possess. The focus of affirmative action is to improve actual participation.

One of the goals of education provision is to have equality within the system. At a basic level, this means ensuring that each child has a school place and can avail of education. In practice, this is achieved. However, for various historical and social reasons, the provision of access (equality of opportunity) does not guarantee that people will take up that opportunity (equality of consumption) or that they will share in the benefits that derive from educational credentials (equality of achievement). There is therefore a demand that people who find it difficult to use their resources in turning the potential of access into the reality of achievement, should get special help to do so. This is seen as a means of empowering people by increasing their social and educational capital. The practical manifestation of this is in grants and programmes for those who are classified as disadvantaged, or who have special educational needs. The aim is to redistribute, within the system, the power and rewards associated with educational achievement.

In theory, the time frame of affirmative action is limited. It is expected that the initiatives will bring about a greater level of equality and then not be needed. However, this gives rise to tensions. Often, designating groups as eligible for affirmative action institutionalises differences and reinforces a degree of separatism which makes reconciliation harder. In some cases, it may promote conflict between groups, making compromise difficult. Groups who benefit from affirmative action may see artefacts (programmes, grants) used as entitlements rather than as means to an end. Individuals not included in the affirmative action may resent the benefits accruing to others, seeing an injustice to themselves. For instance, in a meritocratic system, allocating some places at university or in employment on the basis of gender, ethnic background or some other factor other than an assessment of competence (merit) is seen as unjust.

4.3. INTEGRATION: TRANSFORMATION OF CULTURE

Culture is the framework within which a society finds its identity in relation to other communities. It frames how the world is seen, and incorporates values of how to behave and relate to others. Nations were once seen as stable monocultures; however, globalisation, migration and travel increased communication, and the various crises associated with economics and climate change have all contributed to an increasing interdependence of cultures. This, in turn, has focused attention on the multicultural nature of society itself, with an increased awareness of the diversity of groups within society. This diversity brings challenges about how to maintain a cohesive society which integrates different groups who live in peace with one another, working as partners in a common cause. Whereas the image associated with assimilation is the melting pot, the image that captures the values of integration is the 'salad bowl'. This image seeks to capture the whole rather than focus on individual parts. Each of the individual ingredients contributes to the final product, the result being greater than the sum of these individual parts. The underlying concept is that diversity enriches a society; it presupposes that, if people learn from one another, they will be richer on a personal level and society itself will be more cohesive.

The key to promoting this type of society is building understanding and dialogue. It is based on the belief that everyone is of equal value. It develops by respecting the culture, beliefs and interests of others and gives rise to participation and a sense of belonging. For this to happen, groups need to have a robust sense of identity that values its own traditions yet is open to new ideas. This comes with a trust that civic and political systems work fairly and effectively. In this context, new groups are welcomed with confidence. Citizens focus on the benefits brought by new groups – skills, economic activity, cultural ideas and links. They are not threatened by differences. Integration captures the best of what existed in the past and is open to new developments. This approach is transformative, as the experience of working with others gives rise to new norms that guide relationships and cooperation in the future.

The picture presented of an integrated multicultural society is an ideal. New groups are often welcome in a time of economic prosperity, where their contribution to the overall welfare of the economy is appreciated. In harsher economic times, the presence of 'outsider' groups may give rise to resentment in the competition for benefits, reverting to 'them–us' thinking, where the best one can hope for is tolerance and non-violence. In its optimistic projection, government is seen as being in an interactive dialogue with civil society. It promotes a tolerant, multicultural society through dialogue and participation; it promotes opportunities for dialogue between groups and ensures equality of opportunity and of outcome by enhancing the capacity of citizens; it combats any form of discrimination that might hinder these goals and seeks to remove obstacles to integration. For their part, citizens support the democratic values, comply with the law and are willing to participate in dialogue. Citizens are active rather than passive in the political process.

5. RESPONSIBILITY FOR DIVERSITY

In every society, different interests develop, and individuals and groups have a legitimate expectation that their particular interests will be dealt with in a fair way. Where the vision of society is that of a democracy, there is an expectation that all groups will have an equal right to participate in society. This requires that there are processes by which different interest groups can be heard, and through which their demands are dealt with. This section explores how different individuals, groups, institutions and governments assume roles and responsibility for promoting and responding to diversity.

5.1. INDIVIDUALS AND GROUPS

Individuals have a responsibility for diversity and pluralism in the way they behave towards others. The first responsibility of each person is to accord respect and tolerance to others and not to discriminate against them or treat them badly on the basis of 'difference'. In their pursuit of their own interests, they must also be willing to engage in a respectful way with others who hold diverse interests.

Within civil society, groups form to represent the different interests of some citizens. An essential freedom for individuals to pursue their own interests is the freedom to associate with others of like mind and to support one another in legitimate pursuits. Examples of such groups are political parties, trade unions, churches, support groups and clubs. These groups do not exhibit a full range of pluralism within the group. Their very purpose is to promote a particular interest. In order to do this effectively, there is a restriction on the level of diversity the group can tolerate. These groups naturally restrict membership to those who share their interests. They determine criteria for admission and develop rules and procedures for the operation of the group. These restrictions are based around ideas, beliefs and goals. They cannot be based on discrimination against people. Thus, a political party may restrict membership in terms of political philosophy, but must be open to all people on an ethnic, gender, linguistic, religious or sexual orientation basis.

The existence of such groups is not anti-pluralist or anti-democratic in itself. These groups are part of a pluralist and democratic process. The obligation of the group is to conduct its business in a fair and legitimate manner and to pursue objectives that are not subversive to the values of democracy and pluralism. In their external dealings, they must be open to the process of dialogue with other groups. In this regard, many large companies have a Corporate Responsibility and Public Affairs Department, which oversees diversity issues in recruitment, suppliers, marketing and public relations and ensures compliance with legislation. Their internal organisation will seek to integrate people of different backgrounds into the organisation. This will be seen in:

- **Access, opportunity and outcomes:** Membership of the organisation will be open to all. There will be no discrimination with regard to the rewards offered by the organisation.

- **Recognition and respect:** The institution will be a place that is conducive to different groups to conduct business, embracing the dignity of each person in the workplace. People will be treated with respect and differences will be recognised and valued, not just tolerated. There will be an understanding of different cultural requirements, and the impact of culture on individual attitudes and behaviours. This positive culture will be seen in the physical environment and in policies and procedures, as well as the relationships between people.
- **Building relationships:** In a pluralist organisation, relationships are based on support, respect and trust, rather than on legal requirements. Such an organisation invests in developing integration through good communication that prevents bullying and discrimination. It promotes positive experiences for all and constantly reviews policies to ensure that (a) there are no inequalities in the treatment of different groups, and (b) where inequalities exist they do not persist.

5.2. GOVERNMENT AND PUBLIC INSTITUTIONS

Many business organisations see the benefits of encouraging cultural diversity. Multi-national businesses benefit from having a greater understanding of different cultures in promoting themselves in different countries. Similarly, having a workforce that reflects the cultures of the client base can make an organisation attractive. Others see their commitment to diversity in terms of a civic responsibility and as a way of developing positive relationships in a local community.

The day-to-day work of government is carried out by public institutions, mainly the Civil Service. In representing the State, these institutions play an important role in promoting diversity, both in their own operation and in the service they provide to society. Such public organisations will be expected to reflect the criteria for inclusive and diverse organisations outlined above, thus:

- There will be a conscious effort to ensure that participation in the organisation reflects and is representative of different groups in society.
- Institutions will be encouraged that give independent assessment of diversity issues to the government. These include organisations such as the Equality Commission and the Human Rights Commission.

At times, organisations are slow to respond to diversity issues. It is often only as a result of a crisis or a challenge to their practice that they become aware of issues. It is in this area of contention that people will turn to government for help in resolving conflicts. This will happen in two ways:

- **Specifying rights of individuals and groups:** This will often give rise to legislation so that individuals or groups may claim redress if they have been treated unfairly and principles of diversity have not been upheld.
- **By putting enabling structures in place to promote diversity:** These may include incentives for organisations to promote diversity within the organisation, or they may seek to empower groups who have been disadvantaged to avail of entitlements open to them.

The political agenda is set by the interests of individuals and groups within society, and their expectation that their interests will be catered for. One approach is for individuals to exercise the liberty to pursue these interests. A second is to seek public support to pursue these interests. The education debate in Ireland is an example of this dynamic, characterised as it is by the emergence of different approaches to education and a conflict with the status quo, where most of the schools have been provided by the Churches and there has been a major shift in the philosophy of education to encompass a stronger return on the economic investment of the State. The debate focuses on different dimensions of education policy – order, economic and cultural goals.

At a school level, students are socialised into the norms of the school as an organisation involved in the orderly occupation and organisation of large numbers of people. Order goals are achieved through expectations and regulations for student behaviour in classroom performance, production and participation. These are reinforced through rules and directives and the formal use of sanctions in disciplinary structures. The education system is also part of the order goals of the State. Education is compulsory up to a certain age and the State places obligations on parents with regard to the education of their children. The education system is also a mechanism by which the State regulates the entry of young people into the workforce or the welfare system. A key issue in the management of these order goals, both within institutions and as part of the system, is to ensure that individual rights and choices are respected. Disputes about order goals normally give rise to a discussion of consequences, when individuals find that legitimate procedures within the system or the school have unforeseen and perhaps unwanted consequences for them, and they seek a change of the status quo.

Schools are also involved in economic goals. Under the Education (Welfare) Act (2000), one of the charges made to the National Education Welfare Board was:

> To promote and foster in society, and in particular in families, an appreciation of the benefits to be derived from education, in particular as respects the physical, intellectual, emotional, social, cultural and moral development of children, and of the social and economic advantages that flow there from.

Education is seen as a benefit to the individual. The purpose of the Education (Welfare) Act was to put measures in place to increase school attendance, participation and retention. Although the rhetoric associated with this approach outlines a wide range of benefits to the individual resulting from staying in school, there is a strong focus on the economic benefits as this is linked with better employment prospects. The methods used can be classified, in Etzioni's terms, as calculative. Extra rewards such as enhanced capitation grants are paid to schools to provide extra services for people who are at risk, making staying in school more attractive to them. These include benefits such as school meals, school-book grants and family involvement through the Home School Community Liaison service. There is a particular focus on developing literacy and numeracy skills and a dedicated pathway to higher education. A similar economic model is also used in promoting science subjects within the curriculum. These subjects are seen as being most beneficial in developing the economy, and so bonus points are offered to students who study them. Within secondary schools, the diversity of interests and academic ability is catered for in providing a wide range of programmes and subjects for students to choose from, and also in providing these subjects at different levels. Debates about these issues in education usually occur in the area of distribution – the adequacy of provision for particular needs.

Schools are also agents of socialisation. They are, along with the family, a key agent in the transmission of cultural values and identity. The cultural goals of the education system are promoted through the curriculum. For the most part, the curriculum is set at a national level, and the government plays a role in validating the cultural focus of the curriculum in the compulsory study of the Irish language. At one level, the debate focuses on the legitimacy of the curriculum – the content of what is taught. There are issues with the teaching of religion, the balance between the humanities and science and whether some subjects related to citizenship should be compulsory. At another level, the focus is more on options that are given within the curriculum to cater for diverse needs or on the effectiveness of the curriculum in producing desired results in literacy and numeracy.

Students' experiences of diversity are also influenced by the organisational culture of the school – its hidden curriculum. Cultural and economic goals are reinforced through the reward system, which recognises achievement in academic, sporting, cultural and service activities. Goals can be reinforced through extra-curricular activities such as drama, sport, clubs, tours and exchange programmes. It is within this cultural framework that the debate on the appropriateness of the curriculum takes place.

There are many different perspectives on the legitimacy, distribution and consequences of decisions about education and schooling. This gives rise to diverse interests with regard to the education system. It is one thing for the government to promote the liberty of these groups to pursue their interests; it is something else to mediate between these interests and to actively support them from the public purse. Typically, questions about the governmental role in educational provision focus on issues of legitimacy and distribution:

• If parents are the principal educators, on what basis can a government require certain aspects of education, either in amount or in content? In that context, are schools to be considered 'public institutions' and what degree of government control will exist in terms of (a) the management of schools and (b) the curriculum?

Will the government promote diversity in different types of schools or will it seek to provide a 'one size fits all' approach to schools?

- In terms of the curriculum and the formation of citizens, to what degree may individuals opt out of the public system and undertake 'private' education? And on what basis may this be done – religious affiliation, particular teaching methods, alternative certification, social reasons (schools run for profit)? What are the implications for the size and efficiency of schools, and therefore their number and location?

- In terms of particular aspects of the curriculum, can students 'opt out' of that aspect of study, and on what basis may such a decision be made? For instance, the only compulsory subject in the Irish school system is the Irish language. On what basis might parents opt not to have their child learn Irish? Where conscience is cited as a reason, what constitutes a philosophical position that is linked to conscience and how is this distinguished from more frivolous claims linked to attitudes or opinions?

In seeking to influence decisions in these matters, interest groups use a rhetoric based on the 'common good' or 'individual rights'. In Chapter 1, in discussing Catholic education, there was frequent mention of the common good of society, and the contribution of both the religious worldview and the Catholic school to it. The argument focused on the legitimacy of the denominational approach within society. The documents also focused on the rights of parents to educate their children in a particular way, and the need to provide for that desire by making Catholic schools available. The focus here is on distribution within the system. The question of rights was also raised in looking at the consequences of particular policies, especially in the support given to parents to make their choice real, and also in the quality of religious education that is provided within State schools. This focus on the legitimacy of different positions and demands for access to appropriate provision can also be seen in other approaches to education. The next chapter will examine the way in which the language of the 'common good' and 'individual rights' is used in promoting these positions.

NOTES

1. Amitai Etzioni, *Modern Organizations* (Englewood Cliffs, N.J.: Prentice-Hall, 1964).
2. The *bata scóir*, or 'tally stick', was a device used in primary schools. Students were forbidden to use the Irish language during the day. A 'tick' was notched on the stick for every word of Irish that they uttered during the school day and they received a corresponding punishment at the end of the day for same.
3. Cited in J. F. Healy, *The Sociology of Group Conflict and Change*, sixth edition (Thousand Oaks, CA: SAGE Publications, 2012), Chapter 2.
4. Paul Hersey and Kenneth H. Blanchard, *The Essentials of Situational Leadership: Theories, Concepts, Applications* (New Jersey: Leadership Studies Productions, 1980).

3

THE LANGUAGE OF POLITICAL DEBATE: THE COMMON GOOD AND INDIVIDUAL RIGHTS

Political rhetoric in the West promotes the supremacy of democracy as a form of government. It presents a vision of empowered citizens, each with equal opportunity to participate in the political process and to influence decisions that affect them. There is an assumption of active engagement in public discourse, leading to well-informed decisions that are responsive to the needs of citizens in an inclusive way. The government 'of the people, by the people, for the people' is seen as the best way to respect the dignity of every individual. This rhetoric is also used to justify political sanctions and other interventions against totalitarian states where liberties are not available to citizens.

Western triumphalism is tempered by levels of disaffection with political institutions within democratic states. Recent political and economic crises have given rise to a marked cynicism about politics and politicians, which has had a negative effect on how people see their commitment to democratic values. Many feel that traditional parties and institutions have ceased to take their interests into account. They respond by placing a strong focus on those interests rather than on a common ideal. The introduction to this book quoted comments by John Waters and Fintan O'Toole on the political process in Ireland. Waters focused on flawed models of progress and freedom and a discourse dominated by unchallenged and uncritical opinions; O'Toole promoted the reinvention of Irish democracy based on the rediscovery of the rights and duties of citizens. This critique of politics is not unique to Ireland, and it is often posed as a tension between political philosophies of the 'common good' and 'individual rights'.

Robert Samuelson wrote in *Newsweek* about the US economy: 'We face a choice between a society where people accept modest sacrifices for a common good or a more contentious society where group selfishly protect their own benefits.'[1] Daniel Callahan, writing on the healthcare situation in the US, claimed that what was needed was to replace the current 'ethic of individual rights' with an 'ethic of the common good'.[2] Clifford Longley, writing in the *Tablet* on the European bailout plan, contrasted the European Union's commitment to the 'common good' that is at the heart of the treaty, with the UK's commitment to laissez-faire economics:

> Many on the European continent blame the Anglo-Saxon free-market economies, and especially their hubs in Wall Street and the City of London, for the breakdown of the global banking system in 2008. And they increasingly blame them for the series of sovereign debt crises that have driven one European Union country after another to seek bailouts, backed by drastic austerity programmes. They see, or think they see, Anglo-American financiers in London and New York gambling huge stakes on European economic failure, for the sake of profit at any cost.[3]

The point here is not to agree or disagree with these analyses, but to point to the rhetoric that puts the 'common good' and 'liberal politics' in opposition.

The language of the common good and of individual rights forms the basis for much of the debate on education, with particular reference to denominational education. Chapter 1 outlined the Catholic approach to education. This has many references to the common good, both in terms of the contribution that the specific Catholic worldview can make to society, and the fact that the aim of Catholic education is, among other things, to prepare students for service to their communities. The appeal to the common good is a claim for the legitimacy of the worldview. There are also claims about the right to provide for the distributive good of Catholic education, in its availability to those who want it, and that it be available at reasonable costs. At the core of the argument is the right of parents to choose the type of education they want for their child.

The language of rights and the common good is also used by other education interest groups. The patron body Educate Together presents a philosophy of education that aims at meeting the philosophical position of parents who either want to have no religion in their child's education, or who prefer to have a multi-denominational approach to education. Their position that this is a valid option within the system is widely accepted. In the campaign for changes to the patronage system in primary schools in Ireland, Paul Rowe of Educate Together spoke of the need to 'minimise the deeply worrying infringements of the human and intellectual rights of families' that results from the present distribution.[4] He also appealed to the 'moral obligation of all patrons' to find a solution – an appeal to the Catholic Church to divest their patronage of some schools in favour of Educate Together for the common good:

> Such choice [of different school types] will benefit all in Irish education and society. It is no benefit to Catholic education to have a growing minority of unwilling attendees. In fact, it must be acknowledged that the future health and vibrancy of the denominational option requires that such a choice be available in as many locations as there is viable parental demand.[5]

The question of rights is asserted rhetorically as there is no evidence that any rights are being infringed, although some people may not enjoy the full liberty they have. The position here is a legitimate advocacy position for a particular approach to fulfilling rights. The appeal to the common good is also an advocacy position for the role of Educate Together, even if it does correspond broadly with the Catholic analysis of the situation in Ireland and with their policy perspectives.

The concern in this chapter is not so much to look at arguments that arise in the education debate. This is the focus of the later chapters of the book. Here the focus will be on the language used, especially the language of the common good and of rights. The questions arise from a suspicion that people understand and use the terms in different ways, giving rise to confusion and frustration. For some, the term 'the common good' is the positive basis for political action; whereas for others it is a threat that they will have to sacrifice personal freedoms for an ideology they do not believe in. Others focus on rights language in the same way – as threat or promise. This chapter examines the philosophical understanding of the terms and review how the terms have acquired different meanings over time. It is hoped that the clarification of the terms will serve as a basis for further analysis of the debate in later chapters. The final section of the chapter will look to ways in which the terms might contribute to a fruitful discourse.

I. THE COMMON GOOD

The term 'the common good' has a long history in political thought. This section will trace a brief history and show how the term has developed different meanings over time and the problems that arise from this usage.

I.I. THE CONTEXT OF THE COMMON GOOD

The common good is a notion that originated over two thousand years ago in the writings of Plato and Aristotle. It became the standard approach in political philosophy and was developed in the writings of Augustine and Thomas Aquinas. The common good is seen as the cornerstone of Catholic social teaching, although the term has a wider application in political philosophy. The concept is to be understood as a development of the concept of 'goods'.

The 'good' is what all things desire (Aristotle). At one level, the good is 'anything of benefit'. However, Aristotle enshrined happiness as the central purpose of human life, and a goal in itself. Happiness is an internal condition, which will only exist when it corresponds to an external condition. By reflecting on our actions, we can know which particular actions and external goods make us happiest. In this way, we come to understand the good of individual choices and desires in terms of their contributions to higher goods, such as happiness. We come to know that true happiness lies in the virtuous and just life.

'Common goods' arise from the social nature of the human person. Individuals can achieve their personal good only through the cooperation of others. A common good is over and above the good of individuals in a group; it is the condition that grounds the cooperation of members, thus enabling each individual to achieve his personal 'good'. Material goods contribute to individual happiness. In a group context, the fair distribution of these goods is a 'zero-sum' exercise; the amount to be distributed is finite, and the more one person gets, the less is available for others. Other common goods are immaterial – friendship, knowledge, culture, art, music. An individual's possession of these goods is not diminished by their distribution within the group. Thus friendship and knowledge increase in a society when shared.

The welfare of the State is an example of a complex common good to be achieved by citizens, as it involves both material and immaterial goods. At a general level, it involves peace, security and prosperity. In a modern State, it supposes a just legal and political system, effective public safety and security, accessible education, health and welfare systems, as well as an economic system oriented to growth that allows for meaningful and rewarding employment. At local level, individuals cooperate with one another to promote shared interests – economic, leisure, psychological and social. Examples of this type of cooperation may be seen in the family, in membership of clubs and societies, as well as in collaborative philanthropic activities.

The common good is the all-embracing good that the different common goods both contribute to and participate in. Aristotle distinguished three types of knowledge – theoretical, productive and practical. These give rise to different levels of appreciation of the common good: theoretical knowledge led to contemplation of the unchanging and eternal truths; productive knowledge focused on the needs of daily life and involved the 'how to' of creating artefacts for improved living conditions; practical knowledge was concerned with how to live and act – it involved ethics (which focused on the individual) and politics (which focused on the individual in community). For Aristotle, practical knowledge resulted in citizens living and working together in pursuit of the virtuous life – prudence, patience, justice, fortitude: 'The end of politics is the best of ends; and the main concern of politics is to engender a certain character in the citizens and to make them good and disposed to perform noble actions.'[6]

The assumption behind this statement is that citizens are actively engaged in politics, seeking to define the common good and then organise society around achieving it. It is this engagement in politics and the search for the good that gives rise to the possibility of happiness. However, Aristotle was aware of the difficulties of this position, which he saw as related to the generality of conclusions and disagreement over the starting point of discussion:

> Problems of what is noble and just, which politics examines, present so much variety and irregularity that some people believe that they exist only by convention and not by nature ... Therefore, in a discussion of such subjects, which has to start with a basis of this kind, we must be satisfied to indicate the truth with a rough and general sketch: when the subject and the basis of a discussion consist of matters that hold good only as a general rule, but not always, the conclusions reached must be of the same order.[7]

Aristotle was convinced that what is noble and just is not simply a matter of convention and seeking the 'essential' good constituted the main thrust of politics. However, thorough though this search might be, the conclusions reached would never have the same permanence as the truths of theoretical knowledge, like mathematics, partly because of the variety of instances of practical decisions. Aristotle's optimism that the common good could be discerned by citizens contrasts sharply with the modern diversity of views on what is good for humanity and the suspicion of any attempt to define such a vision. The communal dimension of his assumption also contrasts with the modern emphasis on the individual, and the expectation that politics should protect the individual from intrusion by others.

Aristotle's concept of the common good dominated theoretical approaches to politics up to the fifteenth century. Medieval theologians framed a vision around the purpose of human life as union with God, claiming that all humans share this purpose, whether they realise it or not. The dignity of each person is equal and is the basis for the unity and the interdependence of humanity. This dignity is the cornerstone for the organisation of society, and the promotion of this reality is through the common good. Achieving it calls for cooperation at many different levels – international, national, regional, local, family.

In modern political philosophy, John Rawls defined the common good as 'certain general conditions that are ... equally to everyone's advantage'. This definition focuses on individual benefit as the building blocks of the common good. This benefit is defined in an inclusive way. It acknowledges the social dimension of human existence, and gives rise to two conditions: the first guarantees the basic rights and liberties needed by free and equal citizens to pursue a wide range of conceptions of the good; the second provides equal opportunity in education and employment to enable all to compete for positions in society and guarantees a minimum of means so that individuals may pursue their interests and maintain their self-respect as free and equal.

In a parallel way, the *Catechism of the Catholic Church* summarised social teaching on the common good as 'the sum total of social conditions which allow people, either as groups or as individuals, to reach their fulfilment more fully and more easily'.[8] It consists of three essential elements: respect for and promotion of the fundamental rights of the person; prosperity, which is seen in the development of the spiritual and temporal goods of society and the individual's access to them; and the peace and security of the group and of its members. In describing the common good in this way, there is no insistence on a detailed *a priori* description of what individuals should aim for. There is an assumption that there is some underlying common purpose that is known partially, and that further knowledge can be gained in free and open deliberation about individual interests. What it focuses on is criteria to help us recognise the common good. These criteria include:

- That the benefits include all members of the group.
- That all goods are included.

1.2. DIFFERENT USAGE OF THE TERM 'THE COMMON GOOD'

The term 'the common good' is used widely in political debate, but a close examination of that use shows that the meaning is often inconsistent with the original meaning in classical philosophy. It is important to be aware of nuances in the use of the term in deciphering political positions, as people can use the same term to mean different things. The examination that follows is not exhaustive.

An *a priori* vision: this approach to the common good entails having a vision of a desired State, and eliciting commitment to bringing that about. The vision is sometimes known as the 'public interest' and is seen as normative in its appeal to the cooperation of individuals. Most people involved in education will be familiar with the importance attached to vision and mission statements in school planning. In any cooperative enterprise, it is important that people develop a common understanding of what they are trying to achieve. This is a way of focusing and harnessing energy; it gives purpose and direction to activities and it provides criteria by which achievements can be judged – how well an action contributed to bringing about the vision. In the classical model of strategic planning, such a vision is central to cyclical phases of review, design, implementation and evaluation. The vision aims to be comprehensive and to promote coherence between different policies in the school. It is also important that such a vision is responsive to changes in the environment; otherwise it becomes a straightjacket. Many people nowadays prefer to speak of 'strategic thinking' rather than 'the strategic plan'. This approach focuses on the underlying values that should animate all policies and projects, and which guide responses to unforeseen events.

Marquis's phrase, 'An idea is not responsible for those who believe in it', has already been quoted. It is true that notions of the common good have been used to promote particular social systems and tyrannies. The term has been used as a slogan to justify the actions of powerful elites who have coerced others to be compliant to their vision and wishes. The common good has been promoted as the 'good of the majority' to the detriment of minorities. Even the good of the majority may have been an illusion in some cases, as the interests of the majority were usurped by smaller elites who proclaimed themselves as the 'voice of society'. The modern suspicion of those who propose overarching visions for others is not without a reasonable historical basis.

The aggregate of all goods within a community: this concept of the common good represents 'the greatest possible good for the greatest number of individuals'. The focus is on the sum total of all the private goods of individual members. This concept of the common good relinquishes normative views of goals that people cooperate to achieve; it focuses on the pluralism of interests and values on the basis that individuals act out of self-interests, not out of a moral commitment to do what is in the interests of the community. As the aggregate of individual interests, these interests may not be shared (held in common). From this perspective, politics is more instrumental than normative. The end result is an agreement on procedures rather than a consensus that elicits commitment and cooperation.

In this approach, human freedom relates to an isolated individual, with no ties to others. The approach downplays the social dimension of existence. In its focus on self-interest, it gives little importance to motives such as philanthropy or reciprocal relationships. Although self-interest and the interests of the community may have different bases, it is a mistake to see them as polar opposites. Frequently, self-interest is firmly entangled with the interests of the community, and working for the good of the community is very much in the interest of the individual. Equally, it is disingenuous to describe the aggregate of individual goods as common.

The collective good of a group: this approach is descriptive, without the normative overtones of a vision that promotes action. The focus is on a list of specific goods shared by members of a group, and from which each member benefits. Such goods include language, culture and friendship. Members of a group with these goods in common have a sense of shared meaning and understanding. The focus here avoids seeing the common good in instrumental terms – collaboration to produce goods. Membership of a community is, of itself, a good for persons, not merely because collaboration allows people to achieve more with others than they could achieve alone. Social relations are constitutive of a person's well-being and are not simply instrumental. This allows us to talk of common goods which are only enjoyed by 'insiders'. Our experience of these goods in groups helps us to appreciate the good in itself, and our experience of exclusion from groups helps us to understand the limits of a common good.

The common interests of the group: this approach is also descriptive, but the focus is instrumental. It looks to the conditions that are necessary for the pursuit of individual goals and claims that the maintenance of these conditions is the common good. This approach promotes a level of cooperation between individuals that is instrumental to promoting individualism. The focus is mainly on economic goods but extends also to the protection of individual rights and the provision of basic social goods, such as education, health services and welfare. In seeking what is common between people, the focus is on what might be called a median point, or lowest common denominator. This common denominator is self-interest. It does not presume that any particular good will be shared. It anticipates a conflict situation where the desired goods are different, and often mutually exclusive. Individuals therefore negotiate and compromise, rather than engage in dialogue. This gives rise to the 'median' – I get some of what I want, but not all of it.

A work in progress: This approach seeks to combine elements of the descriptive and the normative. It also seeks to explore the link between a shared good held by citizens and the instrumental procedures used to achieve it. It is founded on the belief that, with adequate procedures of deliberation, it is possible to reach forms of agreement that satisfy both rationality and legitimacy. Rationality is pursued in understanding the interests of individuals and the formulation of these interests as rights or demands within a community. Legitimacy seeks to place this rationality within the framework of a 'popular' community; that is, a community governed by the people. This approach does not accept the existence of an *a priori* overarching vision, but believes that it is possible to ground authority and legitimacy on some form of public reasoning. We know enough about what is good for us to make reasonable, legitimate political decisions and demands on one another. Politics is seen as an exchange of views between reasonable people who seek to be impartial. In that sense, the common good can be seen as a heuristic. *Chambers Dictionary* defines a heuristic as 'adj: serving or leading to find out; encouraging the desire to find out; (of method, argument, etc.) depending on assumptions based on past experience; consisting of guided trial and error' and 'noun: the principles used in making decisions when all possibilities cannot be explored'. Applied to the common good, the heuristic would imply an ongoing process aimed at seeking greater clarity. Any attempt to formulate the common good would be based on past experience and could be judged by criteria that (a) it had been discussed in an inclusive way; (b) that it was of benefit to all members of the group; and (c) did not seek to exclude any other good.

2. INDIVIDUAL RIGHTS

The concept of human rights also has its origins in a philosophical debate that searches for moral standards of political organisation and behaviour. The aim of the search is to eliminate any arbitrary approach by ruling groups to defining what is right or good at a particular time. It seeks to find moral imperatives that bind societies and their governments over time and from place to place. This allows for constructive critique across religious, political and economic divides. The rhetoric of rights, in general, is that they 'trump' other considerations in society.[9]

An appeal to rights is a regular feature of political debate and occurs in three main contexts:

To invoke a right that is established and recognised: in many scenarios, rights are automatically triggered. For instance, when a person is accused of a crime and pleads 'not guilty' to a charge, it automatically invokes their right to a fair trial, and this sets up a series of protocols. When an individual reaches the age of eighteen, they are automatically entitled to a vote. Similarly, when a person reaches pension age, or is made redundant, it automatically invokes their rights to social welfare payments. In these situations, there is no dispute over the right.

To demand that an established right be met, where it seems not to be: the focus is on the conflict that arises when the right is not met. This can happen in a number of different ways:

- When an individual establishes that he has been unfairly treated and that his rights have been denied, he can seek redress for that violation. For instance, if a person was arrested and wrongfully imprisoned based on fraudulent evidence he could then seek compensation.
- When an individual establishes that the distribution of goods or services was unfair, they may seek redress against the discrimination. The focus may be on compensation for unjust treatment or for a redistribution of goods for their benefit. An example of such a conflict has been in differential pay or pension rights for women.
- Another instance is to appeal the scope of interpretation of a right. For instance, in issues related to the provision of education for children with special needs, parents have sought to establish the amount of support they are entitled to under an accepted right of a child to State support in education.

To establish a right where one is not recognised: stating an agenda as a matter of rights suggests its importance and the possibility of realising it through legal or political action. Having it recognised as a right gives legitimacy and promotes the item. This is seen as 'trumping' other positions, thus securing a benefit for the right-holder.

The context in which the debate takes place gives rise to different rhetorical uses of 'rights'. The aim of this section is to explore some of the different connotations of rights from a general philosophical perspective. Firstly, the historical context in which rights emerged will be examined. Different approaches to defining rights will then be considered, followed by looking at the problems such approaches can bring. These will be applied more specifically to religion, education and denominational education in later chapters.

2.1. The Context of Rights

The development of our human rights language and theory from the late seventeenth and eighteenth centuries is linked with the struggle to assert personal liberties against the arbitrary exercise of power: 'Rights are benefits secured for persons by rules regulating the relationship between those persons and other persons subject to these rules.'[10] The definition involves three elements: the benefit, the right-holder and 'other people'. In the development of political theory, there have been major differences in the emphasis placed on each of these elements.

In classical philosophy, the focus of the common good was on the benefit – discerning the good that should be pursued by the individual and by society. The goal of individuals was to lead the good life, and the role of politics was to in some way agree on what that good life was. There was a strong emphasis on the person as a social being. Individual rights, insofar as they were postulated as such, were considered in the context of following this good life as a moral imperative.

In the seventeenth and eighteenth centuries, there was a major shift in the focus of political philosophy from the collective to the individual. Philosophers such as Hobbes, Locke and Rousseau saw little hope in finding agreement on the 'common good' as a means of organising society and focused instead on the individual, describing his ideal development in terms of an independent and autonomous existence. In their view, individuals cooperated with others in society as part of a social contract to better protect and pursue their own interests. These philosophers saw the basis of the social contract in 'natural' rights, although they disagreed over the definition of such rights. The rights proposed included the right to life, liberty, estate, prosperity, security and the pursuit of happiness. Organisation of society was based on developing the consequences of these natural rights in positive law. In this approach, the benefit or good being postulated as a right was important, but it was now to be realised as a project of the individual rather than as a communal project.

Nineteenth- and twentieth-century liberalism saw further developments in approaches to rights. Philosophers such as Bentham and Mill placed the individual firmly in the spotlight. For them, there was no agreement on what constituted natural rights. They focused on the process of choosing and defined the basic freedom of the individual as the freedom to choose, irrespective of the good that was being chosen. For these philosophers, whatever was chosen was good and the only constraint on choice was not to do harm to others. In their view of liberal political philosophy, the main aim of society was to provide individuals with as much freedom of choice as possible. This was partly in opposition to what they termed the 'tyranny of the majority'. Where a majority controls etiquette and morality this often has detrimental effects for those in the 'minority', as their voices are not heard or may be ignored. Although a minority, they must still be treated fairly. In this approach, rights are not benefits attached to individuals, but are legal arrangements around particular goods and services thought to be useful to most people in the pursuit of their individual goals, guaranteeing fair treatment for minority groups.

Undoubtedly, approaches to the common good had been open to abuses of paternalism and dictatorial declarations of that good. In that context, it is easy to see the ready welcome for a focus on individual rights in the seventeenth and eighteenth centuries. These reflected wider philosophical movements that focused on the individual (Descartes) and the rejection of absolute and arbitrary political powers. Their practical application inspired the development of constitutional republics through the English, American and French revolutions. It is also easy to see the attractiveness of the freedom offered by liberal philosophies, both in terms of the optimistic view of the human person choosing what is good for themselves, and the freedom that is implied from State control (or indeed any other norm).

The experiences of two world wars in the early part of the twentieth century deflated this optimism and gave rise to a new focus on rights. In the immediate aftermath of World War II, there was a renewed interest in specifying human rights to protect against any further human atrocities and occurrences of war. The rights were developed as an interpretation of the principles outlined in the Preamble to the Universal Declaration of Human Rights 1948 (UDHR), in the hope that these ideals would be enshrined in law. The formulation, in affirming the ideal, also reveals the stark reality of the context in which these rights were being developed:

> Recognition of the inherent dignity and of the equal and inalienable rights of all members of the human family is the foundation of freedom, justice and peace in the world. Whereas it is essential, if man is not to be compelled to have recourse, as a last resort, to rebellion against tyranny and oppression, that human rights should be protected by the rule of law.[11]

The UDHR was followed by the European Convention on Human Rights, and by various other international conventions and covenants focusing on particular families of rights.[12] States have sought to incorporate the rights into their national laws. Not surprisingly, no country totally abandoned its established legal system. Many of these systems were founded on the basis of some vision of the common good and the integration of rights language has been gradual.

2.2. DIFFERENT RIGHTS

Rights define relationships as they pertain to things, actions and persons. Rights are often described not singly, but in lists. These lists distinguish different classes of rights and different traditions have used different criteria for naming these classes. James Nickel distinguishes seven families of rights in his analysis of the Universal Declaration of Human Rights:

- Security: protecting people against crimes such as murder, rape, torture
- Due process: protecting people against abuses of the legal system

- Liberties: freedom of belief, speech, thought, association and movement
- Political participation: having a role to play in influencing public decision-making.
- Equality: non-discrimination and equality before the law
- Social: that people have access to subsistence, healthcare and education
- Protection of specific groups: a protection that goes beyond non-discrimination.[13]

Nickel argues that rights give a unique perspective of living in community – the perspective of the individual. These lists express various aspects of individual well-being in the community. The different families of rights reflect the diversity of interests within a community, and also different ways in which people are vulnerable to abuse and where they need formal protection. The listed rights seek to identify the basis for the content and scope of public moral norms, providing the context for each individual to live a minimally good life. The list dimension promotes an inclusive and comprehensive approach to rights. Although each right specifies a particular freedom, they are interdependent and some rights cannot be realised without other rights being in place.

The formulation of a right focuses on the right-holder as agent. In most instances this involves a claim against another person or institution, and the other has a duty to respond to that agency. Some rights focus on the way in which the right-holder may respond to the claims of others. This gives rise to four types of benefits (although many commentators tend to classify power and exemption rights as instances of claim rights):

- **Liberty rights** affirm the agency of the right-holder to pursue their own interests. The liberty allows the agent to act as they please; as long as they are not under an obligation, grounded in the legitimate claims of others, to refrain from acting this way.
- **Claim rights** focus on claims that individuals have to goods or services and the duties of other people to act in particular ways for the benefit of the right-holder.

- **Power** affirms a position where the right-holder can act in such a way as to affect a legal relationship with another person. The duty of the other person is to comply with the demands of the right-holder who exercises power.
- **Exemption** rights exist in the context of other people exercising their power rights, but where the right-holder in this case claims to be exempt from the legitimate demands of others and does not have to comply with their intentions.[14]

The distinction between liberty rights and claim rights is important. Liberty rights arise from the capacity to be free, but do not provide the specific means to pursue that freedom. There is no one with a duty to provide for the substance of the right. For example, everyone may enjoy the liberty to live where they want; however, the desire to live in a particular area is contingent on my being able to buy or rent a house in the area – my wealth determines my capacity to use my right and I have no claim against anyone else to help me exercise my liberty in a particular way. Claim rights on the other hand are held against others who have a duty to respond. These claims may be held in general or against specific people. For instance, if I own a house, I have a right for it to be free of trespassers. This right is general, as it is held against all others who are capable of trespassing on my property. Claims for services are directed to specific people – parents, family, business partners or government. Positive claims are regarded as claims for a particular good or service where the other has a duty to supply that good. Negative claims are regarded as claims against interference by these parties in my pursuit of legitimate interests.

The establishment or declaration of rights is not a magical guarantee of their realisation. Rights are applied in specific contexts and these contexts determine the feasibility of many rights. This gives rise to different levels of discourse. The first looks to establish the right in relation to the freedom of the individual to pursue his or her interests as a person (human rights) or as a citizen (civil rights). The liberty, once established, may become a claim right. This changes the language of discourse. For example, in education, the liberty of parents to educate their children in a particular way may become a claim against the State for support in the exercise of that liberty.

For the most part, debates on rights focus mainly on extending the scope of a positive right – seeking even greater support for implementation. Conflict situations arise in a number of ways where this is a conflict over distribution of resources between different rights and when the support of the rights of some people impact on other right-holders. In a time of financial crisis, the application of agreed rights to education, health and social welfare gives rise to competition for scarce resources that impact on the extent of provision. It can be said that the rights are in conflict with one another, not as concepts, but in relation to their distribution. In other instances, the satisfaction of my right may have an adverse effect on the ability of others to enjoy the fullness of their rights. As discussed in the last chapter, governments may undertake programmes of affirmative action that demand that current right-holders cede a freedom to behave in a particular way, find a new way of expressing their beliefs, or agree to a redistribution of benefits such that they may end up with less that they have been used to. Costs have to be taken into account in formulating and evaluating specific rights. A theory of rights that never descends from the heights of morality into the world of scarce resources will be sorely incomplete, even from a moral perspective.[15]

The basis for all rights, according to the international treaties, is the inherent dignity and equal worth of each human person. Rights are described as 'fundamental' and 'inalienable'. They are both descriptive and normative. The named rights specify aspects of human dignity, clarifying what it means in practical terms. Rights also set minimum entitlements and freedoms that should be respected by others, and this becomes an obligation. 'Human rights' are regarded as universal and not related to any particular legal system or cultural tradition. This approach to rights has a moral basis; it assumes a rationally identifiable moral order that is independent of social and historical conditions and applies to all human beings. Human rights amount to universal moral truths about the human person and their validity is not dependent on legal ratification, as some legal systems may in fact deny moral rights. A frequent example used to illustrate this is the case of apartheid in South Africa: opponents argued the legal rights conferred on whites in South Africa and denied to others was a violation of numerous moral rights.

Many political debates focus on establishing a legal basis for particular moral rights. The moral dimension arises from an anthropology that each person has a basic desire to live a good life. Rights are instrumental in securing the necessary conditions of human well-being. These conditions ensure that each person can enjoy their freedom and autonomy to act and to pursue their individual interests, while at the same time respecting the interests of others. This gives rise to different reasons for adopting rights treaties:

- **Moral imperative:** From this perspective the right is seen to reflect a moral norm, based on reason. As a result, people can agree on a specific right for different reasons. The norm is seen in abstract rather than in practical terms, thus the statement is capable of different valid interpretations with regard to practical consequences, depending on the context in which the right is being exercised.
- **Utilitarian:** People judge norms by the benefits they bring to as many people as possible. The criterion that is used in judgment is the consequences for general welfare. When a statement of rights can be shown to contribute to the satisfaction of most people's fundamental interests, then it is deemed worthy of support.
- **Prudence:** Individuals or nations have an interest in enjoying certain liberties or goods. They believe there is a better chance of enjoying them in a community that respects such rights than in a community that does not agree with them. They see in these rights an affirmation of the interests they seek to enjoy, and believe that the rights promote the means to achieving these interests. They realise that others share the same interests and that the best chance of securing the cooperation of others so that they can achieve their interests is to accept these rights as applied to all in the community.

In practice, it is probable that all three motives exist in signing up to particular treaties. Indeed it is not uncommon that people work from different motives simultaneously. The aim here has been to clarify different approaches to rights – what they hope to protect and why they are seen as necessary; to consider different types of rights and the different relationships that exist between the right-holder and others in personal liberties and claim rights; and finally, to look at the basis for these rights, especially in the demand that they be respected by all. The next section looks at some common ground between this approach and that of the common good as a basis for developing a public language.

3. DEVELOPING A PUBLIC LANGUAGE OF POLITICS

The introduction to this book, and also the outset of this chapter, referred to a crisis of confidence in the political process. This crisis seems, at least partly, to focus on the quality of the discourse. Debates on social and political issues reveal different understandings and expectations around concepts of the common good and of rights; people seem to use the terms in different ways and for different purposes. This often happens when people move from a more theoretical discourse aimed at understanding, to a practical discourse aimed at persuasion. For instance, the collectivist approach considers the individual as an element within a social organism; in the heat of debate, this can come across as considering the good of the community without any reference to the free choice and responsibility of the individual. Similarly, the liberal approach that sees the person as unencumbered so that his or her social involvement is not part of the constitution of their identity can come across as considering individuals' choices of ends and goods as a matter of arbitrary preference, involving will and not reason, overlooking inherently communal goods that demand social cooperation. For meaningful debate to take place, it is important that people clearly understand the terms that are being used, and also that they have a positive trust in the motives of other people. This section will explore the common ground between the two approaches, and then examine different ways in which misunderstandings can arise.

Firstly, both approaches are based on the equal dignity of individuals within the community. This leads to both approaches having a moral or normative dimension. They both work from a similar level of commitment to discern lasting and universal values. Secondly, both approaches recognise the social context of existence. In the common good approach, this becomes a value that is promoted in itself, as it is the social context that sets the conditions for personal happiness. Rights also are pursued in the context of other people pursuing their rights, and living in community requires an element of regulation.

Article 29 of the Universal Declaration of Human Rights states this essential social and communitarian dimension of human existence: 'Everyone has duties to the community in which alone the free and full development of his personality is possible.' Thirdly, both approaches seek a balance between the individual and the collective, although there may be differences in the underlying motives. For instance, the common good can be seen as a collective good over and above the good of individuals. However, it is also distributed among the individuals in the group in the form of benefits and goods. Similarly, the rights approach secures the benefits and goods of individuals, and this gives rise to a collective good in the prosperity and peace that exists for the group. Fourthly, both approaches consider themselves as 'works in progress'. The common good approach does not have a blueprint which allows every society to know what it should do in all situations. There is a confidence that elements of the good are known partially and that there are guiding principles of inclusiveness, both in terms of individuals and goods, to promote dialogue, reflection and decision-making. Similarly, in the approach to rights, there a belief in an underlying morality that can be discovered by reason, even if there is not total agreement on it at the moment. This sense of a 'work in progress' motivates participation in public life and is the basis for public political discourse.

These four areas of commonality provide grounds for a fruitful conversation. They point to the common ground in what people are trying to achieve in society. However, they also point to some major differences, particularly in an understanding of what underpins different approaches and in the approaches to be used. It is worth looking at some of the problems in terms of the legitimacy, distribution and consequences model developed in Chapter 2.

Some philosophers contend that the concept of the common good is not a legitimate interest in politics, as it is inconsistent with a diverse, pluralist society. People have different ideas about what constitutes the good life, and the diversity of opinion has increased in recent decades. Even if there is agreement on what is to be valued as public goods to be shared – education, environment, health, welfare – people will differ in their views on what resources should be committed to these goods. Efforts to determine the common good can only lead to adopting or promoting the views of some, while excluding others.

Forcing others to support or participate in a particular notion of the common good violates the freedom of those who do not share in that goal, leading to paternalism, tyranny and oppression.

Other problems are associated with the distribution of goods within a society. When it comes to the distribution of goods within a society, the problem encountered by attempts to promote the common good is a culture of individualism. Rhetorically, we place a high value on individual freedom, on personal rights and on allowing each person to 'do their own thing'. Our culture tends to view society as comprised of separate independent individuals who are free to pursue their own individual goals and interests without interference from others. In this individualistic culture it is difficult, perhaps impossible, to convince people that they should sacrifice some of their freedom, some of their personal goals and some of their self-interest for the sake of the 'common good'.

A third dimension of problem is linked with the consequences of particular political decisions. The pursuit of the common good is sometimes seen as placing an unequal burden on some members of a community, therefore making it unjust. This 'burden' can be seen in two ways – in terms of the extra contribution of some members of the group and in terms of consumption enjoyed by a minority group as a result of the contribution of the majority. An example of this rhetoric can be seen in the debate surrounding a common approach to the debt crisis in Europe. How much should different countries contribute, and on what criteria should their contribution be calculated? Why should certain countries benefit through bailout funds, whereas others try to rectify their economies through austerity measures? Why might Ireland not simply default on her debts and wait to be bailed out? The debate centres on reasons for contributing to the common ethic and also on evaluating the consequences of the possible reaction of other members of the community.

All of these problems pose considerable obstacles to those who call for an ethic of the common good. Behind the disquiet is the need to develop a vision of the type of society we want to become and how to achieve that society. This involves a way of seeing ourselves as members of a community (regional, national, European, universal) and, while respecting and valuing the freedom of individuals to pursue their own goals, to recognise goals that can be shared and to further cooperation to realise these goals. It seeks to develop a vision where the interests of individuals and groups are not seen as being in opposition to the interests of society, but brings them into harmony.

There are similar patterns of objections to the rights approach to politics. One criticism focuses on the legitimacy of universal rights. Moral relativists view morality as a social and historical phenomenon, valid only for those cultures and societies in which they originate. They point to the diversity of moral beliefs, principles and practices in complex multicultural societies, claiming that this pluralism necessarily restricts the scope of political regulation. In particular, the emergence of human rights theories from Western political theories and philosophies poses problems for the universal acceptance of particular lists of rights. Difficulties arise in two particular areas:

- The separation of the individual from their society is not a universal position. There are some collectivist or communitarian societies in Asia and Africa that view the individual as an indivisible element of the whole society. These work harmoniously although not based on concepts of equality or even universal suffrage.
- The particular rights proclaimed have been shaped by the liberalism of the nineteenth and twentieth centuries, and often the rights are seen as a specification for liberal democracy. The rhetoric of human rights is sometimes seen as a vehicle for the values of Western liberalism. As such, their promotion can be seen as ideological imperialism.

There are also distribution problems with rights. As the focus of rights is often on individual liberty and the pursuit of personal interests, this opens the possibility of fragmentation and dysfunction if pursued to an extreme. The argument is that an emphasis on rights seeks to accommodate people in a society rather than integrate them. This can show itself in a number of ways:

- The emphasis is on the benefits to the right holder rather than social responsibilities, thereby promoting egotism and self-centredness. This can skew rights in favour of powerful or rich elites.
- It replaces norms based on love, trust and community, which may be far more useful in ensuring good lives for vulnerable people and integrating them into a society.

- It promotes litigiousness in claiming and pursuing rights, where the resolution of conflict is seen in third-party processes rather than resolving differences between protagonists, thus producing winners and losers, rather than a fair distribution of rights.
- It gives rise to inflated claims which are utopian in the sense of making demands that exceed our moral, institutional and financial resources.

Problems also arise over consequences when rights are interpreted in a strictly legal way. Many people do not see rights as tightly systematised concepts. Frequently, cultural and religious views are loosely organised rather than tightly held categorical imperatives. They are held on the basis that some competing understandings have to be accommodated. For many people, moral principles are seen as ideals or duties which can have exceptions when it comes to particular applications. In that type of culture, rhetorical excess pushes 'all talk of human rights from the morally compelling into the twilight of utopian aspirations'.[16] Also, the expansion of rights has led to rights-inflation, which devalues the currency of rights language. If everything is promoted with the same seriousness and urgency of a human right, then it is hard to distinguish priority areas.

These issues pose problems for those using an ethics of rights. Rights specify liberties but do not confer licence. Since rights are exercised in communities, the social contract balances the freedom of individuals in the pursuit of their own interests with their responsibilities towards others who likewise pursue legitimate interests. There is a vision of a society that is responsive to the interests of individuals, but is also conscious of responsibilities to others. A key challenge is to promote the both–and aspect of rights and responsibilities.

Although problems exist with the language associated with both the common good and with rights, Marquis's maxim that 'an idea is not responsible for those who believe in it' remains pertinent. Problems and difficulties are not an excuse for abandoning the ideas. No organisation will be free of criticism. Individuals and groups can always be called on to explain what they are trying to do, and they can be criticised or praised for how well they do it. For such a discourse to be fruitful, it must be based on understanding and fair criteria. The next part of the book explores how the discourse on denominational education has developed in Europe. It focuses on three developments of the discourse – the legitimacy of different worldviews as outlined in the notion of religious freedom, the socialisation of people through education and the role of education in promoting particular worldviews. This exploration has two aims. The first is to see how the discourse on the common good and rights has been applied. In particular, the aim is to analyse how that discourse has been mediated in the European Court of Human Rights, which acts as an authoritative interpreter of rights, especially in the face of advocacy for particular political positions. A second aim is to provide information and resources on different solutions to the practical dilemmas posed in politics, by bringing together in one place information about the solutions that have emerged in different cultural contexts. The exploration is deliberately limited to developments in the European Union, as this is the immediate international context for Ireland's politics. A similar analysis to different aspects of the education debate in Ireland will be applied in Part III.

NOTES

1. Robert Samuelson is an economic columnist with the *Washington Post*. He also writes regularly for *Newsweek* magazine.
2. Daniel Callahan, *Taming the Beloved Beast: How Medical Technology Costs Are Destroying Our Health Care System* (Princeton, NJ: Princeton University Press, 2009).
3. *Tablet* 17.24 (2011), p. 9.
4. Paul Rowe, 'Response to Patronage Forum Report', *Irish Times* (12 April 2012).
5. Ibid.
6. *Nicomachean Ethics*, 1099b30.
7. Ibid., 1094b14.
8. See paragraphs 1905–12.
9. Ronald Dworkin, 'Rights as Trumps', *Theories of Rights*, J. T. Waldron, ed. (Oxford: Oxford University Press, 1984), pp. 153–67.
10. John Finnis, *Natural Law and Natural Rights* (Oxford: Clarendon Press, 1980).
11. Universal Declaration of Human Rights, Preamble #1–3.
12. Other treaties have been developed that focus on specific groups. Examples include the International Covenant on Civil and Political Rights; the International Covenant on Economic, Social and Cultural Rights (1966); and the Convention on the Rights of the Child (1989).
13. James Nickel, *Making Sense of Human Rights* (London: Wiley-Blackwell, 2007). Others have used different classification systems: human and civil rights, with

social rights; generations of rights – first (civil and political), second (social) and third (solidarity).

14. This classification follows W. N. Hohfeld (1919) and is used consistently in textbooks on political philosophy.

15. Nickel, *Making Sense of Human Rights*.

16. Maurice Cranston, 'Human Rights Real and Supposed', *Political Theory and the Rights of Man*, D. D. Raphael, ed. (Bloomington, IN: Indiana University Press, 1967), p. 52.

PART II

THE EUROPEAN CONTEXT OF DENOMINATIONAL EDUCATION

4

FREEDOM OF RELIGION

The European Court of Human Rights has described religion as 'one of the most vital elements that make up the identity of believers and their conception of life'. In affirming this, the court has also claimed that religious freedom is 'a precious asset for atheists, agnostics, sceptics and the unconcerned'. In effect, the court has opted to protect 'freedom of belief', which expands the popularly understood notion of religion as relating to a belief in God to a 'philosophy of life'. The only limits placed on a belief system that enjoys this projection is that it must be more than 'ideas and opinions'; it must have a 'level of cogency, seriousness, cohesion and importance' and be compatible with human dignity.[1]

The diversity of worldviews raises important political questions about how these views, and the values associated with them, can coexist in society. The development of this chapter has been guided by such questions:

- In what way is a particular worldview a personal or a common good, and what contribution do different worldviews make to the common good?
- How does the vision behind a religious worldview coexist with the vision of the common good of a State which accommodates multiple worldviews? In this context, what is meant by 'the separation of Church and State'?

- What are the implications of seeing the development of a worldview as a right? Is that right to be seen as a liberty, or does it involve legitimate claims? What are the limits of these claims?
- What are the different solutions that have developed in Europe? Are there different approaches to the separation of Church and State?

1. RELIGION AND THE COMMON GOOD

In pursuing their personal identity, individuals ask questions about the meaning of life: where did I come from? Why am I here? What is the origin and purpose of human existence? Why is there something rather than nothing? Is there a God and what is my relationship with him/her/it? How should I relate to others, to the environment and to issues of wealth and power? Religion, broadly speaking, is a free, informed, rational and responsible search for answers to these questions. Such answers have been mediated by different historical and social contexts. Different cultures have developed narratives, traditions, symbols and rituals in order to pass on the core of their worldview from one generation to the next. These worldviews often give rise to a morality or preferred lifestyle that is meant to help individuals live in harmony with the meaning and purpose of human existence as understood by the culture. In particular, people have arrived at very different positions on the existence and nature of God, whether there is a specific revelation from God about himself and the content of that revelation, in particular what it says about human existence or about laws governing relationships between people. Some worldviews have a strong theological base; others reject the idea of God.

1.1. RELIGION AS A 'GOOD'

Religion can be seen as a personal good. In a number of recent books, a positive association between religion and well-being has been asserted.[2] There is wide speculation on the nature of the cause–effect relationship. One suggestion is that the proscriptive aspect of moral 'commandments' sets a tone and helps sustain attitudes that keep adherents away from harmful practices (e.g. drugs, crime, etc.). A second suggestion is that in learning to praise God, individuals develop a sense of gratitude. They are also supported in their lifestyle by a sense of fellowship in community and are encouraged to move away from egoism to focus on others. They develop resilience in the face of trauma, because they can ascribe meaning to facing difficulties, and this deepens their sense of being human. Alain de Botton, in *Religion for Atheists*, proposes that 'religions are intermittently too useful, effective and intelligent to be abandoned to the religious alone'. His approach is to look to religious attitudes and practices and to restate them in secular language; to look for the wisdom behind them freed from their theological infrastructure.

Religion can be seen as a shared or 'common' good in two ways. In the sense that all individuals ask questions about the meaning of life, all share in a common search. There is also a communal dimension to any particular worldview, insofar as it is shared with others and reinforced in common rituals. It becomes part of the cultural identity of the individual and overlaps in personal, family, social, work, church, political and recreational experiences. It consists of multiple beliefs, attitudes and values, making up a complex whole. The religious experience encourages individuals to act humanely and with kindness to one another, giving rise to benefits for the community. It is argued that this communal good arises from the focus on a relationship with God – the vertical dimension of religious experience – encouraging openness to a source of life that embraces the fullness of human experience and sustains our efforts to be human. Improved human relationships – the horizontal dimension of religion – is a by-product of this experience and cannot be achieved by focusing on them as explicit goals in an instrumental way. Without a vertical dimension, reflections on our place in an expanding universe and the random processes of evolution are unlikely to promote a sense of meaning and purpose. Relying on the humanist ideal of respect for one another would truly be, in the words of Samuel Johnson, the triumph of hope over experience.

The tension between religion as a personal good and a common good can be seen in the tension between the terms 'spiritual' and 'religious'. 'Spiritual' is commonly used to express engagement with and commitment to a positive worldview that inspires the individual and gives meaning to their lives. 'Religious', on the other hand, is used to indicate that the spiritual experience is mediated and sustained by a commitment to an organised group. In today's world there is a definite shift towards the spiritual. This has been described as the 'authority of experience', where meaning is validated in one's own experience of what 'is' rather than in authoritative statements of what 'should be'. Some previous experiences of religion, such as those associated with the Catholic Church prior to the Second Vatican Council, can be described as the 'experience of authority'. To some extent, the phenomenon of religious experience is characterised by a tension between individual experience (the 'spirit') and the mediation of meaning by authority (the law). The tendency is to see the two elements of experience as polar opposites, and to opt for one over the other. Both contribute to the richness of religious experience. It is important to be able to freely enter into the fullness of human experience and also to gain from the rich heritage of human reflection in understanding the significance of that experience.

Conflict based on religious beliefs has been a common feature of human history, giving rise to major wars between cultures and within them. Elements of that conflict are also evident in modern political discourse. One focus of conflict is when a group questions the legitimacy of another's worldview. Humanist commentators sometimes characterise religious beliefs as an outdated inheritance, a concession to sentimentality, an irrational answer aimed at simplifying difficult questions, and a denial of the human capacity to control its own destiny through the use of rational processes. They term any effort to pass on religious traditions as indoctrination rather than education, seeing the religious worldview in contrast to their own objective, critical and pluralist worldview. The assumption is that having a religious perspective on life excludes the ability to engage in critical reflection and dialogue with others. Atheistic secularism, seeking a political supremacy of its own position, questions the legitimacy of any worldview that has a theological base and demands its exclusion from public consideration.

A second focus of dispute might be termed conflict over distribution – the number and quality of people's adherence to a particular worldview. This line of discourse can be found between different religious groups and also within groups. For instance, a very high proportion of people in Ireland describe themselves as Catholics, despite the fact that regular attendance at Sunday Mass has dropped considerably. This is sometimes taken as a sign of less-than-adequate belonging to a faith system. For 'outsiders', this throws into question the level and quality of membership, and therefore the claims that a Catholic group may have on the loyalty of its members on any particular issue, e.g. denominational education. 'Insiders' too may question the position of those who claim to be Catholic but are not regular churchgoers. They question whether those who are deemed lukewarm in their approach to their religious affiliation should be allowed benefit from the works of the Church – including attendance at Church schools. There is a problem when judgments about religious affiliation do not allow for the complex interaction between the inspirations of foundational insights (gospel values), the search for truth and understanding (theological doctrines), the development and promotion of human dignity (ethics and social teaching) and community identity (common rituals). Instead, the judgment is based on a single criterion only – attendance at Mass.

There is a serious need for 'outsider' commentators and 'insider' apologists to give credit to the complex realities behind religious experience and how people describe themselves. Pluralism exists within religious groups as well as between them. Conflict can also be generated by commentaries on the consequences of other people's beliefs. For instance, people working from a religious worldview sometimes categorise those with a secular and agnostic perspective as having a deficient approach to some aspects of life. In particular, they look at rituals around bereavement, suicide and other tragedies, claiming that the secular approach simply heightens a sense of helplessness or despair as it presents no hope of an afterlife. On an ethical level, they imagine that atheists think they can do what they want in life as there are no consequences once it is at an end. The assumption is that, if the central inspiration of their own position – a belief in God – is absent from another's position, then that person must be deficient in some, and by exaggerated extension all, other areas of life. However, belief in the sanctity of life, respect for the past, commitment to the good and the rejection of evil are not unique to a Christian religious tradition. One can strive to emulate Christian virtues because of the humanity of Jesus, without accepting that he is God. It is possible to be an atheist and to believe in free will and the need to make responsible, rational, ethical decisions for oneself and in one's relationships with others. Those within a religious tradition can also fail to understand the complexity of elements that make up another person's worldview and the common ground between the human dimension of their own approach and that of a humanist approach.

1.2. Religion and the Common Good

The contribution of religion to the common good arises at two levels. The first concerns the individual and sees religion in terms of a search for ultimate meaning and the attempt to live by that meaning. From the political perspective, this is seen as a positive dynamic, as politics also involved in a search for the best way to organise society so that citizens can find meaning and purpose in their lives. As such, this approach to religion complements the political search for the common good. The second level sees religion as a product, the particular expression of the answers of believers. The diversity of belief systems is seen as enriching society. It is a constant reminder of the search for coherence and meaning in human experience. The different answers that each group has achieved can encourage and challenge other groups. This dynamic, properly understood, can lead to renewed commitment to the search for the common good, and it can bring greater clarity about the depth and the limits of the insights we have achieved. A second dimension of the view of religion as product is its focus on how a particular worldview can contribute to the common good, especially if it speaks with authority on a particular issue and becomes an organised political force. This dimension values the insights that inform religious traditions.

Our beliefs have implications for our private and also for our public lives: if religion is part of who we are, then it is how we contribute to society. For instance, the Christian perspective on human dignity gives rise to a constructive critique of economic systems that overemphasise the market dimension, where people are treated as 'human capital'. It presents 'God and Caesar' as a both–and dilemma rather than an either–or choice. The Sermon on the Mount and the Good Samaritan promote social cohesion and solidarity; final judgment promotes a sense of ethical responsibility on the use of talents and dealing justly with others; the death and resurrection of Jesus encourage a sense of hope and perseverance in the face of difficult situations. These biblical teachings do not provide a blueprint to solving particular issues and problems, rather they promote reflection on what is acceptable and in line with the dignity and equality of each person. As such, they contribute to the common good understood as a 'work in progress'.

People do not fragment themselves, changing their value systems, chameleon-like, in different contexts – family, church, work, politics and so on. They seek values that are consistent and are integrated across the different spheres of their life. Sometimes, individuals have blind spots in the application of values and do not see contradictions in their positions, making it difficult to engage with them in political discourse. At other times, values are poorly articulated and may not be critically examined. There is often a problem of 'insider' language when talking about values, as individuals learn to express the significance of their position within a particular framework – cultural, religious or scientific. In an academic context, it may be easy to distinguish different areas of debate and the technical language appropriate to that area; yet practical life is not debated in the academy, but in the more intuitive experiences of people's lives. The language used reflects the intuitive, and an important skill in an arena of very diverse worldviews is to find a common or public language that promotes understanding when discussing complex issues. In that context, the religious dimension of an individual's values presents a challenge for politics. However, it would be a denial of the democratic process, and it would weaken the notion of the common good, if an individual was excluded from the political process because of the language of expression. The accommodation of language must also be reciprocated in respect and openness to others. If people insist on the authority of their own position from within a particular religious worldview, not shared by others, then that too weakens the notion of the common good.

The Christian tradition has developed ethical, prophetic and transcendent perspectives on human nature that have contributed to the shaping of values across the Western world. The UN Declaration on Human Rights and the European Charter of Human Rights both reflect and affirm basic Christian positions on human dignity. The authority of these documents is not their Christian inspiration but their resonance with an understanding of human nature that transcends different traditions. Other traditions demonstrate similar resonance between the charters of human rights and their worldview, for they too promote similar perspectives on social cohesion, solidarity, ethical responsibility, justice, hope and perseverance, as does the Christian tradition. They offer new perspectives, some complementary, others contradictory to the standard Christian worldview. The issue of religious values in the common good is not that specific values be accepted because they claim a religious authority, but because they reflect deeply held human aspirations and convictions. Attempts to distinguish between these two sources of authority have resulted in efforts to institutionalise the separation of religion and politics.

1.3. THE SEPARATION OF RELIGION AND POLITICS

The separation of religion and politics presents itself at two levels. The first might be termed 'anti-religious', as it seeks to exclude all aspects of religion from the political process. The second can be termed 'anti-clerical', as it focuses on institutional roles, particularly the role of a religious clerical caste, in political decision-making.

The anti-religion approach to separation develops a rhetoric which characterises religion (the Church) and the State as competing power bases, each seeking supremacy over the other. From a political perspective, the Church is seen as undermining the State by using its authority to define behaviour in the civil sphere. As discussed earlier, one approach is to deny the legitimacy of the religious worldview and to characterise it as anti-rational and harmful. A second approach is to recite a litany of intolerance between religious groups, claiming that religion is therefore a divisive force in a society and should not be part of public discourse. Religion is directly connected to hate, discrimination and violence, and history is characterised as exclusive groups competing with one another for domination over the hearts and minds of others, causing destruction and oppression in order to achieve and preserve their goals. This phenomenon seems to be more prevalent with the rise of monotheism, which replaced the polytheistic pantheon of many different gods who were tolerant to one another, as long as each got their fair share of worship. The one God, or at least his representatives on earth, seemed to expect one set of beliefs and one way of worship, all else being heresy. It also seems to be particularly common for religions based on revelation (Judaism, Christianity and Islam) to find in their own scriptures that hatred and violence against enemies is justified. We can find plenty of historical examples of these attitudes from the middle ages, through the Crusades, the religious wars of the post-Reformation period to the present day.[3]

One political response is to isolate religion from the public forum. The scenario is proposed as a choice between an intolerant institution of faith and a tolerant life of secular rationalism. However, this is a naive description of human institutions. Just as there are clear examples of religious institutions that have been intolerant and harmed society, there are also clear examples of religious institutions that have made major contributions to development in healthcare, education, alleviation of poverty, etc. These institutions contribute to a common good that benefits everyone and no one in particular, allowing all to flourish and lead a decent life. In general, a religious approach to morality is based on the principle of 'love thy neighbour' and teaches that we are part of a larger community with obligations to others. Also, in pointing to the rhetoric of tolerant secular rationalism and its power for neutrality and peace between people, we can also find examples of totalitarian regimes that were guilty of inhuman and oppressive practices in the name of non-religious ends.

A strange phenomenon of many human organisations, not just religious ones, is the ability to maintain simultaneously contradictory values. This phenomenon is often linked to insider–outsider dynamics. The appearance of an external threat (the 'other') gives rise to a greater sense of solidarity in defence of the group and a greater commitment and clarity about the identity and values of the group. This fosters a form of elitism, where the authority of one's own beliefs is affirmed, and also justifies the demand that others conform to the insider's worldview. De Bono once termed this phenomenon 'dogmatic ignorance'.[4] This form of group-think can be seen in many groups that have an ideological base – political parties, religious groups, trade unions, etc. It can be seen in business organisations where 'players' get caught up in promoting harmony within the organisation and do not engage in realistic appraisal of their own position or of alternatives.[5] Many commentators suggest that such group-think among bankers was the root cause of the financial crisis in Europe. The purpose of this distinction is not to excuse the bad, or to see the good as somehow lessening the evil that organisations are involved in; it simply acknowledges the complex reality of human thinking, and a similar complexity in organisations. Good ideas often get sidetracked, colonised or corrupted; the response cannot be to outlaw the ideal, but to rediscover its original purpose and reform around that purpose, wiser for the experience.

A more common approach to the separation of religion and politics focuses on the distinction between the religious and civil authority in political decision-making. The main aim is to affirm that the role of government belongs to the laity rather than to a clerical caste. This distinction is often termed 'secularisation', although the term gives rise to confusion. In the Catholic tradition, the term 'secular priest' is used to refer to priests who have certain administrative functions in a parish – registering baptisms, confirmations, marriages and deaths as well as administering the finances of the parish. This distinguishes them from monks or religious orders. In that context, 'secular' and 'religious' refer to functions. This was the original meaning of developing a secular State, and the underlying value is perhaps more clearly understood in the French term *laïcité*, where there was a clear distinction between the role of clergy and laity. The term 'secular' has since come to be associated with secular humanism, which proposes a worldview without God or religious ideology.

In its broadest sense, the separation of Church and State is based on the philosophy that political decisions should be based on the practical consequences for citizen's lives, not the ideological source of the proposals. The beliefs of each individual citizen are equal and are not related to ethnic, religious or other characteristics. This distinguishes the realm of practical decision-making from the realm of theoretical reflection associated with religious doctrine. The philosophy of separation is therefore a protection for both the State and for religious institutions, giving each its autonomous activity and protecting one from interference by the other. It also limits the authority of 'church' to its own members, and allows the State to be the arbiter of the social consequences of many different 'churches' making proposals in the public forum. The separation of politics and religion does not imply that they are necessarily antagonistic towards one another. Frequently, the aims of the two spheres are complementary and there is ample ground for collaboration in achieving mutual aims, once the ground rules on responsibilities and protocols are clear.

The Lisbon Treaty (2007) is an international agreement that forms the constitutional basis for the European Union. Part I of the treaty deals with the principles under which the Union operates. Part II deals with provisions having general application, and it is here that Article 17 states that the Union 'respects and does not prejudice the status under national law of churches and religious associations or communities in Member States'. This recognition is extended equally to recognised philosophical and non-confessional positions. It gives rise to a commitment that 'Recognising their identity and their specific contribution, the Union shall maintain open, transparent and regular dialogue with these churches and organisations.'[6] In affirming its commitment to dialogue, the Union maintains the position of politics as the arbiter between competing values and insists that other organisations have an obligation to respect legitimate political institutions exercising their proper functions.

There is a general acceptance of this relationship in the Catholic Church. A statement from the Commission of Bishops' Conferences of the European Union affirmed the commitment to a process of searching for the best way forward through discernment and engagement. The focus is on promoting an understanding of the social teaching of the Church as a guide in practical matters, and ensuring that its voice is heard and considered in the political process:

> The Christian tradition has a wealth of social doctrine and experience which can be useful for society as a whole. We should note and examine the points of convergence between the Social Doctrine of the Church and the current direction of the European Union. It is not, of course, a matter of wishing for the confessionalisation of institutions, nor to regard political institutions as sacred, but of measuring how the Social Doctrine of the Church can assist both discernment and commitment on the part of citizens of the EU.[7]

The basis of this commitment was made clear by Benedict XVI in 2009 when he wrote his third encyclical to the Church, his first statement on social teaching:

> The Church does not have technical solutions to offer and does not claim to interfere in any way in the politics of states. She does, however, have a mission of truth to accomplish in every time and circumstance.[8]

The challenge for all organisations is to ensure that contributions they make to the political process are genuine and credible. In particular, the Church needs to find a language that reflects its position in a way that engages with and is persuasive in the political process, while at the same time dealing with the baggage of its history where engagement was not respectful of the civil powers.

Ireland is a particular example where there is a tension about Church engagement with political issues. Exchanges over the possibility of abortion legislation illustrate some of the complex issues involved. The focus here is on the early stages of the debate, before any clear directions about possible legislation were given and before the tragic death of Savita Halappanavar in October 2012 focused the debate in a new way. What I want to explore is the way different understandings of the separation of religion, official Church spokespersons and politics have been conceptualised.

In August 2012, Cardinal Brady, the Catholic Archbishop of Armagh, spoke about proposals to find ways of introducing legal abortion into Ireland:

> The debate about these issues is about to intensify in our country over coming months. It is important that we all have the courage to make our voices heard. It is important that we do justice to the logic and human reason behind the values we hold ... They cannot be relegated to the realm of private religious beliefs with no place in our laws or public policy in the name of secularism or tolerance ... These values are rooted in human reason and available to all. They have the same right to be heard, promoted and respected in our laws and to be put to the people in democratic decisions as other, perhaps less representative, views.[9]

When asked in a television interview what the response would be if the government made proposals to legalise abortion, the Cardinal answered by saying that the Church would lobby politicians, launch a media campaign and write a pastoral letter on the issue. In response, the Labour Party minister, Pat Rabbitte, claimed that the cardinal should have no right to engage in any campaigning against legal abortion, and that the Church should not engage with canvassing public representatives on the matter:

> I don't have any objection to any of the Churches stating its position and making it clear, but I think it would be a retrogressive step if we were to go back to the days of the Catholic Church dictating to elected public representatives how they should address an issue.[10]

Other members of the coalition government took issue with Pat Rabbitte. The junior finance minister, Brian Hayes, said the Church was as entitled to lobby for its interests as any other group in Ireland:

> Dictating is one thing, lobbying is another ... They [the Churches] do have a right to make their points of view known on all issues. But people shouldn't engage in a lobbying campaign in a vacuum where there's no report or proposal. But Catholics, Jews and Muslims all have a right to lobby.[11]

In an *Irish Times* editorial, the Cardinal's proposal was also the source of comment. His approach was contrasted with that of the Archbishop of Dublin's approach, suggesting that there was disagreement within the Church on how to handle the issue:

> Last month, Dr Martin confirmed that the Church would reiterate its teaching on abortion and marriage equality, regardless of the progress of legislation on these issues. But, he said, 'before, during or after the enactment of legislation, the Church's teaching is to teach something, rather than to oppose it.' Such a measured approach has now given way to actively lobbying and co-ordinated opposition. Nobody expected the Catholic Church to modify its teaching that abortion is sinful in all circumstances. Neither, however, was it expected to engage in aggressive political lobbying of the kind more usually found in the United States – though that is its right.[12]

The editorial finished by warning politicians that 'They have to decide which takes precedence: canon law or the law of the land.'[13]

The question raised by the Cardinal was the legitimacy of a possible policy direction – to allow abortion. He claimed the need to examine the issue on the basis of 'logic and human reason'. The *Irish Times* editorial saw a possible Church intervention more in terms of a personal and group morality, raising the issue of 'sin'. These perspectives point to different sources of authority on issues. The fear would seem to be that this distinction would not be made by voters, and that any statement by the Church would unduly influence the majority of Catholics to consider the issue as part of the internal morals of the Church rather than as an issue in the public domain, based on reason and logic. In particular, the fear would be that politicians would not make this distinction, and would be guided by canon law – a form of private morality related to Church teaching – rather than by the public 'law of the land'.

The second focus is on Church involvement in canvassing for a particular outcome. It seems to be generally accepted that the Church should be able to state its position freely. However, the degree of engagement in 'persuasion' is disputed. Minister Rabbitte claimed that the Church should have 'no right' to engage in such political activity. His fear seemed to be with a possible abuse of the protocols of political debate – an attempt to 'dictate' to others based on the Church's authority over its members. Others held that as long as these protocols were adhered to, Church involvement in political debate was to be welcomed. The *Irish Times* editorial, however, suggested that the Church should forgo its involvement in such a debate, even though it had a right to engage. It was not clear from the editorial whether the concern was some unseemly image of the Church in Ireland compared to the United States, or some deeper issue. The Archbishop of Dublin would seem to hold some similar reservations, stating that the role of the Church was to teach a positive message rather than to oppose contrary positions.

The debate points to two important issues in terms of the common good. The first is the link between the freedom of individuals to choose and the legitimacy of their choices. This aspect of the debate explores the type of society that individuals want, in particular the limits that are given to diverse views as they affect others. The second is the way that different groups engage in a debate and use their resources to persuade others of a particular direction. It is in working out challenges in these areas that the language of rights becomes important.

2. FREEDOM OF RELIGION AND INDIVIDUAL RIGHTS

Freedom of religion is declared as a right in Article 18 of the Universal Declaration of Human Rights:

> Everyone has the right to freedom of thought, conscience and religion; this right includes freedom to change his religion or belief, and freedom, either alone or in community with others and in public or private, to manifest his religion or belief in teaching, practice, worship and observance.

The religious dimension of human identity is seen to encompass an internal (the mind and heart of the believer) and an external (public display of symbols and rituals) forum. This right gives rise to a liberty for individuals and groups as well as claims that can be made for and against those who hold particular religious beliefs.

2.1. Freedom of Religion as a Liberty

The dictionary defines 'religion' as:

> A set of beliefs concerning the cause, nature, and purpose of the universe, especially when considered as the creation of a superhuman agency or agencies, usually involving devotional and ritual observances, and often containing a moral code governing the conduct of human affairs.[14]

The first section of this chapter outlined a number of basic questions that individuals ask about their existence. The search for answers to these questions is a rational search that exercises individuals and communities. At a personal level, freedom of religion promotes this search as part of an individual's identity. It protects individuals who make this search from any form of coercion, pressure, indoctrination and intimidation. It also protects them from discriminatory treatment by those who do not agree with the answers they reach. At a social level, it respects the diversity of answers arrived at by individuals from their searching and supports their efforts to live in conformity with these answers. This freedom is guaranteed no matter how deficient the search, how lacking in completeness the answers or how inconsistent the behaviour of individuals with these answers. Religious freedom is not a privilege for the committed. It is guaranteed to the apathetic, the confused, the misguided, the zealot and the fundamentalist.

Religious freedom as a liberty focuses on the internal and personal dimension of belief. It has an absolute protection, and attempts at personal intimidation are relatively easy to identify. The individual cannot be asked to deny, adhere to or change any particular personal belief. In some countries, the freedom has been extended so that an individual may not be required to reveal what their beliefs are – thus protecting the personal nature of such beliefs. However, the external and social dimension of religious freedom is more problematic. When individuals manifest their beliefs in particular attitudes and behaviours, then there is a possibility of conflict with others who hold a different perspective. The European Convention on Human Rights (Article 9) echoes the freedom enunciated in the Universal Declaration, and states the basis for limitations to full freedom of religious expression:

> 9.2. Freedom to manifest one's religion or beliefs shall be subject only to such limitations as are prescribed by law and are necessary in a democratic society in the interests of public safety, for the protection of public order, health or morals, or for the protection of the rights and freedoms of others.

These limitations are negotiated as part of the political process – national law and the values of a democratic society. In the context of protecting the rights and freedoms of others, it gives rise to claim rights – claims for and from religion. Freedom 'for' is a positive claim on others to the manifestation and practice of these beliefs, either alone or in community. Freedom 'from' is a negative claim that others should not use their religious beliefs to interfere with your way of life. In a pluralist society both aspects of the freedom are promoted as equal rights, and the freedom is not reduced to one at the expense of the other.

2.2. Religious Freedom as a Freedom From Religion

The right of religious freedom includes a claim on other people that their religious beliefs should not be imposed on or interfere with the right-holder. At a very basic level, this requires others to refrain from coercion, proselytising and indoctrination. All of these terms have a connotation of force and deliberate intention by the perpetrator. There has been a tendency in case law to try to expand the protection to exclude any uninvited contact with the religious beliefs of fellow citizens. This has focused mainly on the display of religious artefacts. For instance, questions have been raised on the display of Christian symbols such as Christmas cribs in public buildings, and whether these breach the negative claims of non-Christians to be free from the religious beliefs of Christians. It has also been used to forbid Muslim women from wearing traditional dress in certain circumstances. One test case in the European Court of Human Rights was *Lautsi* vs *Italy*.[15]

The focus of this case was the compulsory display of crucifixes in State-run schools in Italy. It was taken by a Ms Lautsi, who claimed that the exposure of her children to such symbolism infringed her right as a secular humanist. It its original judgment, the court held that the highly visible presence of crucifixes in classrooms, where their symbolism was predominantly religious, clashed with the secular beliefs of the mother and was capable of being emotionally disturbing for non-Christians or non-believers. This was appealed to the Grand Chamber, and drew a large number of submissions from governments, individual politicians and other organisations. In overturning the original decision, the Grand Chamber stated that the crucifix was predominantly a religious symbol, and therefore had to be used sensitively. Historical values did not remove the obligation to look at the rights of others in a changed cultural context. However, the court claimed that the visibility given to the majority religion could not be seen as an act of indoctrination. The crucifix on the wall was a passive symbol and had not led to any particular teaching practice or proselytising. It had to be seen in a wider context – that the education system welcomed and catered for all beliefs, that recognition was given to other faiths through celebration of their festivals and that religious education was optional. In his concurring opinion to the court judgment, Judge Bonello, the Italian judge in the Grand Chamber, gave a spirited recap of the arguments, moving away from the somewhat formal language used in the judgment itself:

> Millions of Italian children have, over the centuries, been exposed to the crucifix in schools. This has neither turned Italy into a confessional State, nor the Italians into citizens of a theocracy. The applicants have failed to unfurl before the court any evidence at all that those exposed to the crucifix forfeited in any way their complete freedom to manifest their individual and personal religious belief, or their right to repudiate any religion. The presence of a crucifix in a schoolroom does not seem to have hindered any Italian in his or her liberty to believe or to disbelieve, to embrace atheism, agnosticism, anti-clericalism, secularism, materialism, relativism, or doctrinaire irreligion, to recant, apostatise, or to embrace whatever creed or 'heresy' of their choice they find sufficiently appealing, with the same vigour and gusto others freely embrace a Christian faith. Had any such evidence been adduced, I would have been strident in my voting for finding a violation of the Convention.[16]

In looking at the issue of balancing the 'freedom from' and 'freedom for' rights of individuals, the same judge continued:

> The crucifix purge promoted by Ms Lautsi would not in any way be a measure to ensure neutrality in the classroom. It would be an imposition of the crucifix-hostile philosophy of the parents of one pupil, over the crucifix-receptive philosophy of the parents of all the other twenty-nine. If the parents of one pupil claim the right to have their child raised in the absence of a crucifix, the parents of the other twenty-nine should well be able to claim an equal right to its presence, whether as a traditional Christian emblem or even solely as a cultural souvenir.[17]

The judge captures the tension that can exist in a pluralist context. There is a real question as to the standards that are adopted in the degree of discomfort that some individuals have to put up with while others exercise their legitimate rights. The Grand Chamber, in its official judgment, was sympathetic to the tension:

It is understandable that [Ms Lautsi] might see in the display of crucifixes in the classrooms of the State school formerly attended by her children a lack of respect on the State's part for her right to ensure their education and teaching in conformity with her own philosophical convictions. Be that as it may, the applicant's subjective perception is not in itself sufficient to establish a breach of Article 2 of Protocol No. 1.[18]

The Grand Chamber refused to place all use of religious symbolism in the sphere of the private. Freedom of religion allows for public manifestation through symbols. Where tension exists as to their impact, it must be negotiated – by those who do not share them and also by those who do. It is in this tension that real pluralism exists, not in removing the tension.

2.3. THE LIMITS OF FREEDOM FOR RELIGION

The freedom of religion is proclaimed as a liberty which embraces the internal beliefs and the external manifestation of these beliefs. However, there may be limits on the public manifestation of beliefs because of the claims other people have on the believer that their freedom from religion be protected. The case law related to individual freedom focuses on whether other people can curtail the religious expression of believers. The European Convention on Human Rights states quite clearly the basis for any limitations that might be imposed 'in the interests of public safety, for the protection of public order, health or morals, or for the protection of the rights and freedoms of others'.

A distinction can be made between acts which are a direct expression and practice of one's beliefs, and acts that are motivated by these beliefs. For instance, religious beliefs influence attitudes to social issues such as abortion, divorce and same-sex marriage. A key issue for many people in debating these issues is the legitimacy of positions other than their own, and how to allow for alternatives approaches. On some issues, people believe that their position is so fundamental that they campaign quite strongly for its institutionalisation in law. When people engage in such a political campaign, their actions are not just a manifestation of their beliefs, they are political actions motivated by beliefs. For instance, it is one thing to believe that abortion is wrong and to state this in public. Actions such as public demonstrations or passing round pictures of foetuses in public fall under public order legislation and should be judged according to these norms. Such conduct must conform to these norms.

A second area where individuals may be curtailed in acting according to their religious beliefs relates to employment performance and its possible effects on the rights of others. This can arise in public institutions serving multiple rights. The question often arises as to whether employees should have an exemption from certain activities because of their religious beliefs. Case law indicates that Civil Registrars are not free to refuse to officiate at Civil Partnership ceremonies between same-sex couples; social welfare workers must deal equally with single and married parents, even if they have religious beliefs about sexual behaviour outside marriage; freedom of religion cannot be cited by public hospital workers if they object to being involved in treatments they disagree with. This distinction sees the religious freedom of the individual in the context of all other rights. Public organisations must serve the rights of all citizens equally. To refuse these rights, as an agent of the State, would give rise to serious discrimination against the client. It would appear from the case law that if religious beliefs give rise to difficulties in fulfilling the duties entailed in these public positions, then the individual should not be in that position. This case law seeks to balance the rights of different parties and works from two assumptions:

- Clients who have a legitimate claim right to the services of an organisation are entitled to these services without any hindrance or discrimination. Therefore, services cannot be withheld on the basis of the religious beliefs of an employee representing the organisation.
- An employee makes a free choice in entering into employment with an organisation serving such rights. They are not coerced in any way. Therefore, they cannot seek to change the conditions of employment when they are there. They have an equal freedom to work elsewhere, where such behaviour is not required of them.

In other areas, employers are entitled to demand a particular dress code if health and safety concerns demand it, without infringing on employees rights to freedom of religious dress. In the area of education, religious dress has been handled differently by different countries. In France, for instance, the pursuit of the principle of *laïcité* has been used as a justification for refusing to allow any type of religious dress in public schools. In other jurisdictions, this prohibition has been confined to teachers, where the use of symbols (such as dress) could have a pronounced effect (amounting to proselytising) on young minds.

2.4. SUPPORT OF FREEDOM FOR RELIGION

If freedom of religion is primarily a freedom of the individual, what positive support can the individual expect in living out their philosophy? Perhaps the most common instance of such support is in the right of conscientious objection. This is often associated with compulsory military service and the right-holder's claim to exemption from this civil obligation based on their pacifist or non-interventionist religious beliefs. In many countries, conscientious objectors are assigned other roles – farming, fire-service, hospital care assistants or even non-combatant roles in the military service.

The most common form of support for freedom of religion is through religious organisations, rather than through the individual. Arising from the fact that believers form associations based on their beliefs, these associations also acquire rights under this freedom:

> The believers' right to freedom of religion encompasses the expectation that the community will be allowed to function peacefully, free from arbitrary State intervention. Indeed, the autonomous existence of religious communities is indispensible for pluralism in a democratic society and is thus an issue at the very heart of the freedom protected by Article 9.[19]

Thus, religious organisations have a protection (a) in the philosophy they adopt and (b) in expressing and protecting that philosophy. In this context, these organisations include political parties and trade unions, as well as formal religious institutions. Such organisations are characterised by ethical or moral, ideological or religious ideals that pervade all their objectives and activities, and that assume the adhesion on the part of the employee to this inspired concept of the world called 'ethos'. The positive support for 'freedom of religion' works in two ways – in the ability to treat people differently because of their beliefs, and in what can be expected of individuals within the organisation. The approach is *not* to give organisations a licence to engage in discrimination, but to offer guidelines to balance other legal rights of the organisation and of the individual. In effect, it confers exemption rights on the organisation from some civil or legal requirements.

In 2000, the European Council issued a directive on equal treatment in employment and occupation. Directive 78, as it is known, sought to establish the principle of equal treatment and to combat all forms of discrimination on the basis of religion or belief, disability, age or sexual orientation. It defined ways in which direct and indirect discrimination can take place, and then provided specific protection for religious organisations in their selection of employees and their employment practices:

> In the case of occupation within Churches and other public or private organisations the ethos of which is based on religion or belief, a difference of treatment based on a person's religion or belief shall not constitute discrimination where, by reason of the nature of these activities or the context in which they are carried out, a person's religion or belief constitutes a genuine, legitimate and justified occupational requirement, having regard to the organisation's ethos. This difference of treatment shall be implemented taking account of the Member State's constitutional provisions and principles, as well as the general principals of Community law, and should not justify discrimination on other grounds.
>
> Provided that its provisions are otherwise complied with, this Directive shall thus not prejudice the right of Churches and other public or private organisations, the ethos of which is based on religion or belief, acting in conformity with national constitutions and laws, to require individuals working for them to act in good faith and with loyalty to the organisation's ethos.[20]

The protection that is offered is that organisations can set criteria of belief as a legitimate occupational requirement, and that it can insist that an employee act in good faith and loyalty to its ethos. This type of requirement is akin to affirmative action, where an attempt is made to promote a particular group. A key constraint on the organisation in applying this protection is that the occupation be directly related to the dissemination of the ideology of the organisation. Therefore, officers of a political party, a trade union or a faith group can legitimately be expected to believe in the ideology of the organisation. However, applying the same belief criteria to cleaning staff in an office would be regarded as a disproportionate requirement. From the perspective of Directive 78, the organisation must fulfil three criteria:

- The occupation must be related to the legitimate ends of the organisation. That means that it must be connected directly to the ideology of the organisation.
- There must be an objective justification for the requirement. This means that either the belief criteria or the age, gender, health or sexual orientation issues can be demonstrated to be a factor in the occupation.
- There must be proportionality between means and ends. This means that the exemption must be considered within the general legislation of the Member Country, and that it should not be used as a loophole for other aspects of discrimination in favour of the organisation or its members.

In reviewing submissions from fourteen European countries on how such exceptions work, Motilla gave an example of how Education Centres are protected. This summary also illustrates the different types of issues that arise:

Regarding an educational centre founded on an ideology – that is, one with an educational project or line that pervades all of its teaching – the conflict of interests analysed in case law rests between safeguarding the ideology (the right of the founder as acknowledged in educational laws) and the academic freedom of the teacher. In weighing the rights and interests in conflict, in general terms European case law holds that the ideology does not require the teacher to be an apologist of this ideology, nor is he or she required to find inspiration for academic explanations in minimal scientific grounds. Nonetheless, teachers in an ideologically based centre cannot make open or veiled attacks against that centre; they shall carry out their activity in the terms that they judge most appropriate and that, according to a serious and objective criterion, does not run contrary to the interests of the ideology of the centre. As far as the private life of the teacher is concerned, his or her conduct may possibly be considered a violation of the obligation to respect the ideology if, owing to its public nature or intentionality, it affects the educational work for which the teacher has been hired. The director of the centre could thus break the contractual relationship between the teacher and the centre. Naturally the loyalty of the teacher to the ideology intensifies when the subject that he or she teaches is directly related to the teachings of the doctrine on which the ideology is based. A clear example of this is that of teaching the subject of religion in a religious school.[21]

Constitutional contexts can affect organisations differently, depending on whether they are public or private, and if they are in receipt of public monies. As the European Court of Human Rights has pointed out, freedom of religion is essentially an individual freedom. There is no guarantee as to the overall context in which that right will be exercised. States are free to take different positions to the role of religion in public life – what is known as the 'margin of appreciation' of states. The only obligation on the State is to guarantee individual freedom of religion to the individual, and not to discriminate against any organisation on the basis of religious or philosophical belief.

3. FREEDOM OF RELIGION AND THE STATE: MARGINS OF APPRECIATION

The 'margin of appreciation' is a term used by the European Court of Human Rights in assessing cases against individual States. Relying on a principle of subsidiarity, each Member State retains sovereignty and is responsible for the protection of human rights. The 'margin of appreciation' refers to the way in which countries legitimately protect these rights in different ways, reflecting cultural, historic and philosophical positions. It allows for multiple valid approaches to particular issues. In the European Union, it is the discretion that individual countries have with regard to Union law. In human rights issues, it enables a balance between the sovereignty of Member States and the imposition of uniform obligations for all under the Convention. The role of the Strasbourg institutions is limited to ensuring the relevant authorities remain within their limits. In this supervisory role, the European Union promotes a move to the universal application of rights, ensuring that States do not use sovereignty as an excuse for restrictive practices.

In the area of freedom of religion, the obligation of the State refers to its treatment of individuals and also the treatment of religious groups in the public forum. In general, the 'margin of appreciation' is taken to refer to the place of religion in public life rather than to the treatment of the individual, which is taken as a universal freedom. It is worth exploring how different countries exercise their 'margin of appreciation'. This section will consider two concepts that are used – separation of Church and State and the notion of neutrality and equal treatment of all beliefs.

3.1. SEPARATION OF CHURCH AND STATE

The development of Constitutional protection in the separation of Church and State seems to have been aimed at 'denominational' religion, which reflects the history of competing factions within a doctrinal group. In Christian terms, this refers to Catholic and various Protestant groups. In Islam it might refer to Sunni or Shiite groups. In Judaism, there would be distinctions between Orthodox or Reformed groups. In more recent history there has been a focus on inter-faith issues, especially with the spread of Islam to the West. We have also seen the growth of secular humanism as an established philosophy seeking the same rights as established religious groups. A brief historical survey illustrates various aspects of the approach to separate religion and politics.

The origin of the modern concept of separation of Church and State can be seen in the political developments in Northern Europe from the time of the Reformation in the sixteenth century and the development of constitutional law in the emerging States. In general, the concept is linked with the excessive power of the Church and its influence on political affairs. The religious divisions between Catholics and Lutherans were played out in very hostile political confrontations in German territories and gave political rulers an opportunity to assert themselves against Church rule. These were resolved in the Peace of Augsburg (1555) which recognised the equality of the Catholic and Lutheran faiths at the level of the Holy Roman Empire and the right of the ruler of a territory to determine the religion confession of all his subjects (*cuius regio, eius religio*). In cities directly controlled by the Emperor (mainly Lutheran), the minority group was guaranteed rights of worship and property. Subjects who disagreed with the choice of their Lord were given the right to emigrate, essentially recognising that someone could not be forced to change their religion. In 1648, the Peace of Westphalia fixed the religion of the territories as on a particular date, limiting the right of Lord to change religion and allowing minority groups to practice their religion in private. These two principles underpinned later constitutional developments. Equality of treatment of different religions was extended to other groups, firstly to other Christians (e.g. Calvinist and other reformed Churches), then to other faiths and to those with a non-religious *Weltanschauung*, or worldview. There was a gradual disentanglement of State involvement with religious groups, and a freedom for such groups to exist independently. The freedom of individuals to choose any religion was reinforced in their right to practice that religion. The right of the three main groups (Calvinist, Catholic and Lutheran) to public rituals was extended to other groups.

The resolution of the religious wars of northern Europe gave rise to different relationships between Church and State. The first approach was to establish the freedom of different religions with the State, and the role of the State was to be neutral in respect of the different religions. This principle of non-discrimination and fair treatment underpins all States.

The second approach involved the recognition of an established Church within the State. This could be interpreted as the colonisation of the Church by the State. State support can vary from mere endorsement with some financial support to prohibiting any competing body from operating within the State. In Europe, there is a State Church in the United Kingdom, Iceland, Finland and Sweden. The State Church of Norway was disestablished in 2012. In these established Churches, either the monarch or the government has a role in Church governance. In general, the role tends to be symbolic. Decisions on doctrinal matters are decided within the Church and the organisational decisions of internal Church structures such as Synods are endorsed by the political process. In some countries, the political system has a role to play in Church appointments. There is separation of Church and State in the sense that the State does not have power over the internal workings of the Church, or its theology. Lichtenstein, Malta and Monaco have a special relationship with the Catholic Church, as does Greece with the Orthodox Church, but these are not State Churches and their governance is external to the State. Outside Europe, there are a number of countries that have Islam as the State religion, and a number of Eastern countries recognise Buddhism as a State religion. Israel is regarded as a Jewish State.

In some countries, the promotion of the State religion has been quite aggressive. Throughout history, religion has been used as both a means of and a justification for political action. In England, Henry VIII confiscated the property of the Catholic Church and the effect of the Penal Laws is well ingrained on Irish consciousness. The privilege granted to members of the established Church also gave rise to a sense of subordination for other religions. It was partly in order to recover their liberty to worship and to be equal that the pilgrims boarded the Mayflower for the New World.

In practice, most countries have disestablished their Church, or have reclassified them as a National Church, operating in a particular geographical region. These countries work mainly from the principle of State neutrality with regard to religion. In France, the concept of religious freedom has its origins in the French Revolution. Unlike Germany, there was no history of an existing pluralism or equality of religious groups. Catholicism was the single official religion and there was a long history of persecution of those who did not endorse it. In effect, the privileged position of the Catholic Church was seen as closely linked with the aristocracy and a philosophy of absolute power for rulers. In the overthrow of the aristocracy it was natural that the Church and its officials would also be sidelined from political decision-making. The 1905 French Constitution states:

1. The Republic shall ensure freedom of conscience. It shall guarantee free participation in religious worship, subject only to the restrictions laid down hereinafter in the interest of public order.

2. The Republic neither recognises, nor pays salaries to nor subsidises any religious denomination.

Recognition, in this context, means to point out any particular denomination for special treatment. It regards all as equal, and respects all beliefs, but not in a formal way. This was reinforced in the 1958 Constitution, which stated: 'France is a Republic ... secular, democratic and social; it shall ensure the equality before the law of all citizens, without distinction as to origin, race or religion. It shall respect all beliefs.' The focus here is on the equality of the individual citizen, and this is the prime focus of protection. The individual is protected from particular groups rather than groups being protected. This is strictly interpreted, and gives rise to an insistence of a lack of religion in all things public. The State does not recognise any official religion but does recognise as legal entities different organisations that support social activities according to formal legal criteria not related to doctrine or ideology. Organisations may be registered as *associations cult-uelle*. They may also register as *associations culture-lle*, which allows them to promote liturgical services and practices, and be exempt from taxes to engage in other activities such as running schools and hospitals. These are not exempt from taxes and are treated as any other business organisation. A similar situation exists in a number of former Eastern Bloc countries. There is a strict separation of politics and religion. However, some positive support is given to 'recognised' religious bodies. This requires these bodies to be registered and approved by the State.

A fourth situation involves a strong antagonism to religion. This was associated with a totalitarian approach where the State sought to control all aspects of public and private life. In promoting its position, it banned or was antagonistic towards any organisation or philosophy that might oppose it.

An example of the debate on the separation of Church and State can be seen in the discussions about the proposed Constitution of the European Union in 2004 and the Treaty of Lisbon in 2007. Pope

John Paul II, supported by the Greek Orthodox Church, claimed that Europe is based on Christian roots and that the constitution, in its contents, should show respect for the collective consciousness of European peoples to those roots. In response, the phrase 'drawing inspiration from the cultural, religious and humanist inheritance of Europe' was inserted in the final text of the Constitution.[22] There was no favouring of any particular religion or religious denomination. Although signed in 2004, the Constitution was not ratified after defeats in referenda in France and Denmark and the subsequent Treaty of Lisbon has no mention of religion.

The aim of separation of Church and State is twofold: to limit the role of the State with regard to religion and also to prevent particular religious groups having an undue influence on civil decisions. Separation of Church and State prevents the State from giving any formal preference to a particular religious or philosophical position. However, it does not limit the freedom of religious expression in the public forum or prevent individuals or groups expressing opinions based on their religious beliefs, or using their resources to influence developments. However, this engagement does not extend to a formal role in the political infrastructure. The obligation remains with politicians to mediate between different legitimate interests, and there is an obligation on belief organisations to abide by legitimate political decisions. This approach to separation demands that the political system be impartial in dealing with different belief systems.

3.2. IMPARTIALITY AND EQUALITY

The separation of religion from the 'secular' life of a country is not always clear cut. There are often unexamined assumptions or practices in the organisation of a society that are based on a religious approach that was embedded in a historical context. In the United States, this could include the motto 'In God We Trust', which is found on all coins and the preamble to the Declaration of Independence:

> We hold these truths to be self-evident, that *all men are created equal*, that they are endowed by *their Creator* with certain unalienable Rights, that among these are *Life, Liberty and the pursuit of Happiness*. [my emphasis]

In some countries, cultural and religious tradition is often enshrined in different aspects of social life, such as linking holidays to religious festivals and seasons. Elsewhere, the respect for the religious dimension of life is enshrined in blasphemy laws; although in Western countries, the protection is mainly provided under public order legislation in prohibiting speech that 'incites hatred' or vilification.

Perhaps the most contentious issue in politics is not so much the philosophical issues around freedom of religion or the separation of Church and State in policy decisions, but rather the practical issue of disentangling relationships that already exist and dealing with the growing number of groups that have the status of 'religion'. This refers to the relationship that can exist between the State and religious organisations in matters of mutual interest, as they affect social policy within the State. Provocative questions can be asked which clarify the areas of separation. For instance, 'Should the fire brigade (a State service) come to the aid of a religious school?' and 'Should the State provide services such as water, sewerage, electricity, etc. to denominational schools?' are questions that focus attention on extremes of separation. To answer 'no' to these questions would be to promote a position whereby religious organisations would be denied any State services on the basis of their beliefs. This would promote a position where the concept of separation implied antagonism between the State and religious beliefs in all areas of social life. In many countries, there is a positive and mutually beneficial relationship between the State and religious organisations. The State regulates this relationship on the basis of impartiality and equality between different groups. In a political sense, it means that religious beliefs are not criteria for either favour or disfavour in the distribution of goods.

Governments are not impartial with regard to the content of policy but they seek to be impartial in how that policy is implemented. Politicians are elected on the basis of a particular policy platform and they derive their authority to pursue this agenda from the mandate they receive from the electorate. In pursuing their policies, they are required to treat different groups impartially, and must not discriminate against any group. This does not mean that each group has to be treated in the same way in all circumstances. It allows for differentiated treatment of groups for the purpose of achieving social integration rather than simply accommodating groups, as discussed in Chapter 2. Principles of non-discrimination work on two bases. The first is that governments do not act in an arbitrary way, thereby treating groups that are in the same situation differently. In effect, this approach would assign different rights to different groups. The second approach allows a government to treat different groups in different ways as a means to achieving its policy objectives. This amounts to a form of affirmative action. It recognises that groups have the same rights, but that they may need different conditions in order to avail of them. For such an approach to be valid, certain criteria are necessary:

- There should be a rational and objective basis in distinguishing groups entitled to different treatment, and the basis should include characteristics of the group in relation to the good to be achieved.
- The provisions made should be proportionate to the needs of the group in relation to achieving the good.

An example of this type of arrangement can be found in France. Church property that existed before 1905, when a new constitution was written, is owned by the State, having been taken over after the French Revolution. It is leased back to the Church, and for the most part the Catholic Church is the lessee. As part of the landlord–tenant relationship the State undertakes responsibility for the upkeep of the property. After 1905, the State gave assistance to old buildings but not to new buildings. This had a particular impact on new religious groups that have been established in France since that date, and the Catholic Church benefited disproportionately from the provision. As a solution to the dilemmas that arose, the State now helps all groups in establishing places for worship, despite the apparent conflict with the principle of *laïcité*. The basis for the decision is that all belief groups should be treated equally.

In some Churches, there is a requirement that members pay a membership fee. This has its origins in the practice of tithing. Anyone who has done genealogical research on early nineteenth century Ireland will be familiar with the process where the established Church levied 'tithes' on all property without reference to the religious affiliation of the tenant. In some countries, the civil authority collects that membership fee through taxes and passes it on to the Church, charging a fee for the service. This system exists in Norway, Sweden and Germany for some denominations.

One aspect of Church–State relations in many countries has been the involvement of the Church in areas where the State now has core responsibility. Education, health care, social welfare, registration of the population and registration of marriage are examples of such core activities. In some instances, religious groups may feel that, in the activities they engage in, they have acquired rights over time. The issue for the State then is whether to take over the functions themselves, or to extend to other groups the possibility of involvement in these activities, empowering them to do so.

Education is closely linked to religious freedom, in that parents have the freedom to ensure that their children's education is in conformity with their religious and philosophical convictions. For many parents, the development of knowledge and social skills in school would be incomplete without a sense of religious awareness and familiarity with their own religion or beliefs. The growing diversity within societies poses political challenges in renegotiating the roles of those groups that traditionally cooperated with governments in providing religious education, and also for government-run schools to respond appropriately to the rights of all parents. This is the focus of Chapter 5.

NOTES

1.   These statements recur regularly in outlining the context of different judgments.

2.   Martin E. P. Seligman, *Flourish: A Visionary New Understanding of Happiness and Well-being* (New York: Free Press, 2011). Also, Richard Layard, *Happiness: Lessons from a New Science* (London: Penguin, 2005).

3.   George Lundskow, *The Sociology of Religion: A Substantive and Transdisciplinary Approach* (Thousand Oaks, CA: SAGE Publications, 2008), particularly Chapter 5, 'Religious Intolerance and Aggression', pp. 209–44.

4.   Edward De Bono, *I Am Right, You Are Wrong: From This to the New Renaissance: From Rock Logic to Water Logic* (London: Penguin, 1991).

5.   I. L. Janis, *Victims of Groupthink: A Psychological Study of Foreign-Policy Decisions and Fiascoes* (Boston: Houghton Mifflin, 1972).

6.   Lisbon Treaty, paragraph 17.1. Paragraph 17.2 states that 'the Union equally respects the status under national law of philosophical and non-confessional organisations'. Paragraph 17.3 contains the commitment to dialogue.

7. Commission of Bishops' Conferences of the European Union, *The Evolution of the European Union and the Responsibility of Catholics* (2005), p. 15. http://www. comece.org/site/en/publications/pubcomece

8. *Caritas in Veritate* (2009), paragraph 19.

9. *Irish Times* (25 August 2012). Report on the opening of Edmund Rice Summer School in Waterford.

10. Ibid.

11. Ibid.

12. *Irish Times* (28 August 2012).

13. Ibid.

14. http://dictionary.reference.com/browse/religion

15. *Lautsi* vs *Italy*, European Court of Human Rights, Application No. 30814/06. www.echr.coe.int/echr/resources/hudoc/lautsi_and_others_v_italy.pdf

16. Ibid., concurring judgment 2.11.

17. Ibid., concurring judement 3.6.

18. Ibid., paragraph 66.

19. 30985/96 ECHR 2000, XI. Grand Chamber, paragraph 62 .

20. Article 4.2 of Directive 78.

21. Agustín Motilla, 'The Right to Discriminate: Exceptions to the General Prohibition', *Religion and Discrimination Law in the European Union*, Mark Hill QC, ed. (Trier: European Consortium for Church and State Research, 2012), p. 53. http://www.churchstate.eu/

22. European Union, Treaty Establishing a Constitution for Europe, *Official Journal of the European Union*, C310 (16 December 2004).

5

EDUCATION: THE COMMON GOOD AND RIGHTS

Education is the process through which we learn about ourselves, about the world we live in and about our relationship with that world. Education takes place all through our lives – from infancy to senility. We learn from our personal experiences of life mediated by our family, the extended family, our peers, our teachers, the media, theoretical perspectives and a myriad of other factors. Schooling, on the other hand, is the way that society invests in promoting particular types of experiences for young people. As such, it is a major institution in the lives of young people, their families and the State.

In general, politics focuses on schooling – on the choice of curriculum, the distribution of educational opportunity and the consequences of the current status quo on diversity within the State. The choice of curriculum is a discourse on the legitimacy of schooling. If education is seen as inclusive of all aspects of development for individuals and society, the debate on schooling focuses on how well schooling contributes to education. Schooling seeks a balance between meeting the needs of individuals in their psychological development, developing skills to allow them to participate fully in society and to focus on skills that are productive and for the good of that society. The distribution of educational opportunity focuses on access to schooling. This involves the location of schools and the supports given to students and their families such as transport, school meals and so on. It is also concerned with the organisation of the curriculum at different stages, to ensure an inclusive access for all students. The focus on consequences is concerned with the equitable distribution of educational rewards. Policy initiatives often propose different programmes of affirmative action to assist those sections of society that traditionally do not perform well in school. This chapter explores some aspects of the political discourse on education. The first section considers in more detail the cultural context of education. Section 2 looks at how different concepts of the common good frame discourses on education. And section 3 examines how the language of rights has been applied to education.

1. THE CONTEXT OF EDUCATION

The term 'culture' is an abstraction used to label a complex reality of interacting elements. It has been defined as 'the characteristic habits, ideals, attitudes, beliefs and ways of thinking of a particular group of people'. As such, it is built around a configuration of interlocking beliefs, ideas, values, attitudes, meanings, symbols, rituals and behaviours. None of these elements, in itself, defines a culture. Each element can have different appearances, intensities and effects in a group. For instance, Irish people celebrate St Patrick's Day in a variety of different ways. They do not become more Irish on that day, but the intensity of their sense of citizenship is altered.

Culture is non-material. It refers to the complex, coherent and internal reality that is shared by the members. People grow into a culture so that it shapes their identity. Over time, they become accustomed to what it means to be part of the culture. Through the nuances of language, reinforced through symbols and rituals, they learn the meaning and value of different aspects of life, and in turn, share this with others.

Participation in culture has elements of breadth and depth. The breadth of culture embraces a wide range of disparate elements, such as lifestyle, leisure, work, relationships and spirituality. Individuals enter into these areas at different levels of intensity, thus giving the dimension of depth to an individual's experience. Subcultures form around intense experiences of some aspects of community life, giving rise to 'drug culture', 'popular culture', or 'youth culture', where the adjective suggests normative values or behaviours. We talk of specific cultures – 'Western culture', 'literary culture', 'scientific culture' – and we designate some attitudes as 'counter-cultural'. As such, culture is not easy to define. It is not a singular entity and neither is it static. It evolves through interaction with other cultures, borrowing from them and integrating their wisdom with its own in a dynamic way.

Education is closely linked with the culture of a society and how it is transmitted to young people. There are three main sources of transmission – the family, the school and an individual's peer group. There are different dynamics in each of these contexts where the developmental needs of a young person are identified and met. For the young person, these contexts can be considered as different 'worlds', where each world has different concerns and presents different challenges.[1] Together, these worlds contribute to the emerging identity of the young person. Erik Erikson, in *Identity, Youth and Crisis* (1968), described the developmental tasks of young people as identity, intimacy and ideology.[2] Identity issues look to psychological development. The focus is on developing knowledge, skills and attitudes that allow for self-autonomy. Intimacy issues are concerned with social development. This includes the ability to develop intimacy in inter-personal relationships, especially through friendships and cooperation with others. It also develops skills in dealing with power and authority in social settings. Ideology issues look to moral development. The focus here is on developing a reflective and discerning approach to the use of knowledge and influence. This ideology then guides personal decision-making.

The development process is a complex interaction between family, school and peers. Each of these 'worlds' is distinct and has its own set of norms. Young people live in all three worlds and must negotiate their lives in each world as well as their movement between these worlds. Sometimes, the norms in the different worlds are congruent. Other times they clash. For instance, young people may be influenced by peer pressure. The desire to belong to a peer group and to develop autonomy from the intimacy of the home can lead to clashes between the culture of the home and the culture of a young person's peers. Many parents experience this generation gap as a rejection, giving rise to tension and challenges for families. Sometimes there are clashes between the culture of the family or young people, and that of the school. These clashes are referred to in sociological studies as problems with educational capital, which influences levels of success in school, often contributing to the persistence of inequalities in education. Other researchers focus on the alienation of young people from the institution of school and their lack of engagement with learning. Schools contribute to the development of young people in a number of different ways:

> **Learning:** The UNESCO Commission on Education publication, *Learning: The Treasure Within* distinguished four pillars of learning – learning to know, learning to do, learning to be and learning to live together. All four pillars are part of a lifelong process and true education attends to all four.
>
> **Training:** The preparation of individuals for employment in current or emerging occupations – applied learning, problem-solving skills, work attitudes, general employability skills, leading to economic independence as a productive member of society.
>
> **Skills:** The relevant knowledge and experience needed to perform a specific task or job. Skills also constitute the product of education, training and job experience together with relevant technical know-how.

The balance of emphasis on these different elements changes at different levels of the education system. The aims of different stages are outlined in a general way in the International Standard for Classifying Education (ISCED) developed by the United Nations Education, Social and Cultural Organisation (UNESCO). This system is widely used in comparative work undertaken by the OECD. Table 5.1. outlines different aspects of the pre-university education.

ISCED 0 Pre-primary education	The first stage of organised instruction designed to introduce very young children to the school atmosphere. Minimum entry age of 3.
ISCED 1 Primary Education	Designed to provide a sound basic education in reading, writing and mathematics and a basic understanding of some other subjects. Entry age: between 5 and 7. Duration: 6 years.
ISCED 2 Lower secondary	Completes provision of basic education, usually in a more subject-oriented way with more specialist teachers. Entry follows 6 years of primary education; duration is 3 years. In some countries, the end of this level marks the end of compulsory education. 2A – prepares for continuing academic education, leading to 3A 2B – has stronger vocational focus, leading to 3B 2C – offers preparation for entering workforce

ISCED 3 Upper secondary	Even stronger subject specialisation than at lower-secondary level, with teachers usually more qualified. Students typically expected to have completed 9 years of education or lower secondary schooling before entry and are generally around the age of 15 or 16. 3A – prepares students for university-level education at 5A 3B – for entry to vocationally oriented tertiary education at 5B 3C – for workforce or post-secondary not-tertiary education, level 4
ISCED 4 Post-secondary	Programmes at this level may be regarded nationally as part of upper secondary or post-secondary education, but in terms of international comparison their status is less clear cut. Programme content may not be much more advanced than in upper secondary, and is certainly lower than at tertiary level. Entry typically requires completion of an upper secondary programme. Duration usually equivalent to between 6 months and 2 years of full-time study. 4A may prepare students for entry to tertiary level, both university and vocationally oriented education 4B typically prepares students to enter the workforce

Table 5.1. The first five stages of UNESCO's International Standard Classification in Education

Countries differ considerably in the way that education is organised. One difference is the extent of the core curriculum that is mandated at central level. A large core curriculum indicates substantial State control and a drive for uniformity in offering. A lower core curriculum allows for more autonomy at school level or for students in choosing their own direction. A second difference is seen mainly in lower and upper secondary levels and is reflected in the number of students in academic or vocational courses, and the number who enter the workforce. In some countries, this distinction is blurred as academic and vocational courses are offered in the same school (comprehensive education) and the choice is left to the student as to which courses to take. In other systems a clear distinction is made between the two types of education, and there are different pathways both in terms of access to and progress through the strands.

The structure of the education system and curricular provision within it reflects different ways in which the tension between the common good and the good of the individual has been resolved. The provision of a strong vocational base in the education system probably reflects the historical place of industry in a country's economy. The education system played a major role in preparing young people for the workforce, and the clear pathway through the system into the workforce was a motivating factor for students to choose that pathway or to find satisfaction if that was the pathway determined for them. In all systems, there is a growing level of autonomy for students as they move from primary through lower and upper secondary. In general, students are given a greater level of choice as to what subjects they will follow, allowing them to pursue individual interests and talents. This takes place in the general context of a core curriculum that promotes citizenship.

2. EDUCATION AND THE COMMON GOOD

There is a general consensus about the 'good' of education. However, there is less of a consensus about what constitutes a 'good education', much less who should provide for it. This is debated in a number of different discourses. Five of them are explored briefly here. This is not an exhaustive list, nor is the treatment of each exhaustive. Behind each of them is a different approach to what is meant by the common good, and to some extent, this approach legitimises the approach to education.

2.1. PRIVATE AND PUBLIC BENEFITS OF EDUCATION

In political rhetoric, education is heralded as a passport to opportunity. The benefits for the individual are outlined in economic (better and higher paid jobs), psychological (health, longevity) and sociological (prestige, participation) terms. A review of the benefits of education outlined in the OECD *Education at a Glance* has a strong focus on the material economic benefits. Monetary outcomes are easily labelled as material benefit. However, the occupational position a person achieves has material and non-material aspects to it. The non-material is expressed in terms of social prestige, and may be accompanied by greater or lesser material gains. The non-material benefits of education are difficult to measure, and may be culturally dependent. What is valued in one culture or sub-culture may have little value in another. Education is also a 'good' for society, and there are benefits for the State in investing in an education system. These benefits are seen from a number of perspectives and represent different perspectives on the contribution of education to the common good:

- The investment in education produces people who give valuable professional services to society – accountants, doctors, engineers, lawyers, nurses, teachers, etc. They contribute to a definite public good.
- An investment in education contributes to developments in science, technology, medicine, history, culture. This brings practical benefits to all in society.
- Investment in education, based on merit, contributes in an equitable way to allowing all citizens develop their talents.
- There is a return on investment in education in that people with higher levels of education get better paid jobs, thus contributing more in tax revenues, paying back the original investment made in them. This higher tax return is a common good, from which everyone benefits.
- Even if some investment is non-productive – people drop out or do not complete their education – the answer is not to abandon the investment, but to develop efficiencies. The public good is not always measureable in terms of each individual outcome, but in overall terms.

A regular focus of the debate about the good of education is in the tension that exists between the way individuals gain personally and the benefit to the public. The point of contention is often State support for the individual who pursues a costly investment in education. Governments recognise the wider public benefits that higher education systems offer – economically, culturally and socially – and understand that they have obligations to invest in it. One form of investment is directed at helping students by paying or contributing to their fees. The focus of debate is whether such help is promoting the private individual good of the student, or whether it contributes to a legitimate common good. In the UK debate, government officials proposed redressing the balance that existed by cutting student grants:

> It is the students who, regardless of these wider benefits, stand to accrue substantial individual reward through attending university and so it is right that the balance of funding shifts from the State to them in the long term.[3]

This was a justification for asking students to take responsibility for their fees. Help would still be given, but now in terms of a loan, which would be paid back as students realised the benefits of their investment in education in the workforce. This proposal sought to highlight the personal good of education.

2.2. HUMAN CAPITAL FORMATION AS THE 'GOOD' OF EDUCATION

There is a growing trend of defining the common good of education in terms of its link to the economy rather than its link to culture. In that sense, the common good is thought of as the equivalent to GDP, where the addition of the goods held by all citizens is taken to represent all citizens. This use of the term common good does not refer to shared goods or perspectives.

Human capital looks at the development of technical knowledge and the acquisition of skills as a necessary part of economic growth. The common good is seen as the additive effects of individual outcomes, the building up of an infrastructure, a pool of skills resources for the economic system. The underlying assumption is that investment in human beings and their skills increases their capacity for productive work. These benefits lead to increased economic growth at the national level, as well as to personal benefits for those who have the skills. The principal beneficiaries of the human capital approach are employers, who have a ready supply of skilled talent to choose from, thus cutting down their training costs. In an economy where employment is found in short- and medium-term contracts, and the workforce is generally mobile, this is a major benefit. Depending on the market forces of supply and demand, student investment in acquiring a particular skill may give them an advantage over other students in the job market. To some extent, the term 'human capital' has been replaced with the idea of 'knowledge capital' but the argument is much the same. The analysis looks to the skills or knowledge available (product) and has little concern for who has that product and the social basis of its distribution.

From a human capital perspective, investment in education is viewed from the system perspective. It aims at producing a supply of high-quality, desirable skills at the service of the economic system. This may give rise to schools expanding their curricula to cover a comprehensive range of subjects. The student must then negotiate a series of choices and options within the system. Their success depends on their ability to predict the right set of skills for themselves, the market demands for that skill and the durability of that skill over time in changing market conditions.

The human capital approach to investment in education can be seen in a number of different approaches:

- Offering incentives to schools to offer particular subjects, and to students who take them. This has been particularly prevalent in promoting science and information technology.
- Refining the definition of skills required for the workforce, with a growing emphasis on process skills such as critical thinking and creativity rather than on practical skills which may have a short shelf-life.

The contribution of the human capital approach to the common good is debated. A key criticism is that the approach is not inclusive of all aspects of culture; it develops a bias towards certain subjects to the detriment of others, especially the humanities. The critique of the human capital approach is that it sees education in the acquisition of measurable knowledge and skills and has a strong emphasis on short-term relevance of content. This contrasts with other approaches where there is a focus on the moral formation of attitudes, developing process skills that can be adapted to different contexts and a focus on subjects where there are long-term values. Human capital is often characterised more as training than education and its own success is measured in terms of increased 'standards of living', paying little attention to 'quality of life'. The contention is that a genuine contribution to the common good needs to be more inclusive.

2.3. Production Function and the Common Good

The production function perspective looks to the efficiency of the use of resources, seeking an optimum–cost benefit relationship. It is a corollary of the human capital approach, which specifies the product that education should aim for. This approach looks to the means of production. From a government perspective, this is seen as the planning of the provision of schools, where the size, location and organisation of schooling is based on economic efficiencies rather than any educational criteria. The focus is on providing a place in school for each entitled pupil and leaving debates on what should go on within the school to other sources, provided it did not exceed a certain cost.

The production function approach can be seen at a material level – in the design of schools as a multi-faceted community resource rather than a dedicated education centre, in designating desirable sizes for schools, and in balancing the cost of school provision with the operational costs of items such as school transport. This approach can also be seen in certain practices within schools, in the selection of students and their allocation to different courses. Restrictive entry procedures, or streaming policies, are often defended in terms of the efficient use of resources and gaining the maximum benefit from them. In particular, the effect of high drop-out rates in third-level education can be a significant cost to the State as it invests in students who do not finish their courses.

The development of the production function perspective has led to an increased level of managerialism in schools. At one level, this approach makes schools accountable for the efficient use of resources; at another, it can give rise to demands for the standardisation of the school experience for students, making all schools the same. There is a focus on defining a minimum standard of achievement in teaching and learning in all classrooms, thereby protecting the experience of all students from the random effects of being assigned to a particular class in a particular school. The approach is a form of quality control of the educational 'process', which guarantees a minimum standard of the 'product'. The downside of this approach is that it places too much emphasis on reaching minimal standards rather than on promoting excellence.

A by-product of this approach is a focus on results, giving rise to competitive league tables in order to attract new resources or maintain particular levels of support. These have relevance to students progressing to higher education, to schools in attracting students and developing reputation, and also at national level where positions on OECD and PISA tables can often be a spur to policy development.

In this approach, the common good is seen in terms of the common interests of individuals. Education is one of these common interests, as it is instrumental in individuals achieving their other interests.

This approach seeks to ensure that each person has access to that common interest on a fair and efficient basis. It is criticised for its lack of attention to the process of education. However, production function modelling is a vital part of any system where the coordination and allocation of resources is important. In stringent economic circumstances, it is an important part of any political perspective. The key challenge for politics is to ensure that the efficiency sought is governed by the end it serves. Efficiency is a means to an end, not an end in itself. The challenge for government is to have a clear and acceptable statement of the goals to be achieved, and to view the efficiencies in terms of these goals.

2.4. HUMAN DEVELOPMENT AND THE COMMON GOOD

Chapter 1 outlined a particular denominational approach to education based on a particular anthropology of the person. The cornerstone of this vision was the dignity of the human person and their social context. Focus on the person gave rise to an 'inner-directed' education – developing the whole person, with a particular focus on their moral development enabling them to critically analyse situations in terms of a value framework, and freeing them to make decisions in accordance with these values. The focus on the social nature of human existence gave rise to an orientation of responsible service to others and to society in general. The common good is seen in terms of a work-in-progress, which involves individuals in a discourse on what the good is, and in finding an inclusive approach to goods and individuals. The development of the free and responsible person is seen as a good in itself. The quality of person is also a contribution to the common good.

This approach to education is valued for its focus on the individual student and the personal care that is associated with schools that function from this ethos. The inner-direction of education contrasts with the outer-direction of other approaches, which tend to see the person in terms of roles in society. The focus on character formation, personal discipline and social responsibility are valued outcomes. This view of education is also valued for the place of the humanities in its curriculum, and the attempt to cater to a wide range of interests. It is criticised for its lack of focus on sociological issues in the consumption of education, and the apparent assumption that all students have a similar capacity to benefit from such an education.

Although embedded in the concept of the person as a social being, this approach makes little comment on the social consequences of its education.

2.5. SOCIAL EQUALITY, EDUCATION AND THE COMMON GOOD

The focus on diversity in society has led governments to concentrate on the way that different groups engage with the education system and derive different benefits from it. The concern of governments is social cohesion; a key element of policy is the provision of equal opportunity, where all citizens can avail of education and its rewards. The human capital approach opens skills to all citizens and the production function approach ensures that there is a level playing field in terms of access. However, history dictates that not everyone is equipped to play the game in the same way. Major differences still exist in how different groups 'consume' education. Depending on their starting points, some citizens are able to maintain social and economic advantages because of how they negotiate the system.

The negotiation of a system that focuses on a production function approach results in the increased 'commodification' of outcomes – meaning the standardisation of outcomes into discrete units that are easily recognised and compared. An unintended by-product of the human capital approach is an increased credentialism, as users of the system seek to demonstrate their success by accumulating the commodities of education. Credentials are then traded the same as any other product or service. Consequently, success is judged on what you *have* rather than on what, or who, you *are*. In practice, this approach gives an advantage to individuals who have high social and educational capital, as they are able to use the system to their advantage, thereby maintaining their social position.

Responses to these issues take two forms. The first seeks the promotion of groups who traditionally lose out on rewards, encouraging them to achieve more. This takes place through affirmative action programmes, providing extra investment or incentives, which target particular social groups where the uptake of schooling or success within the system is low. The second seeks to develop equality of conditions. This is linked to the production function approach, where there is an attempt to standardise the experience of education. An example of this approach is the 'common school' proposal, which seeks to limit parental choice in education and assign children to local schools on a random basis. The image of the common good in this approach is inspired by an integrated vision where citizens benefit equally from the 'goods' of society and are equipped with the equal opportunities that will allow them to contribute to society.

In measuring participation, this approach is criticised for its focus on economic issues; it is claimed that the economic emphasis is linked to concepts of human capital, where the contribution of a citizen to society is defined in terms of the market – either as a consumer or a producer. It also leads to the designation of certain types of work as high status. Invariably this type of work is linked to high-stake technologies. The roles of caring and social work are marginalised. The approach gives primacy to self-interest and competition, and this has the effect of distancing certain groups who traditionally give care or need it more – women, migrants, those who are disabled. The dream of a society working together from a common base to achieve common goals soon finds itself in conflict with individuals who want to ensure some advantage for themselves.

2.6. The Task of Politics

Five different perspectives have been outlined in the discourse on education and schooling. The focus on the private and public benefits of education highlights responsibility for investment in education. It seeks a balance between the roles of the individual and society based on how they both benefit from having a good education system. Both the human capital approach and the production function approach are firmly rooted in the responsibility of the State for the national economy and the implications of this for an education system. The human capital approach works from promoting individuals as productive members of society, whereas the production function approach looks to economic efficiencies in both the means and end of investment. The approaches that focus on human development and on social equality reflect contrasting perspectives on psychological and sociological concerns of development. The psychological focuses on the personal capacity of individuals with little or no reference to their community context; the sociological looks at how groups are empowered or marginalised in the system and questions the dynamics of personal development.

Each of these approaches is a legitimate perspective on schooling. In practice they are not distinct philosophies but borrow from one another and overlap. Whereas the differences they highlight are real, their contribution is in the emphasis they put on particular issues. Each needs to be complemented by the strengths of other approaches. For instance, the human capital approach needs to take into account aspects of human development and social equality. The production function approach also needs to incorporate a perspective on social equality where outcome benefits are not easily measured. Each of the approaches finds its legitimacy in promoting the common good. However, the concept of the common good being promoted is often different. The human development approach focuses on the individual and the benefits of personal development. This is nuanced by the social perspective of human existence and the moral responsibility of individuals within a society. The human capital approach sees the common good in the accumulation of goods in a society, and views the person more in terms of their productivity. The production function and the social equality perspectives look to the distribution of goods within a society. In these perspectives, the common good is seen in developing equity in education as a means to greater participation. In the social equality approach, the focus is on individuals sharing in the product of education.

The task of politics in education is to negotiate these different concepts of the common good as they are expressed in different discourses. One aspect of the task is to recognise the different perspectives in action. A second is to ensure an appreciation of the strengths and weakness of the different perspectives, and to challenge different groups to be inclusive in their approaches. The third aspect of the political task is to mediate between the different approaches in a fair and equitable way. The political system is often challenged in its task through the use of rights language.

3. EDUCATION AND RIGHTS

The right to education is enshrined in Article 26 of the Universal Declaration of Human Rights. This right has been affirmed in a number of subsequent conventions.[4] In the 1952 European Convention on Human Rights, the right to education was not listed in the main body of the text, but in the Protocols attached to the main text. It is stated quite simply:

No person shall be denied the right to education. In the exercise
of any functions which it assumes in relation to education and to
teaching, the State shall respect the right of parents to ensure such
education and teaching in conformity with their own religions and
philosophical convictions.[5]

In the Universal Declaration of Human Rights, education was
defined in an expansive way as the full development of the human
personality.[6] UNESCO defined education as 'the entire process of
social life by means of which individuals and social groups learn to
develop consciously within, and for the benefit of, the national and
international communities, the whole of their personal capabilities,
attitudes, aptitudes and knowledge.'[7] The scope of the provision is
therefore quite wide, and develops from a worldview that is inclusive
of psychological, economic, social and cultural perspectives.

3.1. The Right, and Who Provides It
From an examination of the different Conventions in the United
Nations[8] and the European Union that promote education as a right,
a number of consistent themes emerge:

- Education contributes to different **personal and social benefits**,
  and these social benefits have both national and international
  perspectives. It promotes the full development of the human
  personality and the sense of its dignity, thus allowing people to
  participate effectively in a free society. It promotes understanding,
  tolerance and friendship among all nations, racial or religious
  groups, and strengthens respect for human rights and fundamental
  freedoms. From the perspectives of the United Nations, it furthers
  the maintenance of peace within and between nations.
- Education is a **freedom for individuals**. It has universal
  application and embraces the concept of life-long learning. It
  focuses particularly on children and on those adults who have been
  deprived of fundamental education. Individuals should be free to
  choose their own education and to establish and direct educational
  institutions as the means to achieving it. In particular, parents
  have the freedom to educate their children according to their own
  religious and philosophical convictions.

- **The State has an obligation** to set up the conditions in which this freedom can be realised. This amounts to a claim that individuals have against the State. It protects the rights of individuals by deciding on minimum educational standards and by ensuring that all schools conform to these standards. It also protects the rights of parents in ensuring that the religious and moral education of children is in conformity with the convictions of the parents.
- **The State also provides an education system**, and there are different claim rights against the State relating to different ages of students. Primary or fundamental education is supposed to be free and compulsory, guaranteeing a student the basic skills to allow them meaningful participation in society. Second-level education, either professional or vocational, should be widely available and third-level education should be available on an equitable basis according to merit. The aspiration of the different conventions with regard to second and third-level education is that they be accessible to all 'by every appropriate means, and in particular by the progressive introduction of free education'.[9]

In the different conventions, education is promoted as an important public function as well as an individual right. The development of rights language in education has seen the emphasis change from the right of the individual and the duty of the parent to the obligation of the State to respect, protect and fulfil the right. The State is regarded as the chief provider of education, often in partnership with non-governmental organisations, the private sector, local communities, religious groups and families. This is done through the allocation of substantial budgetary resources and through legislation. The obligation can be summarised under four headings:[10]

Availability: That there is an infrastructure for education – facilities, qualified staff, resources and materials.
Accessibility: This refers to location and/or transport access. It also implies that the cost of education should not be prohibitive. There should be no discrimination in access, with an active attempt to include marginalised groups. Labour laws should encourage rather than prevent young people attending school.

Acceptability: Education should be relevant and culturally appropriate. It should be free from any bias or indoctrination. It should cover a wide variety of ideas and beliefs. The atmosphere of the school should be welcoming.

Adaptability: Programmes should adjust to societal changes and the needs of the community. The organisation of the school should be respectful of the needs of students and accommodate them (those with disabilities, fulfilling religious obligations, etc).

This is the context in which individuals or groups claim rights, particularly against the State. The focus of these claims will be limited to the European context and to decisions by the European Court of Human Rights.

3.2. Education and Human Rights Case Law

Although each person has the right to education, there are limits to what the individual can claim against the State. In particular, there is no obligation on the State to provide any particular type or level of education. Individuals simply have a right to avail themselves of the means of instruction existing in the State at a particular time. What the State provides is negotiated at a political level, and falls within the margin of appreciation of the State. The only positive claim an individual has is respect for 'religious and philosophical convictions'. This claim does not extend to other cultural or linguistic preferences.[11]

3.2.1. The State and Educational Provision

Although the State is not obliged to provide a particular type of education, there is a consensus that the State has a major role in securing the right to education for individuals. The right to education needs to be practical and effective, not theoretical and illusory.[12] For the most part, the responsibility of the State for education is well established.

[The court] notes ... that all member States of the Council of Europe possessed, at the time of the opening of the Protocol to their signature, and still do possess, a general and official educational system.[13]

Education is seen as an important part of any State, especially in its contribution to the preservation of a democratic society. The court focused on the provision for diversity in the Protocol, seeing the respect given to parental wishes as a key element of a democratic society. It would appear that, because of the complexity of the situation, the only real possibility for such an education to develop is for the State to regulate it:

> The second sentence of Article 2 (P1–2) aims in short at safeguarding the possibility of pluralism in education which is essential for the preservation of the 'democratic society' as conceived by the Convention. In view of the power of the modern State, it is above all through State teaching that this aim must be realised.[14]

3.2.2. THE CURRICULUM IN STATE SCHOOLS

The State has wide powers in determining the curriculum, and the authority of the State is derived from its democratic mandate. The main focus of case law has been on the curriculum as it deals with religion, linking the right to freedom of religion with educational provision. The mandate to respect the philosophical beliefs of parents does not prevent the State dealing with issues where there might be a conflict with such wishes, even in making a particular aspect of the curriculum compulsory. If the State does decide that certain issues are to be dealt with, then the approach must be 'objective, critical and pluralist':

> [T]he setting and planning of the curriculum fall in principle within the competence of the Contracting States. This mainly involves questions of expediency on which it is not for the Court to rule and whose solution may legitimately vary according to the country and the era. In particular, the second sentence of Article 2 of the Protocol (P1–2) does not prevent States from imparting through teaching or education information or knowledge of a directly or indirectly religious or philosophical kind. It does not even permit parents to object to the integration of such teaching or education in the school curriculum, for otherwise all institutionalised teaching would run the risk of proving impracticable. In fact, it seems very difficult for many subjects taught at school not to have, to a greater

or lesser extent, some philosophical complexion or implications. The same is true of religious affinities if one remembers the existence of religions forming a very broad dogmatic and moral entity which has or may have answers to every question of a philosophical, cosmological or moral nature.

The second sentence of Article 2 (P1–2) implies on the other hand that the State, in fulfilling the functions assumed by it in regard to education and teaching, must take care that information or knowledge included in the curriculum is conveyed in an objective, critical and pluralistic manner. The State is forbidden to pursue an aim of indoctrination that might be considered as not respecting parents' religious and philosophical convictions. That is the limit that must not be exceeded.[15]

This problem was tested specifically in the area of a sex education programme in Denmark. In this case, the notion of objective and critical knowledge was developed:

> [C]hildren nowadays discover without difficulty and from several quarters the information that interests them on sexual life. The instruction on the subject given in State schools is aimed less at instilling knowledge they do not have or cannot acquire by other means than at giving them such knowledge more correctly, precisely, objectively and scientifically.[16]

However, the course was not simply about imparting knowledge. It involved evaluation of data and value judgments, and so crossed into the area of moral behaviour:

> By providing children in good time with explanations it considers useful, [the State] is attempting to warn them against phenomena it views as disturbing, for example, the excessive frequency of births out of wedlock, induced abortions and venereal diseases. The public authorities wish to enable pupils, when the time comes, 'to take care of themselves and show consideration for others in that respect', 'not ... [to] land themselves or others in difficulties solely on account of lack of knowledge'.

It also included the direction that schools were required to provide instruction on, inter alia, contraception. Even though this might be against the 'religious and philosophical convictions' of some parents, the court held that there was no violation of their rights by making the course compulsory and not allowing exemptions:

> These considerations are indeed of a moral order, but they are very general in character and do not entail overstepping the bounds of what a democratic State may regard as the public interest. Examination of the legislation in dispute establishes in fact that it in no way amounts to an attempt at indoctrination aimed at advocating a specific kind of sexual behaviour.[17]

In the court judgment, the problems for parents were balanced in favour of the State by two factors. The first was the assertion that there was no interference with the parents' positive freedom *for* religion, that is, their right to pursue their own convictions *outside school time*. They exercised this freedom subsequent to their child's exposure to school information, a process which had limited their freedom *from* religion *during school time*:

> [I]t does not affect the right of parents to enlighten and advise their children, to exercise with regard to their children natural parental functions as educators, or to guide their children on a path in line with the parents' own religious or philosophical convictions.

The second balancing factor was that alternatives were available to the parents, and these were supported by the State:

> Besides, the Danish State preserves an important expedient for parents who, in the name of their creed or opinions, wish to dissociate their children from integrated sex education; it allows parents either to entrust their children to private schools, which are bound by less strict obligations and moreover heavily subsidised by the State ... or to educate them or have them educated at home, subject to suffering the undeniable sacrifices and inconveniences caused by recourse to one of those alternative solutions.[18]

In effect, this judgment made a clear distinction between the liberty of parents to educate their children according to their philosophical convictions and the claim they had against the State to cooperate with them in providing that education. The liberty was supported by the availability of other types of school, or by home education. However, if they decided to send their child to a State school, then their claims to exemptions from courses was limited as long as the teaching was in an 'objective, and pluralist' manner.

The question of a religious education programme (KRL) in Norway's State schools was tested in the court in 2002. KRL had been developed as a core subject in the compulsory programme at primary and secondary level. The design aim of KRL was to provide a meeting place for different religious and philosophical convictions, where pupils could gain knowledge about their respective thoughts and traditions. The methodology was to bring pupils together within the framework of one joint subject, where the different religions and philosophies were to be taught from the standpoint of their particular characteristics and the same pedagogical principles were to apply to the teaching of the different topics. The court affirmed that this was a valid aim for the State and entailed no breach of rights when such a course was made part of a compulsory curriculum. The court held that States could mandate religion and philosophy as part of the curriculum. It also held that, given the place occupied by Christianity in the national history and tradition of the State, devoting a greater part of the curriculum to knowledge about Christianity than about other religions and philosophies cannot, on its own, be viewed as a departure from the principles of pluralism and objectivity amounting to indoctrination. What concerned the court was the different nuances that were attached to phrases such as 'transmit thorough knowledge of', 'know about', 'thorough insight into', 'sound knowledge of', 'learn the fundamentals of', 'study the main features of', 'learn about' and 'become acquainted with', which were used to describe outcomes with regard to different religious traditions. The court had no difficulty with quantitative inequality of topics; the concerns were with qualitative approaches and that the delivery would not be sufficiently 'objective and pluralist'.[19] On these grounds, it granted the parents full exemption from the course.

A similar test case was taken in Turkey against a compulsory religious culture and ethics course.[20] The parents had requested exemption from the course it was 'based on the fundamental rules of Hanafite Islam and that no teaching was given on his own [Alevi] faith'. The request was refused because

> Article 24 of the Constitution has established that religious culture and ethics are among the compulsory subjects taught in primary and secondary schools, and section 12 of Law no. 1739 [states] that religious culture and ethics are among the compulsory subjects taught in primary and upper secondary schools of the equivalent level.

In this case the syllabus and textbooks for the course gave a greater priority to knowledge of Islam than they did to other religions and philosophies. As in the Norwegian case, the court found that there was no difficulty with a quantitative imbalance in the material. Notwithstanding the State's secular nature, with Islam as the majority religion, this was within the margin of appreciation of the State. However, in its treatment of Islam, there was no mention of the Alevi faith or its rituals in any of the lessons, although the Alevi movement differed in many areas from the Sunni understanding of Islam that was in the textbooks. Given the number of Turkish nationals who belonged to the Alevi tradition, this constituted a lack of objectivity. The court held that parents may legitimately expect that the subject will be taught in such a way as to meet the criteria of objectivity and pluralism, with respect for their religious or philosophical convictions, and should not have to rely entirely on their own efforts to enlighten and advise their children *outside* school.

The court went on to consider the issue of exemption, which had been made possible for children 'of Turkish nationality who belong to the Christian or Jewish religion ... provided they affirm their adherence to those religions'. It was judged that the existence of an exemption clause recognised possible clashes between what was taught and the legitimate beliefs of parents. It claimed that limiting exemption to those of other faiths and not to different groups within Islam amounted to discrimination. The court went on to offer an opinion on the onerous procedures that were involved in securing an exemption and stated that the right to freedom of religion should not force a parent to reveal their own religious convictions in order to exercise their right, especially when no alternative course was offered.

3.2.3. STATE RESPONSIBILITY FOR SCHOOL ORGANISATION

According to the European Court of Human Rights, the responsibility of the State in public education goes beyond simply that which is taught – the notion of instruction. The State has responsibilities to ensure that the rights of individuals are guaranteed in all aspects of schooling. This also extends to private schools in the sense that the State regulates and approves them. The basis for this is the obligation of the State to respect the rights of parents in 'the exercise of any functions which it assumes in relation to education and to teaching'.[21]

One of these functions is the development of a discipline system in a school. The court states quite clearly that discipline codes are not merely ancillary to the educational process. Discipline, in terms of expected behaviour and the rewards and sanctions associated with that behaviour, operates at three levels – the character and moral formation of the student, the efficient running of the school and ensuring that the school can achieve its purposes:

> The right to education does not in principle exclude recourse to disciplinary measures, including suspension or expulsion from an educational institution in order to ensure compliance with its internal rules. The imposition of disciplinary penalties is an integral part of the process whereby a school seeks to achieve the object for which it was established, including the development and moulding of the character and mental powers of its pupils.[22]

In the cases of *Campbell and Cosans* vs *UK*, and also of *Costello-Roberts* vs *UK*, the specific issue referred to corporal punishment in a State school:

> Discipline is an integral, even indispensable, part of any educational system, with the result that the functions assumed by the State in Scotland must be taken to extend to question of discipline in general, even if not to its everyday maintenance. Indeed, this is confirmed by the fact that central and local authorities

participated in the preparation of the Code of Practice and that the Government themselves are committed to a policy aimed at abolishing corporal punishment.[23]

That a school's disciplinary system falls within the ambit of the right to education has also been recognised in Article 28 of the United Nation's Convention on the Rights of the Child (1989), wherein it states: 'Parties shall take all appropriate measures to ensure that school discipline is administered in a manner consistent with the child's human dignity and in conformity with the present Convention.'[24]

Another function that affects education is the display of artefacts in schools. In the Lautsi case, discussed in the previous chapter, the issue was the compulsory display of a crucifix in a classroom. The court held that this was permissible, because the crucifix was essentially a passive symbol and, when considered along with other aspects of the education system, did not involve proselytising or indoctrination. In *Dahlab* vs *Switzerland* (2001) the court held that a primary school teacher wearing a headscarf constituted a 'powerful external symbol'.[25] The power of the symbol lay in its potential for indoctrination and related to the impressionable age of the pupils and the influential role of the teacher; the ban on headscarves did not extend to the pupils themselves. There was no suggestion that the teacher had engaged in any proselytising activity. However, the court ruled that it was permissible for Switzerland to make a universal ban on teachers in State schools expressing their religious beliefs through artefacts, given its particular definition of secularism.

In other cases, the court upheld that, in defence of tolerance and pluralism, the display of religious symbols (dress) was not in conformity with *laïcité* and the prevention of indoctrination. In *Sahin* vs *Turkey* (2005) the court held that the ban on a university student wearing a Muslim headscarf was permissible in terms of the protection of others' rights and of public order.[26] In effect, the court endorsed the position that, in the name of *laïcité*, any display of religious artefacts could be banned, simply on the basis of being public. The function of the State with regard to public order legitimately extended to the university, although it was not a State body.

In *Dogru* vs *France* (2008), where a student was expelled from school for insisting on wearing a headscarf in PE classes, which was against school rules aimed at health and safety, and the family refused to engage in any compromise, similar support was given to the French position as part of its promotion of public order according to its philosophy of *laïcité*.[27] The key determining factor in these cases was the 'margin of appreciation' in each State. This is the negotiated approach to diversity within the State, and has its legitimacy in the mandate of the government from the people.

3.3. RELIGION AND EDUCATION

The right to freedom of religion and the right to education cannot be seen as separate or treated differently. The role of the State is to ensure the free exercise of various religions, faiths and beliefs in a manner that is neutral, impartial and fair, within the education system as well as apart from it. Its role is to help maintain public order, religious harmony and tolerance. Politics involves negotiating this order, harmony and tolerance between opposing groups. The judgments discussed above illustrate different ways in which States have solved their issues.

3.3.1. RELIGIOUS SYMBOLS IN SCHOOLS

In France, Turkey and Switzerland the approach is to have a 'secular' public school space. The main focus is on religious symbols, especially the wearing of distinctive religious dress. In France and Turkey, this extends to all involved in the education process and impacts particularly on students. In Switzerland, the claim is only against teachers, and this focuses on avoiding any danger of proselytising due to the vulnerability of children and the influential role of the teacher. The Italian position is to allow all religious groups to display their symbols, and to negotiate the outcome.

The first approach places a strong emphasis on secularism supporting freedom *from* religion in the public arena, while supporting the individual's freedom *for* religion in the private arena or, in the case of education, in publicly supported private schools. The second allows a greater freedom in manifesting one's religion, therefore promoting a freedom *for* religion.

3.3.2. RELIGION IN THE CURRICULUM

A particular conceptualisation of secularism is also evident in the curriculum cases discussed in this chapter. This works from the assumption that it is possible to develop a value-neutral approach to teaching and schooling, one that is 'objective, critical and pluralistic', such that an education 'in conformity with religious and philosophical convictions' can be equally and simultaneously achieved for every parent, regardless of their beliefs. In the three cases discussed, the court allowed the State a considerable margin of appreciation in determining the content of the curriculum and making the curriculum compulsory. Within that margin of appreciation, the State could determine the information to be conveyed, and could also determine the balance of subjects treated. For instance, in both the Norwegian and the Turkish cases, the majority position of Christianity and Islam, respectively, was recognised in the balance of material. What concerned the court was not the quantitative amount of information that had to be negotiated by students of different beliefs, but the qualitative aspects of how the information was delivered. The requirement of the state was to ensure that courses are delivered in an 'objective, critical and pluralist manner' that is respectful of different groups and avoids all dangers of proselytising. In Turkey, omitting references to the Alevi faith was seen as breaching rules of objectivity. In Norway, the expectation of different outcomes when studying different religious groups was seen as a breach of critical pluralism.

The focus of the cases outlined here has been on a single compulsory course in a State-run school. In practice, many States do not depend on this mechanism to teach about religion or to deal with sensitive moral issues. These different provisions are the focus of the next chapter.

3.3.3. Exemptions on the Basis of Religious Freedom

The above curriculum cases made no challenge to the State's right to set the curriculum; their focus was parents seeking exemptions in the face of compulsion. The parents sought to establish their freedom to determine the religious and philosophical education of their child. They sought an exemption from what others studied in order to protect their own wishes. They sought freedom *from* religion, as expressed in the State-sponsored course. In the Danish case, no provision was made for exemption. The court upheld this, based on the State's concern for public welfare. Because it deemed that the curriculum was presented in an 'objective, critical and pluralist' manner and did not advocate any particular approach to sexuality, the compulsory course did not breach a right to religious freedom and it was up to the parents to help their children negotiate and integrate the information given on the course with their own worldview. In the Norway and Turkey cases, some provision for exemptions existed within the system. The court upheld the parents' specific claims because of the way the exemption system worked. In Turkey, exemptions were possible for people of Christian or Jewish faiths, but not for groupings within the Muslim tradition. The court insisted on an objective application of the right to exemption. In Norway, a partial exemption was possible, but the court ruled that this put too much of a burden on parents to anticipate different lessons, and in view of the qualitative deficiencies in the course, a full exemption should be possible.

In the Danish case, the content of the course and its method of teaching made it very difficult for parents to establish a valid objection on the basis of freedom *from* religion. The court held that the course was not 'advocating a specific type of sexual behaviour', nor was it 'exalting sex or inciting pupils to indulge precociously in practices that are dangerous for their stability, health or future or that many parents find reprehensible'. This judgment implied that, unless there was some element of coercion or proselytising on the part of the State, then the individual's freedom from religion was not breached. This placed a heavy burden of proof on the parents if their objections were to be upheld. The court placed an even heavier burden on the parents if they wanted to enact their freedom *from* religion. Although the problem existed in only one subject area – sex education – the court suggested that they would send their child to a private school or educate them at home.

In the Norway and Turkey cases, the court proposed a much less onerous burden on parents. In claiming that exemption procedures should not deter parents from seeking exemptions, it proposed that they should be required to reveal details of their own beliefs in any request. The court also suggested that the State seek to provide options for students of different beliefs, so that an exemption from one course did not force them to reveal their beliefs – that they simply chose one course over another, as they might do in any other part of the curriculum. This proposal endorsed the freedom *for* religion and the freedom *from* religion as equal freedoms.

3.3.4. State Involvement in Religious Education

The Toledo Guiding Principles were developed to assist the States attached to the Organisation for Security and Cooperation in Europe (OSCE) to promote study and knowledge about religions and beliefs in schools, particularly as a tool to enhance religious freedom and to promote public order. They are based on two underlying assumptions: the first is that there is a positive value in courses that emphasise everyone's right to freedom of religion and belief; the second that objective information about other religions and beliefs can reduce harmful misunderstandings and stereotyping. The Principles focus solely on the educational approach that seeks to provide teaching about different religions and beliefs as distinguished from instruction in a specific religion or belief. They recognise religion as a 'cultural fact' and propose that knowledge and understanding of religion at this level is highly relevant to good community and personal relations. Teaching about religion is therefore a legitimate response to concern for public policy. These principles represent the lowest common denominator for all European States.[28]

The Toledo Guiding Principles are designed for a curriculum dealing with religious beliefs, where lessons are delivered in State schools where there is pluralism of religious beliefs among the students. This type of course represents a negotiated approach to providing some education on religion in the public sphere and allowing for confessional groups to add to that teaching in their own way. Religious belief is treated as a phenomenon – the curriculum gives information only. It teaches *about* religion, the assumption being that the information given is neutral and preserves freedom from any form of indoctrination. Nurturing a response to the information is seen as the role of the individual or other groups. A second assumption is that a course which excludes any manifestation of beliefs and practices, or any attempt to critique the holistic link that many parents find between the tenets of their religion and its practices, is a sufficient guarantee for religious freedom as there can be no objection to the objective data. The focus is on protecting the freedom *from* religion in the State school, and assuming the freedom *for* religion can be exercised elsewhere.

There is little dispute about the phenomenon of religion, especially in the history of Europe. There seems to be little argument about the value of students having 'objective and critical' information about different approaches to religion, although when and how they engage with that information may be a question for debate. It would be wrong to suggest that religious groups do not promote critical reflection on their own tradition, encouraging their members to an authentic personal commitment rather than an unthinking compliance in thought and ritual. It would also be a false assertion that religious groups do not give 'objective and critical' information on other religious traditions in their programmes. The issue that many people have with the assumptions of the Toledo Guiding Principles is that they are a form of ideology in themselves. The position promoted is not value neutral, but a worldview of its own. These critics claim that the position is based on a notion of pluralism that assumes a form of assimilation – a melting pot approach to religion, based on the relativism of different religious positions.

Treating religion simply as a phenomenon is at odds with the philosophical position of religion, and strongly reflects the ideology of secularist humanism. To promote such a course would have a powerful symbolic effect on students in the context of a school. It does not encourage a process of integration based on images of the salad bowl or the mosaic discussed in Chapter 2. For these critics, the Toledo approach advocates that the State is obliged to promote a secularist position (treating religion as a phenomenon). As Judge Power commented in her concurring opinion in the *Lautsi* vs *Italy* Grand Chamber judgment:

Neutrality requires a pluralist approach on the part of the State, not a secularist one. It encourages respect for all worldviews rather than a preference for one. To my mind, the Chamber Judgment was striking in its failure to recognise that secularism (which was the applicant's preferred belief or worldview) was, in itself, one ideology among others. A preference for secularism over alternative worldviews – whether religious, philosophical or otherwise – is not a neutral option. The Convention requires that respect be given to the first applicant's convictions insofar as the education and teaching of her children was concerned. It does not require a preferential option for and endorsement of those convictions over and above all others.[29]

3.3.5. THE TASK OF POLITICS

The design of the education system is within the 'margin of appreciation' of each individual State. There is a political mandate to provide a system that, through its curriculum and its structure of delivery, meet the needs of the students and also contributes to the common good. The negotiated system includes personal, social, cultural and economic goals. It encourages some level of engagement with national identity and promotes social cohesion and equality. It helps students develop basic skills of literacy and numeracy so that they can participate fully in society. It also promotes particular types of additional skills in order to direct students to a productive participation in society (human capital). This system is negotiated as part of the normal political process. Education policy changes in response to international, national and regional forces that challenge the legitimacy and distribution within the status quo. It will be part of the manifesto of any party seeking election and is open to the scrutiny of the electorate.

Given its role in relation to the common good, the State has extensive powers in relation to education, and the education system that is proposed has a normative dimension. In other words, there is an obligation at some level on citizens within a State to support the goals of the system for the common good. However, in developing its system, the State is obliged to consider individual rights. On one hand, the State protects the rights of the individual by setting standards within the education system and making a certain amount of education compulsory. It protects these rights by providing an easily accessible system which is inclusive of all its citizens. On the other, education is seen as a liberty, and parents have the liberty – some might say obligation – to educate their children according to their own religion or philosophy of life. In exercising this liberty, parents and students have claim rights against the State.

As the State has designed the education system in the light of the common good, the claims of parents for something different may be difficult to justify unless the State understands its commitment to diversity in allowing differences between groups to be institutionalised in State-supported schools. The Court has made it clear that the State is not obliged to provide any particular system of education, or to cater for any particular philosophy of education. The issue of individual freedom and rights must be worked out in the context of the common good, and the expression of this is the margin of appreciation afforded to each country.

The link between the right to freedom of religion and the right to education points to a particular claim area for parents. The right to education clearly enshrines an obligation on the State that 'in the exercise of any functions which it assumes in relation to education and to teaching, the State shall respect the right of parents to ensure such education and teaching in conformity with their own religions and philosophical convictions'.[30] Many States respond positively to that claim and seek to help parents:

> In many countries religious instruction [in a particular religion] constitutes an integral part of public school teaching and maybe even of the mandatory school curriculum. Such practice may reflect the interests and demands of large parts of the population. Many parents may wish that their children be familiarized with the basic doctrines and rules of their own religion or belief and that the school take an active role in that endeavour. In the understanding of many parents, the development of knowledge and social skills of their children through school education would be incomplete unless it includes a sense of religious awareness and familiarity with their own religion or belief. Hence the provision of religious instruction in the public school system may be based on the explicit or implicit wishes of considerable currents within the country's population.[31]

In a diverse society, this obligation gives rise to problems of logistics, and the State has to ensure there are safeguards for minority religions and belief systems. States have sought to solve the problems by (a) opting out of any involvement in religious education; (b) developing a religious education provision where students have choices either in taking or not taking the programme; (c) developing a religious education programme that allows for exemptions on the basis of religious belief; and (d) facilitating the setting up of alternative schools to cater for particular educational philosophies that differ in some respects from that of the State. Although the State has no obligation to fund private education, when it does so, it must do so without any discrimination:

The situation of religious instruction in private schools warrants a distinct assessment. The reason is that private schools, depending on their particular rationale and curriculum, might accommodate the more specific educational interests or needs of parents and children, including in questions of religion or belief. Indeed, many private schools have a specific denominational profile which can make them particularly attractive to adherents of the respective denomination, but frequently also for parents and children of other religious or belief orientation. In this sense, private schools constitute a part of the institutionalised diversity within a modern pluralistic society. States are not obliged under international human rights law to fund schools which are established on a religious basis, however, if the State chooses to provide public funding to religious schools, it should make this funding available without any discrimination.[32]

The existence of private schools, or the possibility of having them, is not an adequate provision for diversity by the State. The human rights standards outlined by the UN Special Rapporteur, and also the European Court of Human Rights insist on parents' right that their philosophical views be respected within State education, and that they should not need to have recourse to private education.

There is an obligation on the State to respect religious and cultural diversity. In that regard, the UN Special Rapporteur noted the extension of this obligation to cultural preferences such as language,[33] a position that was not upheld in the Belgian Linguistic Case in 1968. The State also has supervisory obligations over private institutions to ensure that the freedom *for* and *from* religion is protected. However, the distribution of rights in private schools has not been tested in the European Court of Human Rights. In particular, there has been no case where parents who opted for a denominational school which was not their own denomination made a claim against the school for particular treatment as a freedom *for* their own religious beliefs. It seems that most were happy to enjoy a freedom from any engagement with the school's religious offering in return for access to other educational characteristics of the school. The main concern of the UN Special Rapporteur was the more difficult situation where parents may not have a free choice of school:

Another caveat concerns situations in which private denominational schools have a de facto monopoly in a particular locality or region, with the result that students and parents have no option to avoid school education based on a denomination different from their own religious or belief conviction. In such situations it falls upon the State, as the guarantor of human rights, to ensure that freedom of religion or belief is effectively respected, including the right of students not to be exposed to religious instruction against their will as well as the right of parents to ensure a religious and moral education of their children in conformity with their own convictions.[34]

In seeking to meet their obligations, States have arrived at different solutions to the political problems posed in their own countries. In the next chapter, these solutions will be explored in a European context in order to provide a resource reference on different possibilities that may contribute to the debate in Ireland.

NOTES

1. David Tuohy and Penny Cairns, *Youth 2K: Threat or Promise to a Religious Culture?* (Dublin: Marino Institute of Education, 2000).
2. Erik H. Erikson, *Identity, Youth and Crisis* (New York: W. W. Norton Company, 1968).
3. Statement by the UK Universities Minister Rt Hon. David Willetts MP at a conference in Warwick (January 2012).
4. UNESCO Convention against Discrimination in Education (1960); International Covenant on Economic, Social and Cultural Rights (1966), Articles 13 and 14; and the Convention on the Elimination of all Forms of Discrimination Against Women (1981).
5. European Convention on Human Rights, Protocol 1, Article 2.
6. The original draft of this article had described this education as embracing 'physical, intellectual, spiritual and moral development of the human personality'.
7. UNESCO, Recommendation Concerning Education for International Understanding, Co-operation and Peace and Education relating to Human Rights and Fundamental Freedoms (1974), Article 1a.
8. The text of the different conventions can be found at http://www.unescobkk. org/education/education-and-human-rights/rights-based-approach-to-education/right-to-education-in-international-instruments/
9. International Covenant on Economic, Social and Cultural Rights, Article 13.2.

10. The 4A framework was developed by the UN Special Rapporteur for the Right to Education, Katarina Tomasevski.

11. Case relating to certain aspects of the laws on the use of languages in education in *Belgium* vs *Belgium*. Application 1474/62; 1677/62; 1691/62; 1769/63; 1994/63; 2126/64, summary of arguments, 1, interpretations 3,

12. *Öcalan* vs *Turkey* [GC], no. 46221/99, §135, ECHR 2005–IV.

13. Belgian Linguistic Case B, Interpretation by the Court, #3.

14. Ibid., #51.

15. *Kjeldsen, Busk Madsen and Pedersen* vs *Denmark*. Application 5095/71, 5920/72 and 5926/72 in 1976 #53.

16. Ibid., #54.

17. Ibid., #51.

18. Ibid., #54.

19. *Folgerø and others* vs *Norway*, Application 15472/02, #98–100.

20. *Hasan and Zengin* vs *Turkey*, Application 1448/04 (9 October 2007).

21. European Convention on Human Rights, Protocol 1, Article 2.

22. Case of *Campbell and Cosans* vs *the United Kingdom*, Application 7511/76; 7743/76 #156.

23. Ibid., #34. See also case of *Costello-Roberts* vs *the United Kingdom*, Application 13134/87.

24. Convention on the Rights of the Child, Article 28.2.

25. *Dahlab* vs *Switzerland*. This case was deemed not admissible. See http://hudoc. echr.coe.int/sites/eng/pages/search.aspx?i=001-22643

26. *Sahin* vs *Turkey*, Application 44774/98.

27. *Dogru* vs *France*, Application 27058/05 (4 December 2008).

28. Robert Jackson, 'Teaching about Religions in the Public Sphere: European Policy Initiatives and the Interpretive Approach', *Numen* 55 (2008), pp. 151–82. This article gives a detailed review of the process and response to the Toledo process.

29. *Lautsi* vs *Italy*. Concurring opinion of Judge Power.

30. European Convention on Human Rights, Protocol 1, Article 2.

31. UN Special Rapporteur on Freedom of Religion, #49.

32. Ibid., #54. Citing Human Rights Committee, communication no. 694/1996, *Waldman* vs *Canada*, views adopted on 3 November 1999, #10.6.

33. Ibid., #55.

34. Ibid.

6

DENOMINATIONAL EDUCATION: A EUROPEAN PERSPECTIVE

Education must ... simultaneously provide maps of a complex world in constant turmoil and the compass that will enable people to find their way in it.

UNESCO[1]

No society survives without providing for the education of its children. In the past, children learned from their families and by participating in the life of the community. Most communities also provided occasions when stories were recounted and ritualised, informing and reinforcing a worldview. In that sense, the institutionalisation of religion predates the institutionalisation of education, and in many ways the two were closely linked.

Until the nineteenth century, literacy was mainly the domain of the elite who had central roles in the administration of society. Most others learned by apprenticeship and imitation. In terms of formal education, the early schools were founded by monasteries and churches and the main focus was on training clergy to read the scriptures and study theology. Other professions were also taught, with a focus on classical texts. Church involvement in establishing schools for the general population expanded just after the Reformation when the printing press made religious texts more widely available and schools were seen as opportunities to teach Christian doctrine.

To a large extent, any analysis of education systems today assumes the heavy involvement of the State. However, this involvement is a relatively recent phenomenon. Prior to the industrial revolution, provision was funded by parents, Churches and philanthropic groups. State involvement sought to impose new systems of 'public' education on an established private system. Initially at least, the nineteenth-century reforms aimed to change what and how people were taught in order to prepare them for a changed economic context. It was much later that the welfare goals of equal opportunity developed.[2]

The cursory history of educational provision demonstrates two sources of authority for establishing the 'map' and the 'compass' of life mentioned in the UNESCO quotation at the beginning of this chapter – the State and the Church. The last chapter outlined how the rhetoric of education invokes different concepts of the common good. The worldview proposed by religious groups has a strong theological framework; the State worldview is dominated by an economic perspective. Although these views are not necessarily exclusive, they give rise to tensions. In some countries, these tensions have been worked out by negotiating common ground and complementary goals between the State, the different religious communities, schools and families, such that all are accommodated within a single system. In other countries, two parallel tracks of Church and State schools exist, with Church schools being supported to varying degrees by the State. The aim of this chapter is to survey how these tensions have been negotiated in Europe. The survey is divided into three areas of exploration:

1. **Context:** This section of the chapter explores different trends in developing meaning across Europe. It looks at concepts of religious education and then considers the different ways the role of religion in education is conceptualised. A final part of the context is an exploration of how Church and State develop different roles in the provision of religious education.
2. **Religious education in State schools:** This section examines the way religious education is provided in State-run schools, with particular emphasis on how the State conceptualises its commitment to the common good, and also how it caters for the diversity of religious philosophies among its citizens.
3. **The State and private provision:** A survey of issues with the provision of private education in the different Member States of the European Union, with particular reference to the provision for separate denominational schools. The aim of the survey is twofold:

- to see how the concepts of 'freedom of religion' and the 'right to education' as outlined in the previous two chapters is applied in different contexts, with a hope of deepening the understanding of these concepts;
- to provide a resource on possible responses to issues that might inform the debate in Ireland, providing a context for the analysis of that debate in Part III.

1. CONTEXT

1.1. CULTURE

The late twentieth and early twenty-first centuries have been characterised as postmodern cultures. This refers to a way of looking at life that is sceptical of explanations claiming to be valid for all groups, cultures, traditions or races, instead focusing on the relative truths of each person. In dismissing metanarratives, the concrete experience of each individual is prized. Each person interprets reality for themselves, and this 'construct' creates meaning. This gives rise to fallible and relative understandings, negating abstract principles and universal truths as valid knowledge. The effects of this postmodern approach can be seen in four elements of modern culture:

Pluralism of belief systems: If one rejects the possibility of a valid metanarrative, then there is a marketplace for different ideas, where different worldviews or meaning systems are in competition with one another. Religion is just one of the items traded. Individuals can choose freely to live without religion and religious groups have to compete for the loyalty of members.

Individualisation: There is a strong emphasis on the individual and on individual choice. Each person makes their own way and is free to choose, at will, what they want to believe in. This has a particular impact on approaches to education, where the child is more and more seen as an agent in the development of meaning for themselves, rather than as a passive recipient of the wisdom of the community.

Secularisation: The rejection of authoritative worldviews takes place in two ways. There is a diminution of the role of organised religion in culture, with more people proposing science and technology as the basis for common belief and public policy. In this approach, any idea of faith is seen as an irrational act and is rejected. On the other hand, there are also movements showing support for religious consciousness, a 'believing without belonging' or what Davie termed 'vicarious religion'.[3]

Radicalisation: Individuals organise around particular shared meanings and often defend or promote these positions using radical and military means. A Centre for European Policy Studies Report claimed that 'Tensions and violence involving people from minority groups of Muslim culture are perhaps the greatest source of societal tensions and violent conflict in contemporary Europe.'[4] Citing evidence from events in Belgium, France, the Netherlands, Spain, Russia and the United Kingdom, it claimed that tensions are fuelled by two issues: economic deprivation and discrimination leads to alienation from society, as demonstrated in a radical rejection of values and norms; and a growth in terrorist violence inspired by radical ideas linked with fundamentalist interpretations of religious texts, the most dramatic examples being the events of 9/11 in the United States in 2001 and the 7/7 bombings in London in 2005.

These different trends shape the cultural life of the countries of Europe and define the landscape in which the politics of educational provision is worked out. The postmodern perspective gives rise to a set of critical, strategic and rhetorical practices that both promote new ways of thinking and theories and also challenge and destabilise some established worldviews. One area that has been affected by these developments is the approach to religious education.

1.2. Concepts of Religious Education

Religious education means different things to different people. The design of religious education courses has been classified as:

Into religion: This typically reflects education through a single religious tradition, usually taught by insiders. It seeks to enable students to come to belief and strengthens them in their commitment. This is the basis for confessional religious education and is sometimes named as religious instruction.

About religion: This approach typically uses descriptive and historical methods, seeking neither to foster nor to erode religious belief. It seeks to develop awareness and appreciation of different traditions, with each being treated from an outsider perspective.

From religion: This approach considers different positions in religious and moral issues. It seeks to promote students to develop their own point of view. In the sense that it may give space for students to be critical of the position inherited from their families, it is termed 'from' religion.

However, this classification needs to be nuanced as good religious education involves elements of all three approaches. Many confessional courses now include sections on religious experience, and also a section on world religions, which means that they have elements of teaching 'into' and 'about' religion. For many Churches, a commitment to ecumenical and interfaith dialogue is seen as an integral part of their own belief system, with a view to promoting attitudes of tolerance:

> In societies where religious indifference, cultural intolerance and rapidly changing norms and values seem to prevail, RE can be the space in which young people learn how to deal with challenges to identity, manage conflict and develop sensitivity in interacting with difference. The task of conceptualising RE in dialogue with other faith traditions is an essential way forward.[5]

Teaching about religion may also seek to understand the way in which religious beliefs, values and practices shapes communities and influences the behaviour of individuals. The 'non-objectivity' of the context of such courses is often a problem, in that pupils have some faith affiliation and there is a demand for more 'authentic' treatment or representation of particular faith communities.

Approaches to morality have also changed within religious groups, with more emphasis on personal discernment and appreciation of values, rather than developing habits based on authority and tradition. For the religious educator, there is a tension between teaching young people to be open-minded and teaching them the wisdom that has developed in their own culture.

Furthermore, there are practical difficulties in the delivery of religion courses, no matter what perspective is taken. In teaching 'into' a religion, there is a tension surrounding the proper relationship between the school and the faith community in the formation of individuals, and in finding a balance for their roles. In the design of courses 'about' religion, a particular weight might be given to one religion or denomination, reflecting the cultural history of the State, reinforcing the concept of minorities and promoting a sense of accommodation rather than integration. In the design of teaching methodologies, 'objective' approaches may militate against active participation, as this may involve students feeling forced to reveal their beliefs and practices or those of their families, violating their freedom. This approach may have negative consequences for student learning.

1.3. THE ROLE OF RELIGIOUS EDUCATION IN SOCIETY

The promotion of peace and cohesion in a pluralist society is a central concern for government policy. In many countries, this has given rise to the development of a new focus on citizenship and the development of courses to promote that citizenship. These courses may be stand-alone courses or may be integrated into other subjects such as religious education or social studies, or they might be designed as cross-curricular projects. In some countries, the focus is knowledge-based, with civics related content; or it may be process led, with interactive, active-learning projects that engage students. Schools are invited to set up democratic processes such as student councils to give students the opportunity for participation and to appreciate the reality of citizenship.

In particular, there has been a focus on the role of religious belief as a divisive factor in many communities. As a result, religious education is seen as having an important role in developing tolerance between groups. In October 2005, the Parliamentary Assembly of the European Council adopted a text prepared by the Committee on Culture, Science and Education on the subject of education and religion:

Education is essential to combat ignorance, stereotyping and incomprehension of religions. Governments must also do more to guarantee freedom of conscience and religious expression, to encourage religious instruction, to promote dialogue with and between religions and to further the cultural and social expressions of religions.

The school is an important element in the education and the formation of the critical faculties of future citizens and also in intercultural dialogue. It shall lay the foundation of tolerant conduct based on respect for the dignity of every human being. It shall teach its students the history and philosophy of all major religions in a measured and objective fashion, respecting the values of the ECHR, and it shall fight fanaticism effectively. It is essential to understand the history of political conflicts in the name of religion.

The understanding of religion is an integral part of understanding the history of humanity and its civilisations. It is entirely different from belief in one particular religion or its practice. Even the countries in which one confession largely predominates must teach the origins of all religions rather than privilege one or promote proselytising.[6]

In this statement, a distinction is made between religion as a good in itself and the role of religious education in the State. As a good in itself, it is guaranteed as freedom of conscience and in its cultural and social expression; it is seen as having its own methods of instruction, whereby believers are inducted into and sustained into the belief system. On the other hand, the aim of religious education in schools is promoted in instrumental terms; the assumption is that a 'measured and objective' approach to the history and philosophy of all major religions will bring about greater tolerance. This type of study is seen as generating knowledge and attitudes outside the particular belief system that any one individual may have or practise. The EU statement seems to give priority to this latter position.

Not everyone is satisfied that religious education should be limited to such instrumental goals. Instead they propose that when religion is properly understood and promoted as a value in itself, goals of peace and tolerance are by-products of religion. In Belgium, the French community developed an understanding of education that related to both the person and to society. It situated religious education within the wider aims of education, and saw much common ground. The context of education was seen as dealing with core issues that were shared in a personal existential search, in different cultures and in religious experience. Education was seen as exposing students to the critical analysis of major metaphysical, social and ethical issues. The document also proposed personal and social values that citizens might hold in common in dealing with these issues and proposed the role of the school as promoting personal human search, as well as being instrumental in developing positive societal outcomes such as greater tolerance and cohesion:

> Whether it is in religious experience, the memory of a people or secular culture, human existence is always confronted by the same fundamental questions. Birth, life and death invariably pose the same great metaphysical problems. Social inequalities, the refusal of democratic rights, and crimes against humanity impose new demands on justice. The progress of technology, medicine, surgery and genetics poses new ethical questions.

> There are values that every one of us, in all our difference, may call upon, ideals that we continue to uphold to unite us in common action.

> • The dynamic of liberation, understood as the liberation of thought, where unfreedom produces a reduction, impoverishment, oppression and negation of the human.
> • The indefatigable quest for peace, fraternity, friendship and love.
> • The development of democratic engagement to develop dialogue and tolerance in the spirit of mutual respect and understanding of differences.
> • An education towards citizenship, understanding of and for human rights and fundamental liberties.

> The school needs to centre on the human being. Ethical and religious instruction is a subject of education which, while respecting all their different convictions, favours integration into a pluralist society. Within a coherent educational action plan, they allow us to fight indifference, fanaticism, dogmatism, intolerance, violence, negativism and other dehumanising evils of our time.[7]

The intrinsic and instrumental approaches to religious education suggest a tension between the freedom of religion of the individual and the needs of the State. One argument is that exposure to a wide range of religious views is in the best interests of children, offering them an important range of alternative worldviews and lessening the chance that parents will 'indoctrinate' them. While parents have a right to provide training and grounding for their children in a particular religion, the State may have an interest in providing children with exposure to a wider range of religious views than those provided or endorsed by their parents as the basis for tolerance and pluralism. At one level, it would seem that the parents' rights 'to bring up their children according to their own beliefs' trumps other concerns of the State, even if the approach of the parents seems to others, perhaps even to the great majority, to be irrational or misguided. Yet, in the organisation of the education system, parents can find it onerous and expensive to pursue their freedom of religion. This tension can, of course, be creative. In practice, many parents agree with goals of tolerance and respect for people of other religions. These goals are part of the religious worldview they have for their children. They see their own goals and those of the State as complementary. Other parents may be more protective, believing that exposure to and acceptance of alternative views can only result in spiritual harm for their child and that tolerance of these views would lead to a decrease in moral behaviour with negative consequences not only for individual children, but also for society as a whole.

Opponents of the instrumental approach argue that its goals are not value-free. The autonomy proposed for children is a value statement of what people should be like or how they should best live their lives. Not everyone subscribes to this ideal, and they argue that it would be wrong of the State to institutionalise this view in policy. The State does not give this level of autonomy for its citizens in political matters and does not promote an examination of different types of political systems with the view that adult citizens can freely choose between them. It promotes liberal democracy as the norm. It is claimed that parents should be allowed the same freedom, as guaranteed by human rights covenants, to determine the religion of the child at family level.

A second aspect of the tension between the intrinsic and instrumental approach focuses on the State's concern for public order and social cohesion. The argument claims that that a well-functioning liberal State, especially one with a diverse population, requires citizens who are respectful and tolerant of a wide range of worldviews and ways of life. Since religious differences are an important and defining aspect of the views and ways of life espoused by various individuals, exposing children to a wide range of religious views would be an important step toward the cultivation of religiously tolerant citizens. This should be done in an objective and pluralist manner.

Opponents of this approach to religious education point to the practical difficulty of delivering a general course on religion in a neutral way, arguing that exposure to a variety of views, by itself, does not automatically result in tolerant children. Knowledge does not necessarily change behaviour, as anyone who has tried to give up smoking may know – the link between smoking and health problems is well established. If children are to learn tolerance, exposure to others' religious views must be positive. Teaching about religion in a comparative way may, either deliberately or inadvertently, lead children to find fault with the beliefs of others. Also, teachers with dogmatic religious views or views that are opposed to all religions may be unbalanced in their approach, which could lead to children becoming less tolerant of others. In some cases, it could lead to conflict in the home, with children becoming critical of the family position. This might have very serious consequences for the welfare of the child.

A third perspective on the tension between the intrinsic and instrumental approaches also focuses on the issue of social cohesion. The intrinsic approach separates children based on their religious beliefs, at least for some classes, and it is suggested that this exacerbates differences. It is pointed out that schools are highly skilled at providing differentiated teaching in many subjects other than religion, and this religious studies approach could provide differentiated experiences for children in their own belief system. Opponents of the instrumental approach claim that teaching religion in a way that pretends there are no real differences may be contradictory to the child's experience outside the classroom. They point to the alternate possibility that schools might turn the experience of difference into a celebration of that difference, making it a positive experience for the school and for the child, who is also affirmed in her religious identity. Such an approach, they claim, is more likely to lead to integration, whereas the instrumental approach is more likely to lead to accommodation.

The promotion of peace and pluralism is clearly linked to a concept of the common good. The achievement of that goal has clear implications for individuals within a society, and calls for their cooperation. In particular, it requires them to exercise their freedom of religion in the education system in a sensitive way. There are also challenges for the political system, chiefly how to convince people of the vision of a tolerant and inclusive society. It must also ensure that the means it adopts to bring this about respects the rights it is trying to promote. In particular, the issue of religious education raises a key question about what is best for the child. It also raises a fundamental question as to who best determines that until the child is able to take a free and informed decision for his- or herself. There is a possible conflict here between the accepted rights of the family and the possible desire of the State to determine the answer. Negotiating this tension for the benefit of the child involves a dialogue between the State, the family, the school and the religious community.

1.4. Provision for Religious Education

The provision of religious education in the different Member States of Europe is based on complex and flexible relationships between the State, religious communities and educational institutions. It often reflects the wider relationship between Church and State and the way that the separation between these bodies works. Jackson has noted three broad geographic patterns – northern Europe which has had a history of links with various Protestant established Churches; southern Europe, where there has been a link with Catholicism; and eastern Europe, where countries formerly under communist rule are now recovering and reformulating mainly Orthodox and Catholic roots.[8] He warns against taking this too literally and describes different approaches to secularisation in Germany (which has recognised both Catholic and Protestant churches); or Norway, which, until 2012, had an established Lutheran Church; in France, where there is a principle of *laïcité*; in Spain, which has had a strong link to the Catholic Church; in Russia, with its link to the Orthodox Church; and in Estonia, with its link to Lutheran Church.

In broad terms, there are three forms of provision. These correspond in general terms to the three concepts of religious education outlined in section 1.2. of this chapter. In this section, the focus is on who is responsible for the RE programme and how it is delivered, rather than the methodology of the programme itself:

Confessional Approach: Religious communities are responsible for religious education. Provision may be made by different religious communities within the State, but in any RE course, the content, teachers and pupils belong to a single faith. The subject may be elective or compulsory.

Religious Studies Approach: The State is exclusively responsible for religious education. This is generally compulsory for all students and focuses on approaches of teaching *about* or *from* religion as discussed above.

Collaborative Approach: The State and religious communities cooperate in the design of syllabi, production of materials, in teacher training and in deciding on the organisation of the curriculum. The State remains responsible for the organisation of education and facilitates the role of religious communities. A second dimension of this type of collaboration is to allow denominational groups set up their own schools as part of the national profile.

The confessional approach is seen as part of the State's neutrality and the affirmation of the individual freedom of religion. The State does not seek to influence the content of the subject. The main issue in organisation is the provision for exemption options for minority groups or providing alternative courses. The religious studies approach also seeks to guarantee the neutrality of the State and the right of individual religious freedom and is carried out under the sole authority of the State. Instruction is not neutral in respect to values but in respect to worldviews, including religion – a demand which corresponds to the religious neutrality of the State. Such neutrality seeks to guarantee that this kind of religious education is equally acceptable to all denominations and religions.

In the provision of education courses that are likely to cause difficulties on the grounds of religious or philosophical beliefs, there are generally two procedures available to the providers – to give students a choice of courses so they can choose one closest to their own beliefs, or to grant exemptions from the requirement of taking the course. Chapter 5, in discussing the particular courses in the Danish, Norwegian and Turkish systems, looked at the issues relating to the power of the State to design curricula and make them compulsory. Exemptions were granted on the basis of defective design, where the delivery of the course was not seen as 'objective and pluralist', or when the procedure for exemptions was discriminatory. In the Danish case, no exemptions were granted and it was suggested that if parents wanted to exercise a freedom of belief in respect of a sex education course, they would have to find a different route other than a State-run school. We now return to the issue of exemptions, and examine the degree of sensitivity to the beliefs of others that is promoted by the European Court of Human Rights.

In Norway, the KRL course was compulsory for all students. However, the State anticipated that some parents might object to parts of the course or certain activities within it. They devised an option for 'partial exemption':

A pupil shall, on the submission of a written parental note, be granted exemption from those parts of the teaching in the particular school concerned that they, from the point of view of their own religion or philosophy of life, consider as amounting to the practice of another religion or adherence to another philosophy of life. This may concern, *inter alia*, religious activities within or outside the classroom. In the event of a parental note requesting exemption, the school shall as far as possible seek to find solutions by facilitating differentiated teaching within the school curriculum.[9]

In reference to the right an individual might have to an exemption, the court discussed three main criteria. The first focused on the qualitative nature of the objection: requiring parents to keep themselves constantly informed about the content of the teaching that went on in classrooms and responsible for singling out incompatible parts, placing an unfair burden on parents in justifying their requests. This would be particularly difficult if the objection was to the general Christian tone of the programme rather than any particular theme or activity.[10] It might also exist if a parent dissented from a particular teaching within his own faith group, and wanted his/her position respected. Here, the court seems to support a very strong freedom *from* religion for parents, with no burden to prove that specific activities within a course constitute some form of coercion. The parents do not have to show a specific 'risk' to their child; they may object to the general religious tone of the programme.

A second criteria applied by the court related to the procedures involved in obtaining an exemption. According to the first criterion, the parent could freely choose to withdraw their child simply on the basis of preference. This freedom would seem to be contradicted if, in seeking exemption, they had to engage in detailed or onerous procedures that forced them to reveal their own philosophy. In the Norwegian case, parents could have their children exempted from clearly religious activities (visiting places of worship, particular services) and did not have to give reasons. This contrasted with the procedures required for a more general exemption from the teaching.[11] If procedures give rise to heavy burdens for parents, the demands are likely to deter requests rather than facilitate them and this does not amount to 'respect' for their wishes.

A third concern for the court was the way that exemptions worked. The court seemed to recognise that there were often organisational constraints in schools when an individual or a minority group were exempt from a particular activity. Resources were not available to offer alternative instruction or, at times, even supervision in a different location. This meant that students remained in the classroom, but did not participate in the work. The exemption resulted in 'observation through attendance' replacing 'involvement through participation'.[12] This gave an exemption from certain activities, not to the knowledge transmitted through the activity. This response diminished the scope of the exemption. Organisational difficulties can sometimes be used as an informal pressure on students to attend religious education, even as observers, against their wishes.

The UN Special Rapporteur on religious freedom has also endorsed these three criteria, or standards, in granting exemptions. A fourth has also been added, which relates to the agent of the request for exemption. In the Convention on the Rights of the Child, parents are seen as providing direction to their child in a manner consistent with the evolving capacities of the child.[13] The concept of evolving capacities is crucial since it acknowledges that the child at some point comes of age and should be able to make personal choices in matters of religion or belief. Due weight should be given to the views of the child in accordance with his or her age and maturity, which need to be assessed on a case-by-case basis.

2. RELIGIOUS EDUCATION IN STATE SCHOOLS

The focus of this survey is on State-run schools and the provision of religious education. It is assumed that private schools have autonomy in how they address the question of religious education, and that denominational schools work from the perspective of teaching 'into' religion, as outlined in section 1.2 of this chapter. A general survey on how religious education is offered in State-run schools in Europe was outlined in the European Court of Human Rights in 2007:

> In Europe, religious education is closely tied in with secular education. Of the forty-six Council of Europe member States which were examined, forty-three provide religious education classes in State schools. Only Albania, France (with the exception of the Alsace and Moselle regions) and the former Yugoslav Republic of Macedonia are the exceptions to this rule. In Slovenia, non-confessional teaching is offered in the last years of State education.
>
> In twenty-five of the forty-six member States, religious education is a compulsory subject. However, the scope of this obligation varies depending on the State. In five countries, namely Finland, Greece, Norway, Sweden and Turkey, the obligation to attend classes in religious education is absolute. All pupils who belong to the religious faith taught in the classes are obliged to follow them, partially or fully. However, ten States allow for exemptions under certain conditions. This is the case in Austria, Cyprus, Denmark, Ireland, Iceland, Liechtenstein, Malta, Monaco, San Marino and the United Kingdom. In the majority of these countries, religious education is denominational.

Ten [*sic*] other countries give pupils the opportunity to choose a substitute lesson in place of compulsory religious education. This is the case in Germany, Belgium, Bosnia and Herzegovina, Lithuania, Luxembourg, the Netherlands, Serbia, Slovakia and Switzerland. In those countries, denominational education is included in the curriculum drawn up by the relevant ministries and pupils are obliged to attend unless they have opted for the substitute lesson proposed.

In contrast, twenty-one member States do not oblige pupils to follow classes in religious education. Religious education is generally authorised in the school system but pupils only attend if they have made a request to that effect. This is what happens in the largest group of States: Andorra, Armenia, Azerbaijan, Bulgaria, Croatia, Spain, Estonia, Georgia, Hungary, Italy, Latvia, Moldova, Poland, Portugal, the Czech Republic, Romania, Russia and Ukraine. Finally, in a third group of States, pupils are obliged to attend a religious education or substitute class, but always have the option of attending a secular lesson.

This general overview of religious education in Europe shows that, in spite of the variety of teaching methods, almost all of the member States offer at least one route by which pupils can opt out of religious education classes (by providing an exemption mechanism or the option of attending a lesson in a substitute subject, or by giving pupils the choice of whether or not to sign up to a religious studies class).[14]

A more detailed investigation of the scenario painted by the court reveals seven different patterns of provision:

a. **No Religious Education:** Religious education is not offered in France, Albania or Macedonia. In France, any mention of religion is in courses on history and philosophy, and then the approach must be informational only.

b. **Confessional Religious Education as a 'Core' Subject:** In this category, religious education is a core subject and is generally compulsory, at least for the majority religious group. Exemption facilities are provided for minority groups, and alternatives are generally not provided.

In Greece, the role of religion is enshrined in the Constitution, and there is a direct link made between the religious consciousness of students and their national consciousness:

> 3.1. The dominant religion in Greece is that of the Eastern Orthodox Church of Christ.

> 16.2. Education constitutes a basic mission for the State and shall aim at the moral, intellectual, professional and physical training of Greeks, the development of national and religious consciousness and at their formation as free and responsible citizens.

This situation is mirrored in Cyprus, which has strong cultural links with Greece. In some countries, like Malta and Portugal, denominational education may be a *de facto* 'core' subject. This reflects the majority position of one religious denomination, and the fact that most schools provide for that group, and do not have alternative courses for minority groups. The State may not require students to take the subject. The requirement comes from the school, which may provide limited facilities for exemptions.

Education in Bosnia and Herzegovina is largely decentralised and policy on religious education is decided at the cantonal level. Normally RE is given according to the beliefs of the majority religious community in the canton. There are four such communities supported by different cantons. Normally, parents have a right of exemption, and in some cantons, provision can be made for a minority religion to be taught in a school, if numbers warrant it (twenty-one in one canton, fifteen in another). However, this is rarely taken up because of the logistical difficulties in finding qualified religious teachers in remote areas.

c. Confessional Religious Education as a 'Compulsory Elective': This category of provision refers to those countries where religious education is proposed as a compulsory component in the curriculum, but there are multiple ways of fulfilling the requirement. The State offers students religious instruction in their own faith as an option among multiple different courses, one of which may be a non-denominational course in ethics designed by the State. The confessional courses are organised and controlled by the different religious communities, who are charged with the training and selection of instructors, the drafting of curricula and the approval of materials. However, the State may be selective about the groups it supports. The other courses are organised by the State.

In Germany, denominational education is taught in State schools. Teachers are paid by the State but answerable to the Churches for the content of their teaching; however they must not teach behaviour widely considered against the law. Children who are part of no mainstream religion or wish to opt out for another reason must usually attend neutral classes in 'ethics' or 'philosophy' instead. From the age of fourteen, children may decide on their own if they want to attend morality classes, and if they do, which of those they are willing to take. For younger children it is the decision of their parents. In practice, the provision has been made mainly by Christian denominations. While there is a large number of Muslims in Germany, mostly of Turkish origin, many of them are not members of large religious bodies, and it is difficult to agree on a RE programme for them. Many Muslims attend separate Qur'an schools.

A similar position exists in Austria, where three categories of religious organisations are acknowledged: recognised societies, confessional communities and associations. Recognised societies are regarded as 'public corporations' and are allowed to engage in a number of public activities denied to other groups. These societies receive support for religious teachers at both public and private schools.[15]

In Romania, since 1995 and the fall of communism, RE is compulsory in primary schools and is offered on an optional basis in secondary schools, although parents have the right to withdraw their children. Seven different denominational syllabi are accepted: Orthodox, Catholic, Reformed, Evangelical, Unitarian, Evangelical Alliance and Islam. Each syllabus has an element of inter-denominational education, especially at senior level.

In Poland, schools provide courses in religion and in ethics if there is sufficient demand for them. On official transcripts, students are given marks for religion/ethics. The transcript does not reveal which option the student took, or indeed whether both subjects were studied and a composite mark given.[16]

In Lithuania, students must take a course in moral education, and the confessional religion course satisfies that requirement. Local government establishments must offer classes in religious instruction upon request of the parents. However, this applies only to the recognised traditional communities.[17] Teachers of religious instruction are authorised by these communities. They are required to have a teaching qualification and they are paid by the State. The Lithuanian Catholic Bishops' Conference distinguishes between religious education in schools and parish catechesis. The school syllabus aims at presenting the basics of the Catholic faith and at analysing existential, moral, social and cultural problems in light of this faith. It is addressed to various groups of students: believers, seekers and non-believers. The focus is on knowledge. This is the basis for further catechesis in parishes, which is linked to sacramental preparation and community life. Approximately 52 per cent of students choose the course in religion over ethics.[18]

A similar situation exists in Latvia, where schools provide non-confessional courses in ethics and the history of religion. All traditional denominations – Roman Catholic, Lutheran, Baptist, Orthodox, and Old Believers – have a legal right to teach confessional religion in public schools. Since the late 1990s the Christian Churches offer an agreed ecumenical course on Christian Ethics and Christian Faith. However, many schools do not facilitate this, either because of financial issues or as a policy of not dividing children according to their religious adherence. The level of provision is worked out at local level, according to the demands of parents, but the uptake is relatively low.

d. Confessional Religious Education as an Elective: In some countries, religious education is an optional or elective subject in public schools. For instance, in Italy there is a concordat agreement with the Catholic Church on the teaching of Catholicism in schools:

The Italian Republic, recognising the value of religious culture and taking into account the fact that the principles of Catholicism are part of the historical patrimony of the Italian people, will continue to assure, among the broader goals of education, the instruction of the Catholic Religion in all schools below university level. Respecting the freedom of conscience and the educational responsibility of parents, everyone is guaranteed the right to choose whether or not to take advantage of such teaching.[19]

The school may also offer a non-religious alternative dealing with issues such as human rights, and this too is an elective. Other religious communities are facilitated in Italian schools in that they may use the public school classrooms for instruction, but at their own expense.

In Spain, every State school is obliged to teach Roman Catholicism. If there is enough demand from other groups, a class in their belief system or an alternative in ethics will be offered. The classes are optional. Over the past five years, there has been an attempt to make a religious studies programme compulsory, with denominational education fulfilling the requirement. The new socialist government aims to eliminate religious studies and make RE a not-for-assessment subject.

In Switzerland, education policy is set at the cantonal level, where most schools teach religious education. Normally, there is a choice between Catholic and Protestant doctrines, and some cantons now offer classes in Islam. In some cantons, classes are entirely voluntary; in others, they are part of the core curriculum, but exemptions are readily granted. In the past five years, a number of cantons have reformed the education programme with non-confessional teachings on religion and culture, either replacing or adding to the previous syllabus. Most cantons would see this type of course as compulsory.

e. Confessional Religious Education is Facilitated: In countries such as Czech Republic, Estonia, Hungary, Latvia Lithuania, Moldova, Slovakia and Ukraine, confessional religious education is offered to students who request it. Students must 'opt in' by declaring their desire to study the subject.

In Slovakia, the Constitution states that religious groups determine the content of religious instruction independent of the State. Groups are allowed teach denominational education in State schools as well as establish their own schools.

In Hungary, schools do not offer RE as a subject, but they are obliged to provide time and facilities. Students take these courses on a voluntary basis and no alternatives are offered. The grades do not appear in school reports and the teacher of religion is not a member of the school staff, but employed by the Church. In practice, many classes take place outside ordinary class time.

In Ukraine, religious education may be taught in State-run schools at parents' request, but only outside the normal class time.

In Moldova, there is a compulsory course in civic education that includes information about religious and belief diversity as well as human rights in general. Since 2010, there has existed a possibility of offering denominational religious education on a voluntary basis and all registered religious denominations have been invited to participate in consultations about the new curricula.

In the Netherlands, State-run schools facilitate confessional education, but parents must fund the teacher. However, this must be understood in the context of the Netherlands' support for denominational schools. The availability of such schools allows this choice to be real for all parents.

f. Religious Studies as an Elective: State-run schools in Slovenia do not offer religious education, although after a recent reform of the public school system, the academic subject Religions and Ethics is being introduced into the primary school curriculum, with the aim of teaching schoolchildren about important world religions. This will be offered on an optional basis.

g. Compulsory Religious Studies: The context of the development of the Norwegian KRL programme was discussed in the last chapter. In Norway, the Lutheran Church is the established Church and its position is stated in the Norwegian Constitution: 'Everyone residing in the Kingdom shall enjoy freedom of religion. The Evangelical Lutheran Religion remains the State's official religion. Residents who subscribe to it are obliged to educate their children likewise.' In the Norwegian Compulsory School Act (1969), the teaching of religion was dissociated from the baptismal teaching of the Lutheran Church and focused on a more general approach, teaching the history of the Bible, the principal events in Church history and basic knowledge of the Evangelical Lutheran faith:

> Primary school shall, with the understanding and co-operation of the home, assist in giving pupils a Christian and moral education and in developing their abilities, spiritual as well as physical, and giving them good general knowledge so that they can become useful and independent human beings at home and in society.[20]

Parents were given the right to opt their children out of some or all of the religion course, and take a course in philosophy in its place. In 1997, after a series of reforms, a single new compulsory course (KRL – Christianity, Religion and Philosophy) was introduced replacing both the courses on religion and philosophy. The new course had the following aims:

(i)   transmit thorough knowledge of the Bible and Christianity in the form of cultural heritage and the Evangelical Lutheran Faith;
(ii)   transmit knowledge of other Christian communities;
(iii)   transmit knowledge of other world religions and philosophies, and ethical and philosophical subjects;
(iv)   promote understanding and respect for Christian and humanist values; and
(v)   promote understanding, respect and the ability to maintain a dialogue between people with different perceptions of beliefs and convictions.[21]

Instruction in Christianity, religion and philosophy is an ordinary school subject, which should normally bring together all pupils. The subject shall not be taught in a preaching manner.

The Norwegian approach to religious studies is strongly influenced by the cultural history of the country and the link with the Lutheran Church. This remains a strong perspective within the KRL course. A similar approach was also outlined in Chapter 5 in looking at the provision in Turkey, where the perspective was dominated by an Islamic perspective.

An overview of the changing approach to RE in Sweden over the past 100 years shows a stronger secularist focus. This can be seen in various curricular statements where there was a deliberate attempt to preserve the unity of the system against denominational fragmentation by moving to a non-confessional approach to religious education in 1919, and since then, moving to accommodate a more pluralistic population, including those who do not believe in God:

1900   Instruction in the Protestant Faith
1919   Instruction in Christianity
1962   Study of Christianity

1969   Study of Religion
1980   Education on the questions of life and existence.[22]

In the United Kingdom, the current requirement in State schools is that RE be compulsory. It is to be taught in a pluralist and non-confessional way. The issues-based approach makes it a mixture of education 'about' and 'from' religion. Exemptions from this requirement exist at a systems level, where 'maintained schools' – a category of State-supported schools – may offer special courses in the religion of the founder of the school.

3. THE STATE AND PRIVATE PROVISION

The State does not have a monopoly right on educational provision. Alternatives to State provision are home schooling and private education. Although there is provision for home schooling in many countries, the focus of this book is on institutional preferences for education. The right to have an education other than that organised by the State is enshrined in the Convention on the Rights of the Child (1989):

> No part of the present article or article 28 shall be construed so as to interfere with the liberty of individuals and bodies to establish and direct educational institutions, subject always to the observance of the principle set out in paragraph 1 of the present article and to the requirements that the education given in such institutions shall conform to such minimum standards as may be laid down by the State.[23]

3.1. CONCEPTS OF THE COMMON GOOD AND RIGHTS

The right to establish schools is not confined to founders who have a religious ideology. Therefore, denominational education must be understood in a wider right to pursue an approach to education that looks at both content and/or methodology as respecting the rights of parents. The Eurydice entry for Germany outlines a philosophy of State support for private education:

> [T]he fact that public-sector and privately maintained institutions exist side by side and cooperate with each other guarantees not

only choice in terms of educational programmes available but also choice between various maintaining bodies, which promotes competition and innovation in education. Through their maintenance of educational establishments, churches and other groups within the community help shape both society and the State.[24]

The development of private education therefore respects the rights of two groups – those who wish to found a school with a particular philosophy, and those who wish to avail of an education with a philosophy different from that of the State. There are four aspects to this right:

a. The right of establishment is the freedom to found schools and provide education, both in form and in content. The autonomy derived from this principle also includes the right to confer legally valid proofs of study and to issue study certificates ratifying those studies. The intention of the provision is to ensure that the State is not the only provider of education.

b. The right of orientation or conviction, which implies that schools can be founded on the basis of either certain denominational or non-denominational philosophies, or certain pedagogical or educational ideologies. In general, privately run schools work from:

- denominational/non-denominational or a particular worldview philosophy
- specific methodologies (Dalton, Freinet, Jena, Montessori, Pestalozzi, Steiner) or language-based schools
- alternative Certification/curriculum (International Baccalaureate)
- private commercial enterprise.

In the Netherlands, approximately 25 per cent of schools are public schools, run by the State. Thirty per cent are Catholic, 30 per cent are Protestant and 15 per cent are based on specific methodologies. Less that 1 per cent are Islamic, although this is changing.

In some countries, especially those with a strong vocational education system at upper-secondary level, different companies will organise schools on an industry or apprenticeship basis, with a focus on a particular skill needed in the economy, and giving a recognised qualification to successful students. In Finland for instance, in compulsory education, approximately 2.8 per cent of schools are private. However, in upper secondary education, in the vocational sector, 20 per cent of the schools are private although they cater for only 10 per cent of the students at that level.

States normally require such schools to be registered. Successful registration depends not just on approving the philosophy, but on the founders showing the viability of the school both in terms of the running of the school and the quality of the education that will be provided for students, and they also set out reporting obligations.

c. **The right of organisation** refers to levels of autonomy in the governance of the school, with regard to admissions, disciplinary rules, employment of staff. The freedom to organise teaching means that private schools are free to determine what is taught and how. The government may set quality standards which apply to both public and private education and prescribe the subjects to be studied. A national curriculum sets the goals and contents of teaching time and allows less flexibility at school level to develop specific aspects of ethos. They set qualitative standards such as the subjects to be taught; attainment targets or examination syllabuses and the content of national examinations; the amount of instruction in each subject; and the qualifications which teachers must have. Private schools are generally open to the same level of inspection as public schools. These requirements may be universal in the case of compulsory education (primary and lower secondary), and be more relaxed in upper secondary, where their application may differ for general, professional and vocational education. The only exceptions to these conditions are the International Schools. They offer the International Baccalaureate and must comply with conditions set elsewhere.

Most privately organised schools seek some control over teaching appointments. In some countries, teacher contracts exist at State or local government level, not at school level. In privately run schools, the contract is more likely to be with the school. Government may set regulations with regard to qualification levels and pay scales as a form of regulation, but it leaves the selection of teachers to the school.

	Publicly Run Schools	Privately Run Schools
Admissions	Open to all children regardless of religion or outlook	Have some control over admitting pupils who do not subscribe to the belief or ideology of the school
Regulations (including employment)	Subject to public law	Subject to private law, and any other conditions that may arise from public funding
Governance	Governed by public legal bodies which are appointed or elected	Governed by a board set up by the founders in accordance with agreed principles
Approach	Provide education on behalf of the State	Base their teaching on a particular worldview

Table 6.1. Summary of some differences between public and private schools

d. The right of parental choice. The basis of financial support for education is not simply that it is a common good and therefore a beneficial investment for the State. In many countries, as in the Human Rights Conventions, the responsibility for education is clearly stated to be that of the parent. In that context, the State supports parents in fulfilling their obligations to their children. A question that arises for many states is the support that should be given to parents who decide to exercise that obligation outside the public education system, the negotiated common good.

The existence of different schools allows parents a real choice when it comes to education, providing the opportunity to invest in an education that is different from that offered by the State. Parents will be influenced by many different issues in their choice of alternatives to the public education system, including:

• The standards and facilities in the alternate systems
• Normative approaches to religious identity
• Beliefs about democratic developments in society
• Beliefs about the social effects of schools.

In general, the attraction of private education will focus on part of the curriculum only, as most private schools will offer a very similar curriculum to that in other schools in the country. The profile of the private sector in each country depends on:

- The history of provision and establishment of the educational system and regulations on who may establish schools. This can be seen in the diversity of the providers of private education.
- The level of funding available for such schools.
- Prescriptions with regard to the curriculum in the schools.
- The level of autonomy granted to private schools with regard to admissions, curriculum, setting fees and employment.

This type of provision is the focus of the next section.

3.2. SURVEY OF PRACTICES

Emer Smyth et al. have developed a typology of funding arrangements for private schools in Europe:

Description of System	Countries
Integrated education systems: private education is more or less on the same footing as public education	Denmark, Finland, Ireland, Netherlands, Poland, Slovakia, Spain, Sweden
Semi-integrated education systems: countries that offer varying degrees of subsidisation to the private sector, but (always) less that the corresponding amount they spend on the public sector	Belgium (Flemish, French and German), Estonia, France, Germany, Italy, Latvia, Lithuania, Luxembourg, Slovenia, Iceland
Faith schools (of some or all faiths) receive more favourable treatment than other schools in the private sector	Austria, Czech Republic, Hungary, Malta, Portugal, United Kingdom
Segregated education systems: countries that fail to make any public funding directly available to the private sector	Bulgaria, Cyprus, Greece, Romania, Turkey

Table 6.2. Typology of provision for private schooling in Europe[25]

An integrated system exists in eight EU countries – Denmark, Finland, Ireland, the Netherlands, Poland, Slovakia, Spain and Sweden. This means that government funding is more or less the same for all schools, irrespective of who the founder of the school is. The status of these schools can be seen in the historical need to accommodate different religious groups. No particular religion or denomination is given special treatment, and so the support is extended to all schools. This philosophy is based on seeing education, in itself, as a public good, and supporting all parents equally in their choice of education experiences for their children. In effect, State support is like an 'education voucher' given to each child. Parents are free to spend their voucher in whatever school they want. For ease of administration, the voucher is paid directly to the school.

In Finland, the Netherlands and Poland, all private schools are 100 per cent publicly funded regardless of ideological, religious, political or ethnic motivation. In Spain, funding schools are divided into three categories – public (67.4 per cent), privately run schools subsidised by the State (*colegios concertados*) (26.0 per cent) and purely private schools (6.6 per cent). Subsidy for private schools may be full or partial. Full subsidy is based on an agreement to provide free education of a comparable nature to public schools. Partial subsidy agreements allow schools to charge tuition fees provided these do not exceed a programme limit set by government. Subsidised schools may charge fees for activities not related to the compulsory programme, provided that these are run on a non-profit, voluntary participation basis outside of school hours. In Denmark, private schools receive grants equivalent to the per capita expenditure on public students, minus the fees paid by parents.

A segregated system exists in Bulgaria, Cyprus, Greece and Romania, where there is no State support for private schools. In these countries, the dominant religion is Orthodox Christianity, where the Church has tended to be a national church. There is a special relationship between the Church and the State and the approach to education is complementary, with the State providing for confessional religious education within the public system. There has been no need to set up a parallel network of schools. In the main, private schools in these countries are commercial enterprises, and there was no rationale for giving support to these schools.

In Bulgaria, all private students in compulsory education receive free schools books, the same as those in public schools. Private schools may apply for project funding on a competitive basis with public schools. In Cyprus, the ministry subsidises the operation of private schools of religious and ethnic minority groups living on the island. In addition, the pupils from these groups are granted subsidies by the government to attend private schools at any level of education.

A semi-integrated system exists in the other fifteen countries where the State offers partial support to private schools in comparison with the support given to public schools. In general, funding issues in education evolve around:

- Investment Issues: capital expenditure on school buildings and maintenance of 'fixed' assets;
- Operational Issues: salaries, resources, support for students, etc.
- Programme Issues: financing of particular projects and outcomes.

Privately run schools are entitled to funding support, which may be full or partial, in some or all of these areas. In general, the return for the private school is some autonomy either in the curriculum – the ability to offer particular subjects such as confessional religion, or to teach according to a particular philosophy. A second area of autonomy may well be in employment of teachers. For instance, in some countries, teachers' contracts are not with the school but with central or regional government; hiring and deployment is done at this level, with the school having no autonomy. A third area of autonomy is in the allocation of budgets; this is considerable in some countries where expenditure, even at school level, is determined centrally. In most countries, the schools have autonomy to spend monies they receive. In some countries, a fourth area of autonomy is in admissions criteria, especially where the allocation of school places takes place at a regional level. This autonomy allows schools to determine criteria with regard to support for the ethos of the school.

In some countries, the funding of education is divided between different authorities – national government and local authorities. The funding of operational aspects of the school is done at national level. The regional level is responsible for investment in capital and for special projects. In terms of capital expenditure, local authorities are treated as 'founders' in the same way that an individual legal entity might found a private school. The only difference is that the local authority receives money from general public funds whereas private founders must provide for capital expenditure either through fees or donations.

The most common focus for government funding of private schools is in support for operational aspects. In Lithuania, for instance, the operational costs of education is known as the 'student's basket'. This includes costs of teachers' salaries, in-service and inspection, curriculum development and resources. This is provided by the national government. In other countries, this cost is estimated on a per capita basis, with different formulae being used for varying levels or programmes of education. In some countries, all schools are entitled to the same support from national government. In Norway, private schools get 85 per cent of that amount, in Iceland 75 per cent, and *sous contract* schools in France get approximately 60 per cent of their costs.

Government support often comes with organisational conditions that go beyond curriculum targets and standards. In Slovenia, schools get 85 per cent of the per capita cost of public pupils, and their fees are limited to 15 per cent of costs at that level. In Portugal, government funding is based on supporting particular criteria. The criteria governing the grant are always the student and not the school. This can lead to all or some of the students in an individual school being subsidised.

The existence of a **faith school** system refers to those countries that make special arrangements with one or some denominations. In Hungary and Malta, religious schools may enter into an agreement with the State based on their cooperation in public affairs and receive higher subventions that other privately run schools. In the Czech Republic, private schools generally receive 60 per cent of costs and cover other expenses through fees; however, some denominational schools receive extra subventions, up to 100 per cent, on condition that they do not charge fees. In Austria, as outlined above, the thirteen recognised religious communities receive special treatment with regard to State support. In countries like Germany and Austria, there is a mandatory donation to Churches which is collected through the tax system and passed on to recognised Churches to fund their different works.[26] Some of that money is allocated to education, making for low fees in some schools.

In Scotland, there are a number of denominational State schools. In 1918, the Catholic Church handed over the properties to the government in return for full funding and guarantees, with legal provision, for the Catholic ethos and certain rights of appointment in religious education, guidance or senior management. In England,

Wales and Northern Ireland, there are different types of privately owned but State-maintained schools. These voluntary aided schools are owned either by school trustees or by the founding body of the school (such as the Church of England or the Catholic Church). Both types of school receive full funding for revenue expenditure but are generally expected to contribute a small proportion of capital costs (around 10 per cent). Faith schools are mostly run in the same way as other State schools. However, their faith status may be reflected in their religious education curriculum, admissions criteria and staffing policies, all of which are determined by the Board of Governors.

3.3. Ireland in Context

The survey of provision in Europe was undertaken as a way of situating Ireland in a European context. Part 3 of this book will look in more detail at the Irish context. Two of the chapters focus on the historical context and the way the current system evolved; the primary and post-primary sectors are very different, and these are treated separately. The other two chapters focus on current issues in the education debate, with specific reference to issues that affect denominational education. One chapter focuses on the Forum on Patronage and Pluralism set up by the Minister for Education and Skills in 2011. The aim of this chapter is to explore the concepts of diversity in use in the Forum Report and to situate them in a European context, with particular focus on how proposals are justified by reference to the common good and to rights. Chapter 10 examines issues that arise in government financial support for schools and also in proposals on admissions policies for schools. These are ways in which private education is regulated and they have a major impact on denominational schools.

NOTES

1.   UNESCO, *Learning: The Treasure Within* (Paris, 1996), p. 85.
2.   Ernest Barker, *Church, State, and Education* (Ann Arbor: University of Michigan Press, 1957).
3.   Grace Davie, 'The Significance of the Religious Factor in the Construction of a Humane and Democratic Europe', *Legal Aspects of the Relation Between the European Union of the Future and the Communities of Faith and Conviction*, Symposium Report, W. Burton and M. Weninger, eds (Brussels: Group of Policy Advisers European Commission, 2002), pp. 11–14.

4. Michael Emerson, ed., *Ethno-Religious Conflict in Europe: Typologies of Radicalisation in Europe's Muslim Communities* (Brussels: Centre for European Policy Studies, 2009), introduction.

5. World Council of Churches, 'Concepts on Teaching and Learning in Religions', EEF-Net 6 (2000), pp. 10–11.

6. Decision 1720, Parliamentary Assembly of the Council of Europe (October 2005), pp. 6–8. http://assembly.coe.int/Main.asp?link=/Documents/AdoptedText/ta05/EREC1720.htm

7. Cited in R. Jackson, S. Miedema, W. Weisse, and J. P. Willaime, eds, *Religion and Education in Europe: Developments, Contexts and Debates* (Münster: Waxmann, 2007), pp. 57–66.

8. See also, Robert Jackson, 'European Institutions and the Contribution of Studies of Religious Diversity to Education for Democratic Citizenship: The International Context', *Religion and Education in Europe*, pp. 27–55.

9. *Folgero and others* vs *Norway*, #23.

10. Ibid., #97.

11. Ibid., #98.

12. Ibid., #99.

13. Convention on the Rights of the Child, Article 14.2.

14. Report of the Special Rapporteur for Freedom of Religion, #51.

15. There are fourteen such societies in Austria: Roman Catholic Church, Old Catholic Church, Lutherans (Augsburger confession), Methodist Church of Austria, Presbyterian (Helvetic confession), Islam, Judaism, Eastern Orthodox Church (Bulgarian, Greek, Romanian, Russian, Serbian), Syrian Orthodox Church, Coptic Orthodox Church, Armenian Apostolic Church, New Apostolic Church, Church of Jesus Christ of Latter-day Saints (Mormons), Buddhism.

16. *Grzelak* vs *Poland*, Application 7710/02 (15 June 2010).

17. In Lithuania, Roman Catholics make up 80 per cent of the population. Other recognised Christian groups are Russian Orthodox, Old Believers, Lutherans and Uniate Christians. Other religions recognised are Sunni Islam, Judaism and Karaism.

18. Briefing document, Lithuanian Catechetical Centre: www.chiesacattolica.it/cci_new/PagineCCI/.../30/Lituania_ingl.doc

19. This agreement was made in 1884 between the Italian Republic and the Vatican, modified by the Lateran Concorde of 1929, and ratified in a new law in 1985.

20. Norwegian Constitution, Article 2.

21. Quoted in *Folgero* vs *Norway* (2007), #11.

22. Quoted in *Folgero* vs *Norway* (2007), #23.

23. Convention on the Rights of the Child (1989), Article 29.2.

24. https://webgate.ec.europa.eu/fpfis/mwikis/eurydice/index.php/Germany:Organisation_of_Private_Education

25. Emer Smyth et al., *Religious Education in a Multicultural Society: School and Home in Comparative Context* (2011): http://www.esri.ie/research/research_areas/education/Remc/

26. Individuals may opt out of this payment by making special application.

PART III

IRELAND IN CONTEXT

7
PRIMARY EDUCATION: HISTORICAL PERSPECTIVE

The earliest attempt at State educational provision in Ireland originated in an Act of 1537 where the State recognised parish schools licensed by the local Anglican bishop claiming to have a national outreach. Despite laws banning them from being educated, Catholics set up an alternative network called 'hedge schools'. It has been estimated that in 1826 there were 11,000 schools in Ireland with a total of about 500,000 children in attendance. The Kildare Place Society had 1,600 of these schools and educated 140,000 children on large grants from the government as well as charitable donations. Those Catholics who could afford the fees of the master attended the hedge schools. In these schools, pupils were given the rudiments of the 3Rs, along with instruction in religion and Irish history. In advanced schools pupils learned the classics:

> By stealth they met their pupils in the glen's deep – hidden nook,
> And taught them many a lesson was never in English book;
> There was more than wordy logic shown to use in wise debate;
> Nor *amo* was the only verb they gave to conjugate ...
> And through the dread, dread night, and long, that steeped our island then,
> The lamps of hope and fires of faith were fed by these brave men.[1]

The government of the time was prompted to set up a board in 1831, the Commissioners for National Education, to promote a State-sponsored system. The organisation of the system was outlined in a letter written by Edward Stanley, the Chief Secretary for Ireland, a cabinet position in the British government. It was written to the Duke of Leinster, who was to be appointed as chairperson of the Board of Commissioners, and it outlined the objects and aims of the proposed education system.

1. THE PROPOSALS OF THE STANLEY LETTER

The Stanley Letter began by outlining the reasons for the failure of the Kildare Place Society. This failure was seen as having a twofold basis. The first focused on the fact that the Kildare Place Society was a private organisation, and that it did not have responsibilities that it was accountable for to government: 'No private society ... made the channel of the munificence of the Legislature, without being subject to any direct responsibilities, could adequately and satisfactorily accomplish the end proposed.' The second focused on the society's approach to religious education. The rules of the society insisted that scripture be read without note or comment, a position that had been assumed as value neutral. In some ways, the approach might be characterised as religious studies in a Christian context. However, Stanley pointed out that this 'overlooked the principles of the Roman-Catholic Church which denied even to adults, the right of unaided private interpretation of the scriptures with respect to articles of religious belief'.[2] Stanley's letter understated the context of religious divisions and the tensions between denominations at the time. Catholic emancipation had been achieved two years earlier in 1829 but memories of the Penal Laws and attempts at proselytising were still strong. The Anglican Church of Ireland was the Established State Church and people of all persuasions had to pay tithes or taxes towards its upkeep.

Stanley's solution was simple, radical and, in hindsight, politically naive. All schools would be required to accept both Catholic and Protestant children who would be taught secular subjects together. The children would be separated only for religious instruction which had to take place at specified times. When religious instruction took place for one group, pupils from other denominations would not be required to attend.

The letter set out in detail how these schools would be established, or in the case of established schools, be recognised for State support. There were three aspects to the process: a local patron, a financial contribution to the establishment and running of the school, and regulations about the curriculum and conduct of the schools:

Local patrons: the system depended on an application from local patrons. Patrons could be 'Christians of all denominations'. In order to support the aim 'to unite in one system children of different creeds', priority was to be given to applications of mixed patronage, with a preference for the involvement of clergymen.

Financial contribution: this local contribution covered capital and operational issues. The site, which had to be approved by the commissioners, was to be provided locally. Also, one third of the estimated cost of building the school had to be raised by the patron. When complete, the building and furniture would be vested in trustees approved by the commissioners, ensuring that the building would be used for educational purposes. The local community also contributed the salary for the master, a fund for the full cost of repairs of the building and furniture, and a fund for the purchase of books and school requisites. This latter contribution would be matched by the commissioners.

Rules and regulations: the Board of Commissioners would exercise 'complete control' over the internal running of the school. The main focus of this control was focused on the curriculum where 'moral and literary education' would take place together and 'religious education' separately. It delegated the supervision of religious education to the clergy of the respective persuasions. This was to take place at certain fixed times – either within the week or within the school day. The board also decided on the textbooks to be used for combined moral and literary and also separate religious education (although this latter choice was determined by different denominational subcommittees). Furthermore, they conducted inspections of the schools to examine their state of repair and also to report on the quality of teachers with the power to fine, suspend or remove them.

The hiring of teachers was delegated to a local manager, although the board set criteria for who could be employed. The most contentious of these criteria was that new teachers would have been trained in the Model School system run by the board, although it did allow for recognition of those teachers already in place. Managers were also required to keep a register in the schools recording the attendance or non-attendance of each child at divine worship on Sundays.

Not mentioned specifically in the Stanley Letter are the other regulations of the commissioners. Instruction was only through the medium of English. The use of the Irish language was forbidden even in Irish-speaking areas. It was not until 1883 that the use of Irish was allowed as a medium of instruction in the Gaeltacht, and then only 'as an aid to the elucidation of English'.[3] The history taught was the history of England. If Stanley's intention was a national system, then he was thinking solely in terms of geographical distribution, not language and culture.

In comparison with modern issues related to diversity and integration, the politics outlined in the early nineteenth century were very different. Here, the aim was to integrate a largely alienated majority into a system that had been designed for the minority. Usually, the problem is getting a majority group to cater for the minorities. The Stanley Letter contained a mixture of approaches to the common good and to rights, although the terms are not used specifically. The vision behind the initiative was partly based on a reaction to the widespread 'hedge schools' and the risk that a nationalist, revolutionary spirit might be encouraged by some masters. Induction into the anglicised education system was seen as mutually beneficial to the State and to the individuals who would benefit from a fundamental approach to literacy. The other concern could be termed a welfare concern that the provision in Ireland should be on a par with what was proposed in the rest of the kingdom. In proposing a high level of local involvement in the provision and management of the schools, education was seen as both a personal good and a personal freedom. There was no compulsion to attend. The approach was to help groups achieve their interests by some State support. The board directed aspects of the common good by its control of the curriculum.

Stanley's approach was respectful of the right to freedom of religion. There was a strong prohibition on using schools as places of proselytising or coercion. In terms of the survey of different European countries in Chapter 6, the approach was to give denominational education to each child within a school that was open to all denominations.

2. THE IMPLEMENTATION OF STANLEY'S PROPOSAL

The development of policy is like any lesson that is taught in a classroom: there is the policy that is intended in the planning and implementation, full of good intentions and commitment to the common good. Then there is the policy that is delivered, with a special emphasis on some aspects of the policy and other parts being underprovided. The delivery of the policy may be affected by various aspects of the context, often resulting in compromises in what is expected and demanded of the different stakeholders. Thirdly, there is the policy that is received, and how the different stakeholders operate the policy. They may understand the values of the policy, agree with them and implement them fully. However, the reception can be dysfunctional at the level of understanding, commitment or implementation. This can lead to very different outcomes than those originally envisaged. At times, the subversion of policy initiatives is deliberate. More often, it happens in the cut and thrust of action. Practical responses are made to concrete situations without considering all the implications; directions are taken and precedents set before the consequences are noticed. Often, the cost of reversing these directions is prohibitive, and the unintended consequences become institutionalised. In truth, the implementation phase of politics is often messy and unpredictable and not always guided by reason. The implementation of Stanley's proposals is an example of such a process. This section will examine how, in at least two instances, the intended outcome of his policies were subverted by the very provisions of the policy itself.

2.1. THE DENOMINATIONAL ALIGNMENT OF THE SCHOOLS

The attempt to build a non-denominational system of provision was based on two approaches – the separation of secular and religious instruction and the support of the local clergy. In the latter, Stanley seems to have underestimated the momentum developed by Catholic leaders in the campaign for Catholic Emancipation. This campaign gave the Catholic Church a very different relationship with its members than the one developed in France at the time of the French Revolution. There the Church was closely identified with the ruling elite and was sidelined after the revolution. In Ireland, the Church was closely identified with the political struggles of the people and built on this relationship to promote its people, politically and socially. It had already been involved in promoting education for the poorer population, indirectly through its support for the hedge schools and directly in the work of new Irish religious congregations – the Christian and Patrician Brothers, Presentation and Mercy Sisters. The growth of these congregations was to become more spectacular. In 1800 there were approximately 120 women in Irish convents; in 1850 their numbers had increased to 1,500 and by 1900 there were 8,000 sisters as well as 1,100 teaching brothers. This growth took place in post-famine times, when the overall Irish population declined by more than 50 per cent.[4] This new energy, along with the antipathy to the Established Church because of the collection of tithes, contributed in no small way to a focus on having their own denominational schools. These schools were as much a symbol of the new political identity as they were a product of theological reasoning.

In the rest of the United Kingdom, parallel systems of local authority schools and voluntary schools developed. Stanley's approach depended on the voluntary application from the local area rather than any direct State initiative in setting up the schools. This had the potential for an uneven distribution of schools and a lack of access in remote areas. However, in 1870 the Powis Commission concluded that the voluntary effort had adequately met the need for schools. It was to some extent because of the responsiveness of Church structures of parish and diocese that the pattern of universal provision emerged. It also contributed to the large network of small rural schools which are still a feature of the Irish system. This dynamic of provision cemented the relationship between the Church, the school and the local community. There also seems to have been an element of 'identity competition' at local level where the preferred local solution was for separate schools for Catholics and Protestants where demographics allowed. This was later exacerbated by an exclusivist theology in the Catholic Church that insisted on separate education for its members. It also meant that the school was very closely identified with the local parish. This identification is not unique to schools, as many aspects of social life in Ireland are organised around the Catholic parish (e.g. the GAA).

2.2. The Local Contribution

Perhaps the most telling feature of local involvement was the extent of the local contribution. The capital requirement meant that the site had to be contributed locally and, at least in the case of new schools, one third of the costs of buildings. In some cases, the direct purchase of land was negotiated; in others, there were complex trust relationships relating to the use of the land. In some cases, vesting leases were negotiated with the Commissioners, in others they were not. Where leases were negotiated, they were often long-term (ninety-nine years). This gave rise to complex relationships between owners, patrons, trustees and the State. That complexity is enshrined in civil law and, in the case of Church property, trust obligations are also established in Canon Law.

With these arrangements for property, it was difficult for anyone other than a corporate body like the Church or the local landlord to meet the requirements. This acted as a disincentive for 'private' schools run by individuals or small groups. There was also an obligation to make a financial contribution to the building and running of the school. In the aftermath of the famine period, the Church was in a good position to develop normative community support for schools and to seek support that was not related to a family-based fee-per-child system. At times, the support would come from outside the immediate parish boundaries, at diocesan level. This ensured that many poorer children had access to a school.

Undoubtedly, involvement in acquiring land and gathering finances to establish and maintain the schools gave a sense of ownership among the Church officials who negotiated and administered these affairs. The building of a church and school also contributed to a sense of local identity, which was probably reinforced in the agitation over land ownership in the late nineteenth and early twentieth century.

In the initial commissioning stage, little support was given to the operational side of the school other than through textbooks. The operational costs of the school were carried mainly at local level. State support gradually increased, first in giving support for teacher salaries, including the infamous payment by results approach and later other grants. The local clergyman also acted as the manager of the school, paying bills and dealing with the Board of Commissioners. This was done on an unpaid basis, and was part of the responsibilities associated with being the patron.

2.3. CONSEQUENCES

The unintended outcome of denominational alignment and local contributions was a strong sense of corporate ownership by local patrons, not the Board of Commissioners. The ownership issue, and the relationship between the State and the patron of the school, has been an underlying issue in the development of primary education. On it hinges, the conceptualisation of the system is as a State system of education run on principles of subsidiarity by local managers or, alternatively, as a private system run by the patrons with State support. The relatively non-controversial involvement of the State in setting the rules for schools and in determining the curriculum would seem to indicate that this was intended mainly as a State system, although the Christian Brothers clearly dissented from this endorsement of the Board of Commissioners by refusing to bring their schools into the scheme. However, the board functioned in the practical politics of give and take, where local patrons entered into beneficial agreements on the provision of schools while compromising on some of the cultural goals, especially with regard to language. Indeed, there were some practical trade-offs on these cultural goals in preparing people for emigration in the years immediately after the famine. In some functions, such as the appointment of the teacher and the organisation of religious instruction, the local patrons and managers had autonomy in return for their local contributions. In practice, the role of the local manager became more central. Issues that had been delegated to local autonomy, as secondary to the issue of provision, soon became the identifying feature of the system.

It is possible to trace aspects of the common good and/or rights language in the development. However, reference to the common good is scarce. There was certainly a strong sense of education as a good, something desirable for an individual, and to be encouraged. It was also promoted as *a* common good for particular groups, and certainly the Catholic Bishops promoted it as a good for their members, and sought to protect their religious freedom in the provision of education.

However, there is little evidence of the debate being raised to the level of *the* common good, to be inclusive of different groups in the country and of different cultural values, particularly that of language. Engagement at this level was more the exception than the rule. In general, the focus was on asserting and maintaining rights.

3. PROVISION IN A NEW IRELAND, 1922–

In many ways, the transition from British rule to independence was a seamless transition for the education system. There was little change in the way the system was provided for and managed. However, there were a number of key changes in the curriculum, with a major focus on developing a strong Gaelic identity through an emphasis on the Irish language, culture and history. The vision of a Gaelic Ireland was in many ways a reframed vision of the common good, and the State found in the Church a ready ally in implementing this in the schools. In focusing on educational developments over the past ninety years, four main themes are outlined here: the patrons of the schools and the gradual provision for diversity; the religious dimension of the curriculum and the challenges to that vision; the provision for Irish language schools; and the provision for social diversity in Special Needs education. The aim of the review is to give a background for issues dealt with by the Forum on Patronage in 2011. Some of these issues will be taken up again in dealing with the issues raised by the Forum.

3.1. PATRONS

With independence, the new Irish government inherited a ready-made infrastructure for education, supported and managed by the Churches. It accepted this as a given and did not question its legitimacy. Despite a commitment to free education, government support was always less than the full cost. The requirement of a local contribution in the establishment and maintenance of schools remained and the government continued to rely exclusively on the Churches as the corporate entities that could meet these requirements. Up to 1999, a per capita contribution from the patron was still required for the running costs of schools, although the amount played a less significant role in the school budget. The Department of Education and Skills website in 2013 claims that a local contribution is still paid for the running costs of primary schools. It was up to the patron to decide how to collect the money – as a local charge on parents or from other 'membership dues'. No matter how small the overall contribution was in terms of the running of the school, the psychology of the payment, and the unpaid work of the manager, established the patron as having ownership rights in the schools.

This dependence on the corporate capacity of the patron, and the corporate organisation of the Church, was seen as late as the 1980s and 1990s in the Archdiocese of Dublin, where a second collection at all masses was partly related to supporting new parishes in poorer areas to make a mandatory local contribution to the schools. To this day, the redeployment panels for teachers in primary schools are set up according to diocesan rather than local government structures.

The new government committed itself to the support of education. The 1922 Constitution had only one short statement on the right to education: 'All citizens of the Irish Free State (Saorstát Eireann) have the right to free elementary education.'[5] The government made some changes on the basis of its support for schools. In particular, it moved from a 'payment by results' to a 'per capita' basis for funding. The first focused on product – the teacher was paid according to the results and achievements of the students. The second focused on consumption, and was based on the number of students in a school, no matter how successful they were. This approach allowed for a more stable and predictable level of support of individual schools. The 1937 Constitution gave a fuller account of rights and obligations in education:

1. The State acknowledges that the primary and natural educator of the child is the Family and guarantees to respect the inalienable right and duty of parents to provide, according to their means, for the religious and moral, intellectual, physical and social education of their children.
2. Parents shall be free to provide this education in their homes or in private schools or in schools recognised or established by the State.
3. 1° The State shall not oblige parents in violation of their conscience and lawful preference to send their children to schools established by the State, or to any particular type of school designated by the State.

4. 2° The State shall, however, as guardian of the common good, require in view of actual conditions that the children receive a certain minimum education – moral, intellectual and social.

5. The State shall provide for free primary education and shall endeavour to supplement and give reasonable aid to private and corporate educational initiative, and, when the public good requires it, provide other educational facilities or institutions with due regard, however, for the rights of parents, especially in the matter of religious and moral formation.

6. In exceptional cases, where the parents for physical or moral reasons fail in their duty towards their children, the State as guardian of the common good, by appropriate means, shall endeavour to supply the place of the parents, but always with due regard for the natural and imprescriptible rights of the child.

The Irish Constitution predates the major covenants on human rights that we rely on today. It is interesting to note that the provisions with regard to the primary role of the family, and by implication the secondary role of the State, are consistent between these documents. Parents are responsible for all education of the child in the Universal Declaration of Human Rights (Article 26.3). According to the European Convention on Human Rights, the State must ensure that any involvement in education is in conformity with the religious and philosophical convictions of the parents (Protocol 1, Article 2). The International Convention on Civil and Political Rights guarantees that moral and religious education will be in conformity with the wishes of parents (Article 18.4). The role of the State is in terms of the common good, and it establishes a minimum level of education and intervenes in circumstances where parents fail in their duty.

The Constitution envisages education taking place in three ways – at home, in private schools and in schools run by the State. It does not oblige the State to set up schools and run them. The mandate is to *provide for* free primary education. The mandate is couched in the form of a positive obligation – *shall provide* for and *shall endeavour* to 'supplement and give reasonable aid' to private and corporate initiatives. This is balanced by the guarantee of a negative freedom, that the State would not oblige parents to send their children to a State school. What was clearly contemplated was that the State would subsidise the schools that existed at that time, set up mainly on a denominational basis. It was not envisaged that the State should become the sole provider of education, thus forcing parents to send their children to State schools. The idea of parental choice was core.

In the Preamble to the Constitution, religion is recognised as having played a major role in the development of the country and Article 44.1 outlines a positive disposition to religious belief. Article 44.2 outlines a standard understanding of both freedom *for* and freedom *from* religion for the individual. It further outlines the separation of the powers of Church and State, where the two are cooperating in a common enterprise but with distinct responsibilities. Paragraph 4 outlines this cooperation in terms of education, and paragraphs 5 and 6 protects religious groups from arbitrary interference by the State:

> 4° Legislation providing State aid for schools shall not discriminate between schools under the management of different religious denominations, nor be such as to affect prejudicially the right of any child to attend a school receiving public money without attending religious instruction at that school.
> 5° Every religious denomination shall have the right to manage its own affairs, own, acquire and administer property, movable and immovable, and maintain institutions for religious or charitable purposes.
> 6° The property of any religious denomination or any educational institution shall not be diverted save for necessary works of public utility and on payment of compensation.[6]

The degree of cooperation that is permitted by the Constitution has been tested in the courts, where it was claimed that the provision of support to denominational schools amounted to endowment of religion. This was rejected emphatically by the court.

> [Article 44.2.4°] makes it clear beyond argument, not merely that the State is entitled to provide aid to schools under the management of different religious denominations, but that such schools may also include religious instruction as a subject in their curricula. It is subject to two qualifications; first, the legislation

must not discriminate between schools under the management of different religious denominations and, secondly, it must respect the right of a child not to attend religious instruction in a school in receipt of public funds.[7]

In practice, the constraints of having to organise a local contribution was a major disincentive to groups who wanted to establish new schools. The Churches were the preferred providers for the government and for most parents. An example of the difficulties faced by new providers, and the opposition from government sources, can be seen in a case tested in the High Court in 1999. A group of parents had set up a Steiner school. A request for official recognition of the school – thereby making it eligible for State funding – was turned down. The parents argued that they had a right to support for this type of education. The Department of Education argued that it was fulfilling its obligation to provide for free primary education as there were enough other schools in the area. It also claimed that the teachers in the school did not have a recognised State qualification, specifically relating this to teaching the Irish language:

> In its entirety, [Article 42] is imbued with the concept of parental freedom of choice. While parents do not have the choice not to educate their children, it recognises that all parents do not have the same financial capacity to educate their children. It is in this overall context that the obligation is imposed on the State to 'provide for free primary education'. In my view, it would pervert the clear intent of the Constitution to interpret that obligation as merely obliging the State to fund a single system of education which is on offer to parents on a 'take it or leave it' basis. In the case of parents of limited or modest means unable to afford, or to afford without hardship, fees charged by private schools, it would render worthless the guarantee of freedom of parental choice, which is the fundamental precept of the Constitution. If the defendants' stance – that it has discharged its constitutional obligations to the plaintiffs by providing financial aid for fifteen denominational schools within a twelve-mile radius of Cooleenbridge School – was tenable, it would render meaningless the guarantee of parental freedom of choice in the case of the parent plaintiffs. It is not

tenable. Moreover, it is clear from the evidence that it is not the stance adopted by the Minister in practice, as the past recognition of multi-denominational schools and Gaelscoileanna indicates.[8]

In her judgment, Judge Laffoy outlined the positive obligation of the State to support parents, especially those who cannot afford it, in realising the child's right to education. Given the role of the parent in education, the State was obliged to cater for parental choice in the development of the education system; this was not to be equated with schooling, which the State seemed to be saying when it pointed to the availability of places in other schools in the area. However, there was no guarantee that all possible choices would be available to all parents, for provision is made within reasonable guidelines based on rational foundations and proper criteria for eligibility based on need, viability and accountability. If any judgment was to be made, it was on the fairness of these criteria. The complicating factor in this application was the failure of the teachers to meet the requirements to teach Irish.

The judgment cited above mentioned that the Minister for Education was promoting some freedom of choice within the system in recognising multi-denominational and Gaelscoileanna. The provision of non-denominational or multi-denominational schools had become a political issue in the 1970s. The movement started in a modest enough fashion in Dublin with a clear focus on one school in Dalkey where parents sought a different type of school environment for their children. Some rejected a religious worldview. Others rejected the narrowness of the worldview on offer in the denominational schools at the time. Others sought a more democratic form of governance where parents played an active role. The school opened in 1978 and the difficulties the Educate Together movement had in securing government support for a new type of school, in face of the expense of providing a site and in competition with an established level of provision, are well documented.[9] The Celtic Tiger years saw a major boost in demand for Educate Together schools, reflecting changing religious sensibilities in the Irish population and a growing multi-ethnic group. The Educate Together movement now provides an effective patron service as part of the infrastructure of school provision and has sixty-five schools.

A second community initiative in setting up schools was the Gaelscoil movement. These schools aimed to provide an immersion experience in the Irish language, while teaching the national curriculum, in schools set up outside Irish-speaking areas. As with the multi-denominational sector, there is an effective patron body to support these schools, Foras Pátrúnachta, although some schools are supported by diocese or religious congregations. There are currently 141 Irish medium primary schools and thirty-six second-level schools in Ireland compared with twenty-one and nine, respectively, in 1980.[10] Supporters claim that the early acquisition of the Irish language is of general intellectual benefit and also facilitates the acquisition of other languages later. They claim that bilingual children have a benefit over those with only one language. Critics point to the 'positive social selection' of these schools.

Government support for Gaelscoileanna and for multi-denominational schools required a new arrangement between the State and the patron body. The State now purchases the site for and builds new schools. These are then leased to the patron for educational purpose. The scheme was brought in to facilitate the multi-denominational and Irish language schools, but it benefits all patrons equally. However, the scheme applies only to new schools. In areas where there is surplus school accommodation but a reconfiguration of educational demand with new patrons seeking to establish themselves, the reallocation of facilities to new groups gives rise to major difficulties. This was one of the issues dealt with at the Forum on Patronage in 2011.

3.2. THE RELIGIOUS DIMENSION OF THE CURRICULUM

The historical survey of the establishment of the primary education system shows that the initial intention was that all children in an area should be educated in the one school and that diversity would be catered for within the school. The Rules for National Schools from 1831 to 1965 stated: 'The system of National Education affords combined secular and separate religious instruction to children of all religions, and no attempt is made to interfere with the religious tenets of any pupils.'[11] Even today, the current rules for National Schools include provision that:

a. no pupil shall receive or be present at any religious instruction of which his parents or guardians do not approve

b. that the periods of formal religious instruction shall be fixed so as
   to facilitate the withdrawal of [such] pupils.[12]

Given the demographic distribution of the population and the way in
which provision had been negotiated locally, the schools were, *de facto*,
denominational. Attempts to have that written into law were resisted.
They kept open the requirement that pupils of all persuasions could
be educated in the one school. However, a significant change was
made to the status of religion in primary schools by the inclusion of
what has become known as Rule 68:

> Of all the parts of the school curriculum Religious Instruction is
> by far the most important, as its subject matter, God's honour and
> service, includes the proper use of all man's faculties, and affords
> the most powerful inducements to their proper use. Religious
> Instruction is, therefore, a fundamental part of the school course
> and a religious spirit should inform and vivify the whole work of the
> school. The teacher – *while careful in the presence of children of different
> religious belief, not to touch on matters of controversy* – should constantly
> inculcate, in connection with secular subjects the practice of
> charity, justice, truth, purity, patience, temperance, obedience
> to lawful authority and all the other moral virtues. In this way,
> he will fulfil the primary duty of an educator, the moulding to
> perfect form of his pupils' character, habituating them to observe
> in their relations with God and with their neighbour, the laws
> which God both directly through the dictates of natural reason
> and through Revelation, and indirectly through the ordinance of
> lawful authority, imposes on mankind.[13] [my emphasis]

Historians of Irish education claim that the inclusion of this rule
had the effect of changing the character of the school from a secular
school with religious instruction, to a school imbued with a particular
religious outlook. However, the text of Rule 68 does not explicitly
adopt a denominational position. It certainly advocates a worldview
that has a theological framework, as the human person is defined in
relation to God's honour and service. The religious spirit that should
inform and vivify the work of the school is outlined in terms of *moral*
virtues – charity, justice, truth, purity, patience, temperance and

obedience to lawful authority. These virtues are regularly portrayed as the virtues of citizens, although undoubtedly they had become coloured with particularly religious overtones. In many ways, this is the same position as held by Stanley, where he saw 'secular and moral' education combined, and distinguished this from religious instruction. In Rule 68, the theological framework for promoting the moral formation of students seems to have been uncontested at the time, a situation that no longer pertains. Religious instruction was seen as the 'most powerful inducement' in bringing about moral formation and reinforcing it through prayers and devotional practices. The assumption that different belief groups would be together in the school is evident in Rule 68 in the admonition that teachers had to be sensitive to different groups and not deal with controversial topics.

In 1965, the Department of Education revised the Rules for Primary Schools. In effect, this revision had the effect of classifying the school in terms of the patron rather than in terms of its role in the local community. It was seen as a way of recognising a de facto situation: 'In pursuance of the provisions of these Articles [Articles 42 and 44.2.4°] the State provides for free primary education for children and gives explicit recognition to the denominational character of these schools.'[14] Rule 68 was amended, removing the requirement for sensitivity to issues herein emphasised in the previous version of the rule. However, it would be wrong to assume that teachers abandoned the spirit of the rule and understood the change as giving licence to be aggressively exclusive in schools. The evidence would be contradictory to that and would be particularly evident in the quality of care that primary school teachers have shown in adapting to the needs of different ethnic and religious groups in schools in recent times. If the early history of the system was a movement from *de jure* non-denominational to *de facto* denominational schools, the more recent history has been an example of *de jure* denominational schools providing a *de facto* multi-denominational service, although the extent of this provision may be limited. Undoubtedly, there are contradictory instances of over-zealous applications of denominational rules.

In 1971 a new curriculum was introduced which encouraged the integration of both religious and secular subjects:

> The decision to construct an integrated curriculum ... is based on the following theses ... that the separation of religious and secular instruction into differentiated subject compartments serves only to throw the whole educational function out of focus ... The integration of the curriculum may be seen in the religious and civic spirit which animates all its parts.[15]

While the option of exemption from religious instruction still remained, a child was open to the religious influence that might permeate the secular subjects throughout the day. There is a specific link made between the religious and civic spirit, suggesting common ground in terms of the 'moral formation' of the student. As outlined in the discussion of Rule 68 earlier, the main impact of this approach in secular subjects would have been in terms of general virtues associated with citizenship rather than formal religious practices. There is little evidence to show that a theological framework for these virtues is articulated in the planning of primary school classes. However, in the changing social and religious climate of the 1970s this caused genuine ideological and practical differences for parents who did not want a denominational education for their children. It was exacerbated for parents who did not support the religious assumptions associated with moral or citizen values.

In 1999, there was a revision of the primary curriculum. The aim of the curriculum was 'to nurture the child in all dimensions of his or her life – spiritual, moral, cognitive, emotional, imaginative, aesthetic, social and physical.'[16] The focus on the spiritual was not grounded in any particular theological framework, but a more general social and cultural phenomenon:

> For most people in Ireland, the totality of the human condition cannot be understood or explained merely in terms of physical and social experience. This conviction comes from a shared perception that intimates a more profound explanation of being, from an awareness of the finiteness of life and from the sublime fulfilment that human existence sometimes affords. The spiritual dimension of life expresses itself in a search for truth and in the quest for a transcendent element within human experience.[17]

This aspect of children's lives was also developed in the Strategy for Children policy document *Our Children – Their Lives:*

> Spiritual and moral well-being covers feelings, experiences and beliefs that stimulate self-awareness, wonder, reverence, moral and aesthetic sensibility, and questions about the meaning and nature of life and death. For many children, the experiences and questions of life are supported by traditions of belief, observance of religious duties and attendance at designated places of worship. For all children, the spiritual dimension of their lives needs to be validated by their peers, parents and significant adults.[18]

There is a clear distinction here between 'spirituality', which involves every child, and a 'religious tradition' which supports that spirituality in a particular way. Some people would argue that the school has no role to play in nurturing a spiritual sensibility in students, as this is the role of the family. They argue that the school cannot hope to carry out such a task given the diversity of views that exist. Others contend that it is possible, even a duty, for the school to promote this sensibility, at least by dealing with certain key issues in an objective and pluralist way. Others would promote a positive link between school and the support of traditional beliefs for individual children. They contend that denominational schools offer this dedicated service to them.

Denominational schools are criticised in that the general worldview they espouse pervades the whole school day, making it very difficult for those who are not of the denomination to feel comfortable within the school. Although the impact of a 'religious ethos' in secular subjects is hard to pin down, denominational rituals in schools are easier to identify as sensitive points. This has a particular relevance for Catholic schools in Ireland where the schools have played a major role in preparing children for the sacraments. The difficulties that arise in this dimension of schooling were also addressed by the Forum on Patronage.

3.3. THE IRISH LANGUAGE ISSUE

A second feature of cultural transmission in Irish education is the Irish language. Since 1922, Irish has been a compulsory subject to be a recognised pupil for the purposes of government support. Indeed, the high level of compulsion is often said to have been a negative effect in the development of the language. At one stage, a student had to get a pass in the subject in order to be awarded any certificate of completion. This is no longer necessary; however, it is compulsory to have a passing grade in the subject for entry to many third-level courses.

The status of the Irish language is seen in Article 8 of the Constitution:

1. The Irish language, as the national language, is the first official language.
2. The English language is recognised as the second official language.
3. Provision may, however, be made in law, for the exclusive use of either of the said languages for any one or more official purposes either throughout the State or in any part thereof.

The objects of the Education Act (1998) include specific responsibilities with regard to the Irish language:

a. to contribute to the realisation of national policy and objectives in relation to the extension of bilingualism in Irish society and in particular the achievement of a greater use of the Irish language at school and in the community
b. to contribute to the maintenance of Irish as the primary community language in Gaeltacht areas
c. to promote the language and cultural needs of students having regard to the choices of their parents.[19]

A recognised school also has special functions in that the education provided will:

d. promote development of the Irish language and traditions, Irish literature, the arts and other cultural matters
e. in the case of schools located in the Gaeltacht area, contribute to the maintenance of Irish as the primary community language.[20]

Government policy recognises different levels of commitment. The first is to promote the Irish language in the context of a general

Irish culture, which is a mainly English-language base. The second recognises that, within that culture, there are those who want a deeper experience of the language and culture, while still living in the English-speaking environment. A third level exists where the Irish language is the primary community language. In relation to the second level, there is a special policy commitment to promote all-Irish medium schools:

> **Objective 6** A high standard of all Irish education will be provided to school students whose parents/guardians so wish. Gaelscoileanna will continue to be supported at primary level and all Irish provision at post-primary level will be developed to meet follow-on demand.[21]

The Strategy Document notes that 'the education system is one of the critical engines for generating the linguistic ability ... given the critical importance of the school in influencing language awareness and behaviour.' This is very similar to the aims of any religious organisation – generating spiritual sensibility and awareness and influencing moral behaviour.

In the Forum on Patronage and Pluralism, a special place was given to all-Irish schools as a symbol of pluralism. There was an undisputed endorsement that all demands for such schools should be met as long as the proposed school was viable, no matter what the effect on other schools might be. There was even a degree of special pleading for such schools. Despite the clear statement that the economy could not sustain adding to the stock of schools in some areas in order to promote religious diversity, the report noted that 'many all-Irish medium schools tend to start out from a small parent base, but subsequently thrive' and recommended that 'the DES should analyse the pattern of such experience, as a guide towards evaluating future applications for such schools'.[22]

No parallel recommendations were made for other school types. It would appear that promoting diversity of religion on the same basis does not merit the same type of financial investment.

3.4. Providing for Social Diversity

Diversity within a State is not confined to issues of religion and language. In particular, the education debate has centred on two areas of diversity – special needs education and social disadvantage. To a large extent, the issue of special needs education was worked out in the courts, whereas the issue of social disadvantage has been an ongoing issue focusing on how the State should invest in education. It is beyond the scope of this book to examine these areas in detail; however, a brief glance at the political process involved illustrates the dynamics applicable to all appeals for recognition in public policy and will be helpful in the analysis of how the Forum on Patronage and Pluralism framed the issue of religious and cultural diversity.

The first stage in the political process is to establish the legitimacy of one's position. This process often challenges assumptions held in a society at a particular time and can focus on perceptions of (a) the people who are to receive the education or (b) the concept of education itself. In the case of special needs education, the appeal is to the duty of special care based on a vision of the common good that promotes the dignity of all children, cherishes them as equals and integrates them into society. The focus is often on the needs of the individual child. In social equality cases, the focus is on groups within society. Education is not a neutral process. It reflects and reinforces patterns of social and cultural reproduction. It mirrors and produces notions of 'advantage' and 'disadvantage', which means that children are not treated with the same dignity. Behind both approaches is a vision of the common good – a society that is inclusive and responsive to diverse needs.

The vision of an inclusive society can also challenge the concept of education as it applies to individuals. This is particularly relevant in the case of special needs students, where a distinction was made between education and schooling:

> [Education] involves giving each child the advice, instruction and teaching that will enable him or her to make the best possible use of his or her inherent talents and potential capacities, physical, mental and moral, however limited these capacities may be.[23]

In his judgment in the *O'Donoghue* vs *Minister for Health* case in 1999, Justice O'Hanlon clearly stated that the right to free primary education was not simply a right to the scholastic teaching related to the primary school curriculum for children between the ages of four and twelve. The court pointed to the personal 'good' of education as a right that was prior to other issues of contributing to economic welfare. All children were educable and primary education had to be appropriate to the needs of the child.[24] This has become known as a landmark case in terms of the provision of special needs education. In the case of social equality, the focus is on affirmative action and providing resources that help the target group improve their achievement in education.

The second aspect of the political process is to negotiate the amount of support that is given in particular circumstances. Negotiations are often framed in terms of rights, although this can often have limited success.[25] In the special needs debate, a key case was the Sinnott case in 2001, which sought to extend the State's duty of care to a severely handicapped young person beyond the age of eighteen. It was contended that educational and support needs were related to need, not age. Although supported in the High Court,[26] this approach was rejected in the Supreme Court,[27] based on the wording of the Constitution. Whatever the legal merits of the interpretation, defining children according to the quantitative measure of age with little or no regard to qualitative issues such as the capacity for independence and autonomy expected in adults gave rise to heated debate. There were strong political objections to the way the Department of Education had handled the case, and advocacy groups pointed out that the court judgment did not prevent the department making a more generous response, although not legally obliged to do so. They argued that the Constitution did not restrict the State to the provision of primary education, particularly the provision for educational support to people who are under eighteen, as was evident in the support then being given to post-primary education, third-level education and further education of adults.

In terms of politics, when the rights approach had failed, advocates tried to persuade the Minister by appealing to a vision of the common good that allowed for a greater element of care for vulnerable people.

In the case of social equality, the approach has been to fund particular types of intervention: the Disadvantaged Area Scheme (1984), Breaking the Cycle (1996) and Giving Children an Even Break (2001). Resources are allocated based on availability in the central budget. The politics of this situation is a delicate balance between promoting a vision of the common good based on solidarity and equality and the establishing rights to such funding. The distribution debate here accepts the need for intervention but focuses on the effectiveness and consequences of particular interventions, especially when there seems to be little change in patterns of social stratification and mobility. A frequent criticism is that interventions work from impoverished assumptions; rather than examining system issues, interventions tend to work from 'social deficit' models of disadvantage – there is something wrong with the patient – and then produce a technicist solution that seeks to 'normalise' the disadvantaged group. Commentators also point to the lack of coherence in conceptualisation of inclusion. At one level, it is promoted as providing opportunities for employment – a standard of living approach. At another level, it promotes empowerment and self-determination, facilitating individuals to take charge of their own education. Providers are challenged to reflect on whether they are working 'for' or 'with' the excluded. Working 'for' implies a level of paternalism, that the provider knows what is best for the learner. Working 'with', a collaborative approach, might well focus on the lived experiences of disadvantaged groups and develop creative alternatives to the current curriculum, teaching practice and assessment procedures. This latter approach challenges the current vision of education, and how it contributes to the common good.

4. POLITICAL CHALLENGES

The politics of the debate highlights the tension between the common good and individual rights. The political debate seeks to establish a vision of a caring, inclusive society, and to work out the consequences of what that looks like. These consequences look at the redistribution of resources within the community. This tension was highlighted in an exchange between Justice Denham and Justice Hardiman in the Sinnott case mentioned earlier. Justice Denham examined the promise of educational provision in terms of a normative approach to the moral good:

> The Constitution is a constitution of the people expressing principles for its society. It sets the norms for the community. It is a document for the people of Ireland, not an economy or a commercial company ... [Article 42 represents] the promise given by the people of Ireland to future generations that the State would provide for free primary education for its children. The promise is an acknowledgement of the great importance placed by the people of Ireland on the education of children.[28]

Justice Hardiman linked this normative approach to the issue of distribution of resources:

> In reaching the contrary conclusion Denham J. in a memorable aphorism says that the 'Constitution of Ireland is a constitution for the people of Ireland, not an economy'. It may not be necessary to distinguish so rigidly between the people and their economy. I would prefer to say that the Constitution is not solely or primarily about the economic as opposed to other attributes of the people. But the Constitution is directly concerned with such economic topics as natural resources, with the gathering and allocation of public money, with the human rights to earn a livelihood and hold property and with the regulation of these rights in the interest of the common good.[29]

For Justice Hardiman, the issue was mostly the separation of powers between the political and judicial branches. Whatever the Court might have liked to happen, it could only issue judgment in terms of the law. Decisions on the use of national resources for the common good was for politicians.

The discourse on the common good takes place in the political arena. What we constantly learn is that what is often considered the common good is not so common, as some people are excluded from it. We are often challenged to review our perceptions to be more inclusive of particular individuals and groups. Claims are made for inclusion in the common good based on 'human rights' – because their dignity as individuals is at stake – or on the basis of 'civil rights' because their equality as citizens is being denied.

The discourse on education can also challenge us to think differently about what education is. Frequently, we are caught up in models of schooling, where we compete for position and credentials on a given curriculum. The challenge of special needs education has forced us to look more closely at the personal good of education adapted to the needs of the individual. The challenge of social equality forces us to look at paternalistic approaches to different groups in an effort to normalise them to a majority, and not allow for diverse views and needs. Culture issues, such as religion and language, also challenge a worldview of what real education is and seek to allow individuals to pursue a vision that includes personal and common benefits arising from that vision.

There are striking similarities in the language used to promote inclusion of disadvantaged groups, special needs groups and religious and culture values in schools. In all areas, there is an attempt to develop a vision of a caring, accepting and equal society. There is a focus on the rights of those who feel excluded and a willingness to be advocates for these rights. There are also striking differences in the way that the status quo is treated, and how the rights of the current 'in-groups' are challenged and confronted. Before dealing with some of these issues, the different issues that arose in provision of post-primary education will be considered.

NOTES

1. Seumas MacManus, 'The Hedge Schoolmaster', *The Story of the Irish Race* (New York: Devin-Adair Publishing Co., 1921). Brian Friel's play *Translations* also gives a perspective on these schools.

2. The full text of the letter can be found in *Irish Education Documents*, Vol. 1, Áine Hyland and Kenneth Milne (Dublin, Church of Ireland College of Education, 1987), pp. 98–103. It can also be found in *We Declare: Landmark Documents in Ireland's History*, Richard Aldous and Niamh Puirseil (London: Quercus, 2008).

3. John Coolahan, *Irish Education: Its History and Structure* (Dublin: Institute of Public Administration, 1981), p. 21.

4. Maygray (1998); Corish (1985).

5. Irish Constitution (1922), Article 10.

6. Irish Constitution (1937), Article 44.2, paragraphs 4–6.

7. *In Campaign to Separate Church and State Ltd* vs *Minister for Education* (1998), 3 IR 321, (1998) 2 ILRM 81, Part of judgment of Judge J. J. Keane, pp. 84, 360.

8. *O'Shiel* vs *Minister for Education* (1999), 2 IR 321, (1999), 2 ILRM 241.

9. Áine Hyland, 'Educate Together, Schools in the Republic of Ireland: The First Stage 1975–1994', http://www.educatetogether.ie/reference_articles/Ref_Art_001.html

10. http://www.gaelscoileanna.ie/about/statistics/?lang=en

11. Department of Education, Rules for National Schools (1947).

12. Ibid., 69.2.

13. Ibid., 68.

14. Rules for Primary Schools (1965).

15. Integrated Curriculum (1971).

16. DES Primary School Curriculum (1999), p. 34.

17. Ibid., p. 27.

18. *Our Children, Their Lives: National Children's Strategy* (2000), p. 27.

19. Education Act (1998), section 6.

20. Ibid., section 9.

21. The Strategy for the Irish Language 2010–30 (2010); Government Statement on the Irish Language (2006).

22. Ibid., p. 69.

23. *O'Donoghue* vs *Minister for Education* (1992), 2 IR 20 at 62 per J. O'Hanlon.

24. *O'Donoghue* vs *Minister for Education* (1992), 2IR 20. Also *Comerford* vs *Minister for Education* (1997), 2ILRM 134 and (2001), IR 724.

25. *O'Carolan (A Minor)* vs *Minister for Education and Science & Ors* (2005), IEHC 296 (15 June 2005). Here, the court rules that the therapy proposed by the State was 'adequate' and satisfied the obligation of the State, although the parents deemed it inadequate.

26. *Sinnott* vs *Minister for Education* (2001), 2IR 545 at 583–84.

27. Ibid., 683–90. There was only one dissenting judgment to this position, that of Judge Kean, who held that the age threshold had no meaning, and that the entitlement was for 'as long as he could benefit from such education'.

28. Ibid., 664. Justice Denham.

29. Ibid. at 712. Justice Hardiman.

8

POST-PRIMARY EDUCATION: HISTORICAL PERSPECTIVE

Provision for secondary education has been a very different story. We can distinguish three different strands to that history – the voluntary secondary schools, vocational education and the more recent community/comprehensive schools.

1. SECONDARY EDUCATION

From the early part of the nineteenth century, small privately owned schools were unevenly distributed around the country. Where the Catholic Church was involved in such provision it was mainly through the religious congregations rather than through diocesan or parish structures. Dioceses tended to found minor seminaries where non-clerical students were taught. Many religious congregations came from Europe to set up schools here, and the indigenous congregations also set up secondary schools.

There was a very different dynamic in the secondary sector when compared with the primary sector. Religious congregations do not have the same relationship with local Church members as diocesan priests have. Diocesan priests collect monies and dues and distribute them according to the various works of the parish and diocese. They have a strong sense of identity with the local place, be it parish or diocese; their identity is built around that place and service to the people of that place. In religious congregations, identity is around the inspiration of a founder rather than a particular place. They may be inspired to work in a school or a hospital or at other works, but that work could take place in any location where the need exists. The attachment to any work is as a sense of family pride in the work itself, rather than the place.

The congregations depend on the approval of a local bishop in order to operate in a diocese but most of them have a governance structure that crosses diocesan, and at times national, boundaries. Financially they depend on different sources of income – philanthropic legacies, donations, stipends for services or on the 'dowries' that many sisters brought with them from their families on entering the convent.[1] This is reflected in the provision of schools, which were owned and set up by individual congregations and run on the basis of fees paid by students and the investment of the congregation from its own resources. The schools selected the students and the teachers.

There was no State involvement in secondary education in Ireland before the Intermediate Education Act of 1878. However, from the early 1870s there had been a growing demand in Ireland for a competitive examinations system which would allow Catholics in particular to enter the newly created jobs in the civil service and careers in the professions. The Act was responsible for:

1. Instituting and carrying on a system of public examinations for students.
2. Providing for the payment of prizes and exhibitions, and the giving of certificates to students.
3. Providing of payment to the managers of schools complying with the prescribed conditions of fees dependent on the results of public examination of students.
4. Applying the funds placed at the disposal of the board for the purposes of the Act as hereby directed: provided that no examination shall be held in any subject of religious instruction nor any payment made in respect thereof.[2]

Many of the early schools were boarding schools and the timetable for students was heavily coloured with religious routines and prayers. The curriculum was mainly a classical education with priority given to Latin, Greek, English and mathematics. These subjects could score 1,200 marks; German and French could score 700 and Irish 600. Scholarships were awarded on aggregate marks. This was the beginning of a system of using the results of standardised school examinations as a criterion for entry into other positions. The results were used mainly for the distribution of prizes and scholarships but also were the basis for civil service calls. At the initial Bill stage, the provisions of the Intermediate Education Act applied to boys only, but by the time it was passed as an Act, equal opportunities were given to girls.

The Act focused deliberately on 'secular subjects' and excluded any focus on religious instruction in the examination system or as a basis for payment to schools. It was also keen to protect the religious affiliation of individual students and to ensure, as had been the case in primary education, that there was no encroachment on personal beliefs:

> The board shall not make any payment to the managers of any school unless it be shown to the satisfaction of the board that no pupil attending such school is permitted to remain in attendance during the time of any religious instruction which the parents or guardians of such students shall not have sanctions and that the time of giving such instruction is so fixed that no pupil not remaining in attendance is excluded directly or indirectly from the advantages of the secular education given in the school.[3]

In general, teachers had always been paid from schools' fees. This Act provided serious funding for schools on a payment-by-results basis, easing the burden of fees on parents. In 1921–2 there were 274 recognised schools with 20,776 recognised students. The schools received £97,153 in 'payment by results'. The commissioners also contributed some additional sums – amounting to £38,520 in 1921–2. In total, this amounted to an average of just over £6 per student.

After independence, the Irish government in 1922 abolished the payment by results scheme and a capitation scheme put in place, as they had done for primary education. This gave schools a guaranteed payment based on pupil attendance, not results. A scheme was put in place where the schools paid a maximum amount of £200 to each teacher and the State paid the rest of their salaries and allowances. A major focus of educational policy was the Irish language, and the government gave extra grants to schools that taught some (B schools) or all (A schools) of the programme through Irish. Incentives of extra marks for students who answered their examinations in Irish were also put in place.

By 1957–8 there were 489 recognised secondary schools with 66,221 recognised students receiving £638,907 in capitation grants. The State contributed £1,562,740 in salaries and allowances. This amounted to an expenditure of approximately £33 per student, of which less than £10 went to the school. A further 5,367 students were receiving secondary education in the primary schools (secondary tops). This total represented approximately 16 per cent of the school-age population, indicating that secondary education was a relatively privileged pathway. In 1958, 14,293 sat for the Intermediate Certificate and 7,820 the Leaving Certificate, indicating that the general trend was for completion of education around sixteen and a transition into the world of work. For those with a secondary education the focus would have been on the clerical and commercial jobs.[4]

The schools were mainly founded by Catholic religious orders, although over fifty were founded by lay Catholics.[5] A striking feature of the schools was that they were small and mostly single-sex. In many small towns there were three schools – boys' secondary, girls' secondary and the vocational school. The majority of teachers were members of the founding congregation, and this gave rise to a position whereby lay teachers were regarded as 'helpers' rather than full colleagues. This history was to have an impact on the way the system later developed and on the internal politics of secondary schooling.

Major changes in educational provision took place in the late 1960s, based mainly on the Investment in Education Report, commissioned by the government and carried out by the OECD. The report heralded a major change in the State's attitude to involvement in post-primary education and it was now prepared to take a more proactive approach. The first initiative was to provide capital grants to secondary schools to improve their facilities, particularly in the area of science provision. This provision was made just prior to the 1964 general election and caused reactions of relief, delight and some apprehension as to what reciprocal concessions would have to be made by a sector that had largely been independent of government. The newly elected government showed a commitment to changing a system that had been dominated by, from the State's perspective, an unsuccessful mission to restore the Irish language. The first 'reform' focused on the curriculum and the need to align the secondary and vocational systems to provide a different kind of service – one that was more responsive to individual needs and to the developing economy. In announcing the changes in a letter to school authorities, the then Minister of Education George Colley placed the initiative in both a social and an economic context. He gave an analysis of the effect of educational provision at the time and indicated the benefits of moving to a more integrated system:

> For reasons that it is not necessary to examine here, Secondary schools and Vocational schools pursued their educational endeavours along widely separate paths; indeed they formed two separate systems, each with its own schools, its own curricula and courses of study, its own examinations and its own cadre of teachers. The secondary system offered courses of an academic nature almost entirely while those offered by the vocational system were mainly of a practical nature. The student opting for either system was required to take the options of the system of his choice regardless of where his abilities lay. Those suited to the system received an excellent educational service; those not suited, in numbers not inconsiderable, made the best of it.
>
> There are two good reasons for urging that the barriers between the systems be broken down. First, the denial of a suitable education tends towards frustration in the pupil; second, our national survival depends of making the full use of all the talents of our citizens.[6]

Less than a year after this announcement, Colley had been replaced by Donogh O'Malley as the Minister for Education. O'Malley continued the drive to implement aspects of the Investment in Education Report and announced a new scheme that would make post-primary education free for parents. It was initially proposed that this would be up to Intermediate Certificate only, but by the time the scheme was introduced it included all students. This was introduced in 1967 linking greater access to education with economic and social development:

> Every year some 17,000 of our children finishing their primary school course do not receive any further education. This means

that one in three of our future citizens are cut off at this stage from the opportunities of learning a skill and denied the benefits of cultural development that go with further education. This is a dark stain on the national conscience. For it means that some one third of the people have been condemned – the great majority through no fault of their own – to be part-educated unskilled labour always the weaker who go to the wall of unemployment or emigration.[7]

From a political perspective, the focus was on a new vision of the common good where all citizens would have a greater share in the wealth of the country and also make a new contribution to it. Rights language was not used, although O'Malley's outrage at the injustice suffered by one third of primary school leavers implies a rights issue. The reaction was positive and school authorities worked enthusiastically to respond to the Minister.

The approach to development was to build on the infrastructure in place in the secondary and vocational schools and also to develop new schools run entirely by the State – comprehensive schools. The main State initiatives included:

- Major capital grants to schools to expand the number of places available for students.
- Payments to schools as 'grants in lieu of fees', in return for which schools agreed not to charge fees to parents. The response to this was almost universal with almost 90 per cent of schools opting into the 'free education scheme'.
- A major reform of the curriculum with the introduction of new subjects in science, technology and business. Within established subjects there was a changed emphasis on outcomes, with a focus on integrating practical and academic knowledge. There were also changes in the modes of assessment within the existing certificate examinations.

The effects of these initiatives were immediate. The number of students attending secondary schools increased dramatically over a very short period. There was also an influx of lay teachers into the schools, as the religious congregations could not provide for the expanded service needed, coupled with the decline in vocations to religious congregations that began in the wake of the Second Vatican Council. A new focus in provision began to emerge:

- A major increase in school size and the expansion of the curriculum within each school.
- A gradual move towards the amalgamation of small schools in order to be viable. This heralded a move towards co-education. In many cases it meant that schools became community schools under State control rather than secondary schools.
- The replacement of the school manager with a board of management with representatives of the teachers and parents. This promoted principles of participative democracy.

It is perhaps worth noting that some issues arose in the area of maintaining diversity within the system, although from very different perspectives. Problems arose early for the Protestant schools. The grant-in-lieu-of-fees was lower than the fees charged in these schools, many of which had boarding facilities to cater for a dispersed Protestant community. In response, the government developed a special means-tested grant for students in these schools. In the interests of fairness and promoting diversity, Protestant pupils who had no option but to attend a boarding school in their own ethos received higher grants.

A second manifestation of diversity occurred in the Catholic sector. Many of the negotiations about changes and the impact of changes had taken place between the Government and the Catholic Bishops. However, the Bishops had very little knowledge or involvement in post-primary education, and when the religious congregations came to discuss issues with the government, they found that decisions had already been made. What emerged was a high level of diversity within the Catholic sector – differences between the bishops and the religious congregations, and also differences between congregations themselves. This led to the setting up of what later became the Association of Managers of Catholic Secondary Schools (AMCSS) and the Joint Managerial Body (JMB) – organisations representing the secondary sector. Some of the same tensions with regard to diversity within the Catholic sector were seen more recently in the setting up of various cooperative trusts between religious congregations to deal with the growing complexity and duplication of patron services to schools. This has resulted in the establishment of new organisations such as Association of Trustees of Catholic Schools (ATCS), Catholic Schools Partnership (CSP) and the aspiration of a Catholic Education Service (CES), to coordinate all the educational and pastoral initiatives of the Church.

2. VOCATIONAL EDUCATION

The Vocational Education Act (1930) set out the formal approach to State involvement in post-primary education. The Act focused on 'continuation' and 'technical' education; these were defined as follows:

> For the purposes of this Act the expression *continuation education* means education to continue and supplement education provided in elementary schools and includes general and practical training in preparation for employment in trades, manufactures, agriculture, commerce, and other industrial pursuits, and also general and practical training for improvement of young persons in the early stages of such employment.
>
> For the purposes of this Act the expression *technical education* means education pertaining to trades, manufactures, commerce, and other industrial pursuits (including the occupations of girls and women connected with the household) and in subjects bearing thereon or relating thereto and includes education in science and art (including, in the county boroughs of Dublin and Cork, music) and also includes physical training.[8]

The right to establish, support and maintain schools was given to local authorities in the Act. The focus of the curriculum in the vocational schools was to be as a practical support for those who would go on to employment, and was to be linked to the employment available in the area:

> Where a continuation school or a course of instruction maintained or provided by a vocational education committee is attended by young persons who have the prospect of employment in a particular trade, business, or occupation, it shall be the duty of such vocational education committee to register and classify such young persons and to provide in the curriculum of such school or

in the instruction given in such course (as the case may be) for the educational requirements of such young persons having regard to the nature of the said employment.[9]

The freedom of curriculum in vocational schools allowed rural and urban schools to cater for the specific needs of local students. Courses lasted approximately two years and students sat the Group Certificate examination at the end of that time. Some subjects were suggested by the Commission of Technical Education, including English, arithmetic, algebra, woodwork drawing, mechanical drawing, rural science, domestic science and bookkeeping, as well as having some emphasis on the Irish language.[10] Initially there was no provision for religious instruction in vocational schools. Hyland maintains that the 'emphasis on occupational training was conscious and deliberate and was motivated largely by the concern of the government not to antagonise the Catholic Church by providing general education'.[11] There seems to be a general consensus that the curriculum of the vocational school was deliberately limited by an assurance given by the Government to the Catholic Church that vocational education 'would not be allowed to develop so as to impinge upon the field covered by the denominationally run secondary schools'.[12] However, the distinction between the two sectors began to break down in the early 1960s. As part of the changes mooted by Minister of Education Patrick Hillery in 1962, it was proposed that the vocational schools would begin to offer a wider range of subjects that would allow students sit for the Intermediate Certificate and well as the Group Certificate. This became embedded in the system and the two systems were soon offering the same curriculum.

In 1942, Memorandum V.40 reaffirmed the vocational role of continuation education. However the picture painted of what was needed was more holistic. There was a clearer picture of the student as having wider personal needs, these being related to age and also to the uncertain external environment. The role of education was seen not just in terms of skill training but also of moral formation. As in the Rules for National Schools, there was a focus on citizenship, but with a link to national traditions and language. There was a very strong theological structure to the framing of the values. A selection of passages from the Memorandum gives a sense of the vision behind education:

The memorandum is intended to not only place on record what is of permanent value in the experience gained so far but also to define clearly the fundamental aims of continuation education ...

Continuation education must be in keeping with the Irish tradition and should reflect in the schools the loyalty to our Divine Lord which is expressed in the Prologue and Articles of the Constitution. In all schools it is essential that religious instruction be continued and that interest in the Irish language and other distinctive features of the national life be carefully fostered. The integration of these elements with one another and with the body of the curriculum is a task calling for the cooperative effort of all teachers. In the good home – the model for ordered social life – tradition, faith, work and recreation blend naturally and easily with one another and it should be the aim of those in control of continuation education to secure similar unity within the school so that pupils may go out well prepared to play their parts as members of society and guardians of the national inheritance.

It is neither possible nor desirable to fit every young person for a specific occupation. The child's inclinations and hopes are far from fixed when he leaves the elementary school. Neither he nor his parents are certain what he will want to do when he reaches sixteen years of age. Further, his opportunities for finding the work he wants are no more certain ... the [subject specialisation] situation is best dealt with by group specialisation.

The bulk of the time must be allotted to practical subjects because of the urgency of the economic end for the young persons for whom the courses are designed but this makes it all the more necessary to safeguard the general purpose of the education which is to develop, with the help of God's grace, the whole man with all his faculties, natural and supernatural, so that he may realise his duties and responsibilities as a member of society, that he may contribute effectively as a member of society to the welfare of his fellow man and by so doing attain the end destined for him by his Creator.

For this development it is essential that all pupils with due regard for the rights of parents should receive instruction in the fundamental truths of Christian faith. Vocational Education Committees should provide facilities for religious instruction and incorporate it into the general class timetable for all continuation courses. The local ecclesiastical authorities should be approached with regard to the provision of the actual teaching. The teachers appointed should be accorded the same privileges as the other members of the staff and every effort should be made to collaborate with them. This collaboration is essential to the production of really fruitful results from vocational education. It is necessary that not only is religious instruction given at certain times, but also that every other subject be permeated with the spirit of Christian charity and that the whole organisation of the school, whether in work or recreation, be permeated with the same spirit. In the nature of the case all teachers have opportunities each day of showing the practical application of religious doctrine and can do much to form the character of the pupils by inspiring them to acts of supernatural virtue and self-sacrifice.[13]

In a memorandum from the minister setting up Boards of Management in vocational schools (Circular 73/74, July 1974), one of the functions of the board was to see that religious instruction of 2.5 hours per week took place for each student, other than those withdrawn by their parents. The link with the moral formation of the person and religious instruction was regarded as unproblematic and axiomatic. There was a recognition and respect for different approaches to religious instruction, but there is an assumption that there will be some. The authority to design and deliver the system rested with the local ecclesiastical authorities, which meant that there would be a strong involvement of the Catholic Church in the overall provision. The teachers too would have been drawn from a mainly Catholic background.

The Investment in Education Report had a major impact on vocational schools as well as on secondary schools. In small towns, schools were amalgamated into community schools and passed to direct government control, although the VEC was still involved in appointing people to the board of management of these schools. At this time, many VECs became very active in 're-branding' their schools and promoting the vocational sector as a provider for the unified curriculum. A cursory examination of the list of vocational schools that existed in the 1950s shows that they were invariably named 'Vocational School [town name]' or '[town name] Technical

School'. The current list of vocational schools is hard to distinguish from the voluntary secondary sector – they have saints' names and often have the title 'College'.

3. COMMUNITY AND COMPREHENSIVE SECTOR

With the announcement of the Free Education Scheme, the Minister for Education announced a new State initiative in establishing secondary schools. Four issues were uppermost in the mind of the minister. From the student perspective, the issue was access to schools and a suitable curriculum that respected the diversity of talent. From a systems perspective there was concern for equity in the distribution of schools and the efficiency of how resources could be allocated:

1. The provision of free post-primary education to all children irrespective of ability and without regard to selective tests as part of the transition.
2. Supporting the unified system with no barriers between secondary and vocational education.
3. The provision of comprehensive facilities in all areas of the country so that schools could cater for a wide range of abilities and needs.
4. Elimination of waste and duplication in the provision of services.

3.1. COMPREHENSIVE SCHOOLS

The concept of the comprehensive school was established in the aftermath of the Investment in Education Report. The schools were to combine the subjects traditionally taught in the secondary and the vocational schools. Initial focus was on areas where children were not served by any school. Also, the State wanted to support secondary education for Protestant children. The comprehensive schools were established between 1966 and 1970, with the exception of one Protestant school opened in 1987. They are all managed by a board of management appointed by the minister. The board represents the Department of Education and Skills, the VEC and a relevant religious authority. Of the current schools, eight are classified as inter-denominational, five are Protestant and one Catholic.

The concept of the community school was developed shortly afterwards, particularly in relation to possible amalgamations between schools.

3.2. COMMUNITY SCHOOLS

All schools tried to respond to the access and curriculum issues within their current situation. The need to look at equal provision of schooling throughout the country and the efficiency of that provision gave rise to discussion on the ideal size of schools. The first issue had a solution in new 'green-field' schools and the second gave rise to amalgamations of smaller schools – often with denominational single-sex secondary schools and the vocational school coming together. As more schools looked for amalgamations, the concept of a community school developed. This was based on the idea of a unified comprehensive curriculum and incorporated the idea of school facilities being available to the local community as part of life-long learning. The State took on full responsibility to provide the facilities and to fund the ongoing costs. The schools are governed by a board of management appointed on a collaborative basis by the joint patrons, who are the relevant VEC and Catholic partners (diocese or religious congregation). The current structure reflects the history of amalgamations where the patrons were drawn from the schools being amalgamated. The model of involving religious groups as patrons was also used in new green-field schools, where congregations offered or were invited to be trustees and patrons.

The focus of the school is on providing a comprehensive curriculum to all students. Although religious groups are involved in the patronage of the school, the model of provision is inter- or multi-denominational. The religious congregations were given some guarantees as to the provision of religious instruction and the support of a paid chaplain, but not the right to a Catholic ethos as might exist in a secondary school:

> [The Trustees] hold the Trust property upon trust for the purposes of the School (to be established with the object of providing a comprehensive system of post-primary education open to all the children of the community, combining instruction in academic and practical subjects and ongoing education for persons living at or near aforesaid and generally for the purpose of contributing towards the spiritual, moral, mental and physical well-being and development of the said community) ...[14]

As well as the 'secular subjects', religious instruction is offered as part of a holistic education, contributing to the spiritual well-being and moral development of students. The role of this subject was clearly outlined in the Articles of Management of the school and closely followed the guidelines for vocational schools, with a commitment to respect the denominational affiliation of parents in its delivery. There is also a clear understanding that the contribution to spiritual welfare is more than just information, as it allows for other supportive practices and rituals as well. Some excerpts from the Articles of Management illustrate this point:

11. (i) In exercising its general control over the curriculum and conduct of the School, the board shall ensure that there is religious worship and religious instruction for the pupils in the School except for such pupils whose parents make a request in writing to the Principal that those pupils should be withdrawn from religious worship or religious instruction or both religious worship and religious instruction.

(ii) The religious worship attended by any pupil at the School and the religious instruction given to any pupil shall be in accordance with the rites, practice and teaching of the religious denomination to which the pupil belongs. Religious instruction as aforesaid of the order of two hours shall be given to all the pupils in the school (except those who are withdrawn from religious instruction in accordance with the provisions of sub-clause (i) of this clause) in each week during which the school is in session.

(v) The Minister and the board shall ensure that there are at all times sufficient teachers in the school to give religious instruction. Depending on circumstances and requirements, teachers of religion may be appointed in a permanent whole-time, temporary whole-time or part-time capacity.

(x) The board of management will appoint a chaplain nominated by the competent Religious Authority who shall be employed outside the normal quota of the school. He shall be a full-time member of the staff and shall be paid a salary equivalent to that of a teacher in the school.

(xi) Inspection of the teaching of religion shall be the responsibility of the catechetical inspectorate. Such inspection shall be carried out in consultation with the board and shall be conducted in accordance with agreed procedures.[15]

There are seventy-nine community schools currently recognised by the Department of Education and Skills. In practice, there is provision for the teaching of religion within each of these schools, and it is to be delivered in the faith of those who attend. Any parent has the right to opt out of such provision. This provision has been facilitated by the development of an inter-religious course by the National Council for Curriculum and Assessment which allows for some shared modules and some modules specific to the faith of individual students.

The provision of chaplains in community schools was challenged as unconstitutional, as it involved endowing a religious group. In giving judgment in the case, Justice Barrington outlined the constitutional position:

> Article 42 of the Constitution acknowledges that the primary and natural educator of the child is the family and guarantees to respect the inalienable right and duty of the parents to provide for the religious and moral, intellectual, physical and social education of their children. Article 42.2 prescribes that the parents shall be free to provide 'this education' (i.e. religious, moral, intellectual, physical and social) in their homes or in private schools or 'in schools recognised or established by the State'. In other words the Constitution contemplates children receiving religious education in schools recognised or established by the State but in accordance with the wishes of the parents.[16]

The Supreme Court reiterated the point already made about primary education and also enshrined in the human rights covenants, that the parent has the first responsibility for deciding on the education of the child. It was parents who decided what was appropriate in spiritual and moral education and that the State had a positive duty to assist parents in this aspect of education, as in others. It followed that the Constitution permitted:
- The general State funding of denominational education.
- Religious instruction in State-funded schools (subject to the right not to attend such classes).

- State funding for religious instruction in denominational schools.
- State funding for the supply of chaplains in State schools.
- The display of religious artefacts (crucifixes and statues) in State-funded institutions.[17]

Payment of such chaplains is not an endowment of religion, no more than the payment of teachers in a denominational school, or more particularly, the payment of religious personnel; payment is being made to help the school run according to its ethos, including pastoral as well as academic functions. A proviso is that a chaplain would not provide religious instruction to a student that was not approved by the parent.

3.3. COMMUNITY COLLEGES

The community schools created a challenge for many of the VECs as they were losing schools through amalgamations. Many of the VECs indicated their willingness to run amalgamated schools, and rather than setting up community schools directly responsible to the government, they set up community colleges in which they were the sole patrons. In a number of cases, an agreement was made with religious authorities that they would have a number of places on the board of management of the college and that paid chaplaincy services would be provided, as in the community school. Such colleges were known as 'designated community colleges', where the designation referred to the denomination of the patron with whom the VEC cooperated. However, the school makes arrangements for the religious instruction of all students, in line with the VEC commitment to cater for all students. Most of the designated community colleges have a Catholic partner; however, one community college in County Donegal has representation from the Catholic, Protestant and Quaker communities, reflecting the diverse religious composition of that local community.[18]

4. DEVELOPMENTS IN POST-PRIMARY PATRONAGE

Since 1970, there has been a steady decrease in the number of schools and an increase in the number of students attending post-primary schools (Fig. 8.1.). The overall figures do not show the full extent of closures (often through amalgamations) and new schools opened.

What is clear however is that when the denominational secondary schools closed, the students tended to move to State-run schools.

	Number of Schools				Number of Students			
	Sec	C/C	Voc	Total	Sec	C/C	Voc	Total
1970/71	599	6	*300	*900	150,642	1,592	*57,578	*209,812
1979/80	491	63	252	808	213,788	40,139	85,205	339,132
1990/91	478	68	248	794	213,047	42,139	86,428	342,416
2000/01	419	85	247	751	197,376	51,168	96,842	345,384
2010/11	383	92	254	729	186,622	54,724	114,761	356,107

Figure 8.1. The number of different types of post-primary schools and the students attending them in selected years. (Source: Department of Education and Skills, Statistical Reports.) The 1970–1 figures for vocational schools were collected on a different basis than in other years. *The number of vocational schools is estimated from other sources and the number of students refers to full-time continuation students. No statistics were published for 1980–1.

Since 1970, over two hundred voluntary secondary schools – mainly denominational – have been closed. No new denominational school has been opened in over twenty years. In the establishment of new schools, there has been a marked preference for the vocational sector Of the thirty-five new second level schools established between 1992 and 2009 a total of twenty-eight were under the patronage of VECs (fourteen Gaelcholaiste and fourteen community colleges). The others were community schools arising from amalgamations.[19]

In June 2011, the Minister for Education and Skills, Ruairí Quinn, announced a fresh approach to the appointment of patrons in new primary and secondary schools. The department was to take a more proactive role in designating when and where schools would be built; and it would be involved in choosing the patron on a competitive basis according to (a) the need for diversity and (b) the demand from parents. Minister Quinn had already signalled his intention in this regard shortly after assuming office, when he announced that he was recognising Educate Together as a possible patron at post-primary level, where, to date, it had acted at primary level only.

Any prospective patron was required to meet a range of different criteria related to the organisation of the school – size, curriculum, co-educational, language, admissions, special educational needs and diversity in faith provision. The criteria outlined here illustrate the DES approach to the common good in education, based on the efficient use of resources and focusing on the needs of particular local community area. The school is seen as an effective economic unit responding flexibly to changing local demands. All patrons have to be able to respond to this vision before they will be considered. The minister's document developed the process. The main criterion for the decision on patronage in an area was linked with diversity of patronage:

> Whether the establishment of the proposed school model would result in greater diversity and plurality of second-level school patronage and provision in the area (having regard to neighbouring areas) where there is demand for such diversity and plurality. In this context individual patron bodies from the one faith group will be regarded as representing the same school patronage type for assessing plurality.[20]

The second criterion related to parental demand:

> Patron bodies proposing schools will be asked to provide evidence of parental demand. Patrons will be asked to sign up lists of parents who indicate interest in having their children educated in their new school. These lists are to be broken down by the age of the children, including year of proposed entry to school, and by where they are living, having regard for the area to be served by the school.[21]

The first assessments using this process were announced in July 2012. Some aspects of the assessments raised concerns about both these criteria.

4.1. ASSESSING DIVERSITY

One of the proposed new schools was for Maynooth in County Kildare. It already had one vocational school in the area. Two groups applied for the patronage of the new school – Kildare VEC and the Loreto Education Trust, a Catholic body. As part of the assessment, it was wrongly claimed that the current school in Maynooth was a 'designated community college with a Catholic ethos'.[22] The patrons being equal in their ability to meet the other criteria of running the school, this became a crucial element in providing for diversity. Two aspects of the assessment are important:

- The existing school in Maynooth is not, and never was, a designated community college. It did not have any arrangement to have a religious group on its board of management and it did not have a paid chaplain in accordance with the terms of the Model Agreement for community colleges.
- As a vocational school, the school could not be said to have a 'Catholic ethos', at least in terms of the diversity issues with regard to patronage promoted by the process. It would be against the Vocational Education Act (1930) for a vocational school to act in such a way.

It is interesting to speculate on how such a basic error arose, especially in the Department of Education and Skills. One could speculate on a mischievous intent where the term was used to eliminate the Catholic applicant from consideration by claiming that there was a faith school in the area already. This could be related to an anti-Catholic bias, or it could be sharp practice to promote the VEC case for a second school. Either of these would be a serious betrayal of the protocols of public discourse and would have the potential of undermining confidence in this application process into the future.

A second explanation might be to look at the failure to make some basic distinctions between a school with a Catholic ethos and a school serving a community that had a majority of Catholics. This failure has also been evident in a recent document published by the Irish Human Rights Commission, which stated that the vocational and community schools were, *de facto*, denominational.[23] From a governance perspective, the remit of vocational schools is to cater to all groups. The confusion arises, it seems, because the schools respond to religious needs on a confessional basis; this makes the schools multi-denominational in their provision. If demographics dictate that a majority of students are from one denomination, then their exercise of a right does not change the status of the school. The problem would arise if this right meant that minority groups were denied their legitimate rights under the same charter. There is no evidence that this happens. To call this in question is to declare the normal political process of representative democracy (in terms of the voices on the board of management) to be dysfunctional and not capable of delivering on the charter of these schools. Confusing the commitment of the school to providing for diversity for all groups with the visible outcome of its provision for a majority group is problematic. The problem is exacerbated when the DES, which is championing the policy of diversity, seems to have a very flawed notion of what that means.

A second curious issue arose during the application phase of this process, relating to diversity. Clarification was sought as to whether the department's policy was to promote single-patron schools or whether new community schools could be opened. The response indicated that joint patronage between a faith group and the VEC would be considered

> only when a single national Catholic patron body or Protestant patron body for community schools is in place. The Department's policy approach is for a single national Catholic patron body to represent all of the Catholic trustee interests in the existing community schools.[24]

This approach is remarkable in the way that different trustees are being treated. Each of the VECs retains an individual identity. The faith groups must form into one body and speak with one voice, although each of the new trusts are separate legal bodies in civil law with the same status as Educate Together and Foras Pátrúnachta. It would appear on the surface that there can be diversity in the VEC sector but not in the denominational sector. It might be argued that the VEC is being treated as a single sector as each VEC acts under the one piece of legislation – the Vocational Education Act (1930). If that is so, then the misunderstanding concerning the school in Maynooth is more difficult to explain.

In clarifying the error that was made in the Maynooth situation, the Department of Education stated that the error did not 'impact the outcome of the assessment'. It is hard to see how it could not have had a major impact on the deliberations and on the expectations of the parents and patrons involved in the process. It can only be that the second factor of parental demand played a deciding role.

As part of the application process for a new school, prospective patrons must demonstrate support for their application among those who are likely to attend the school. In Maynooth, the Kildare VEC submitted 641 names, of which 429 were from the specified area. The Loreto Education Trust submitted 186 names, 147 from the specified area. Applying this criterion, it would seem that there was a 3:1 support for the VEC school, and on the surface at least, justifies the decision.

4.2. Assessing Demand

The new process looks like a poll where parents can choose between patron candidates. Parents are asked to indicate their preference based on what they know about the patron, just like they do when choosing a candidate at an election. However, the outcome in this case is not based entirely on the weight of votes – either as a straight vote or as a 'quota' to be reached. The determining factor in the published criteria is 'diversity'. Yet there is no clarity as to what 'quota' a particular patron might need to gain recognition in a particular area – e.g. 35 per cent in a two-school area, 25 per cent in a three-school area, 20 per cent in a four-school area, etc. This lack of clarity could lead to the appearance of arbitrariness in decisions.

A comparison between the appointment of patrons and a political election can also clarify some issues about the status of parental choice in education. Parents choose patrons; as in a representative democracy they select people who will be responsible for the schools rather than make decisions about the school itself. Insofar as the patron is linked with a particular ideology, they choose that ideology. In politics, election promises are not always fulfilled in the short term. Similarly in education, not all ideologies are realisable immediately. Decisions are made to accommodate different viewpoints within the school. Some supporters will feel betrayed; others will be happy with the compromises that are made. Some who did not 'vote' for the successful patrons may be satisfied with the new reality and become supporters; others will simply 'put up with those who got in'.

There are also key differences in the procedures. For instance, in the appointment of a patron, the 'voting unit' is the child. The preferences are counted in terms of the number of children, not the number of families, thereby giving some families more influence in the process. Names of children not of immediate school age are counted, despite the fact that some families may be mobile and relocate before their children even go to school. The term of office for the patron is approximately twenty-five years, which is much longer than any politician might dream of. The patron is not subject to regular reviews, whereby voters can change their minds as they often do in the political arena.

4.3. THE TASK OF POLITICS

On the surface, the process involved in choosing a patron for a new school gives greater voice to parents and is responsive to diversity within the local community. However, given the need for stability and continuity in the running of the school, there is a delicate tension between the local community, the patron and the Department of Education and Skills. The patron does not run the school directly but appoints a board of management which has elected representatives from among the teachers and the parents, promoting a level of responsiveness to changing community needs and the arrival of new voices claiming their rights. This structure protects to some degree the developmental vision of the common good. Also, the community and the patron are both constrained in their actions by the decisions of the department in line with the common good as seen from a national perspective. The politics of education provision have had a more public face in the primary sector where there is less choice of school types available to parents. The next chapter takes up some of the issues in the current debate as focused on in the Forum on Patronage and Pluralism.

NOTES

1. Caitriona Clear, *Nuns in Ireland* (Dublin: Gill and Macmillan, 1988).
2. Intermediate Education Act (1878), #5.
3. Ibid., #7.
4. Joseph Lee, *Ireland 1912–1985: Politics and Society* (Cambridge: Cambridge University Press, 1979).
5. Eileen Doyle, *Leading the Way: Managing Voluntary Secondary Schools* (Dublin: Secretariat of Schools, 2000).
6. George Colley, Letter to the Authorities of Secondary and Vocational Schools (January 1966), extracted in *Irish Educational Documents*, Vol. II, Áine Hyland and Kenneth Milne, eds (NAIRTL, 1992).

7.   Donogh O'Malley, speech announcing the introduction of free post-primary education (10 September 1966), extracted in *Irish Educational Documents*, Vol. II, pp. 263–67.

8.   Vocational Education Act (1930), Articles 3 and 4.1.

9.   Ibid., Article 33.

10. Commission on Technical Education Report (1927), pp. 44–5.

11. Áine Hyland, 'The Curriculum of Vocational Education 1930–1966', *Teachers Union: The TUI and its Forerunners*, 1899–1994 (Dublin: A. & A. Farmar, 1999), John Logan, ed., p. 134.

12. John Henry Whyte, *Church and State in Modern Ireland: 1923–1979* (Dublin: Gill and Macmillan, 1980), pp. 37–8.

13. Extracts from Memorandum V.40 (1942), *Irish Educational Documents*, pp. 224–31.

14. Model Lease for Community Schools, ACCS, Deed of Trust for Community Schools, section 1, http://www.accs.ie/content/publish/ch1/1_2_The_Deed_of_Trust_for_Community_Schools.php

15. Articles of Management of Community Schools, ibid., section 3. The Second Schedule: Articles of Management.

16. *Campaign to Separate Church and State Ltd* vs *Minister for Education* (1998) 3 IR 321, emphasis in the original; (1998) 2 ILRM 81.

17. Ibid., 2I.L.R.M 181.

18. Briefing Document, Description of School Types at Post-Primary Level: http://www.education.ie/en/Schools-Colleges/Information/Establishing-a-New-School/

19. Ibid.

20. Invitation for Applications for Patronage of new Post-Primary Schools 2013 and 2014: http://www.education.ie/en/Schools-Colleges/Information/Establishing-a-New-School/New-Post-Primary-Schools/

21. Ibid.

22. Clarification note re. Maynooth: http://www.education.ie/en/Schools-Colleges/Information/Establishing-a-New-School/

23. Irish Human Rights Commission, *Religion and Education: A Human Rights Perspective*, http://www.ihre.ie/publications/list/religion-and-education-a-human-rights-perspective (2011), paragraphs 26–31. This document also erroneously claims, in reference to Community and Comprehensive Schools, that the vast majority of patrons are Roman Catholic Bishops. The main non-VEC patrons are, in fact, religious organisations.

24. Clarification of Patronage Models for New Second-Level Schools, statement issued by the Forward Planning Section, DES (1 December 2011), http://www.education.ie/en/Schools-Colleges/Information/Establishing-a-New-School/New-Post-Primary-Schools/Clarification-of-patronage-models-for-the-new-second-level.pdf

9

CONTEMPORARY ISSUES: THE FORUM ON PATRONAGE AND PLURALISM IN THE PRIMARY SECTOR

In 2011, Ruairí Quinn, then newly appointed Minister for Education and Skills, set up a Forum on Patronage and Pluralism in the Primary Sector. Four key issues were identified:

- The large number of small schools and their distribution.
- The level of provision by Church groups and the problems this causes to a significant number of parents.
- The uneven distribution of alternatives to denominational schools.
- The particular problem of 'stand-alone' schools. This refers to areas which have the capacity for one school only to serve many different needs.

As discussed in Chapter 2, the role of politics is to facilitate the dialogue between competing interests and to ensure that everyone adheres to the rules of negotiation. The outcomes seek to ensure that diverse interests can co-exist; the focus is on 'what will work'. The more theoretical approach starts with different concerns, seeking coherence with theoretical frameworks. The Forum dealt with the practical; it brought different interest groups together in the context that some political decisions had already been taken. Guidelines about assigning patrons to new schools in developing areas had been issued prior to the Forum coming together, and there had been considerable discussion between the Department of Education and Skills and the Catholic Church on the process of divesting schools in areas of stable population. In its submission to the Forum, the Church claimed that it had initiated these discussions. The Forum sought to formalise these developments in the public arena; it also sought to raise public awareness of the issues and to forge a broad consensus about how to promote diversity.

1. CONTEXT

The minister had announced his own expectation that the recommendations of the Forum would allow approximately 50 per cent of the schools to be divested from Catholic patronage within a very short period. In many ways, the desired solution had already been established before the Forum met. What was also striking about the terms of reference was the assumption that such a large-scale change process could be carried out on a 'cost-neutral' basis, where there might be transfers of land and property giving rise to possible compensation claims. There was also an assumption that the desired diversity could be achieved within the current system of patronage by simply finding different patron bodies or promoting Educate Together as a competitive alternative to the Catholic Church.

A general analysis of the proceedings of the Forum distinguishes two different paradigms at work. The first focused on rights, and this was the underlying paradigm in analysing the current situation; the second was the common good, and this was evident in the discussion of different recommendations. In some parts of the report, the two different paradigms were confused. Sometimes rights language was used as an advocacy position to promote legitimate interests; at other times, an appeal to the common good seemed inappropriate if the issue was an established right. This remedy would normally be a legal one.

The Advisory Group in the Forum understood their role and deliberations as a response to rights issues:

> It is also the case that over recent decades a number of international conventions has been agreed, to which Ireland is a signatory, which set out the rights of children and which highlight the human rights of all citizens, including their educational rights. There is now a mismatch between the inherited pattern of denominational school patronage and the rights of citizens in the much more culturally and religiously diverse contemporary Irish society.[1]

This statement was taken as a given, with little discussion of the way these rights are grounded, how the rights are claimed and the consequences of these rights in the current configuration of Irish primary education. The concern here is not the recognition that there may be significant consequences to Ireland in signing various international conventions, but the logical leap that is made in claiming that there is now a mismatch between the inherited pattern of school patronage and the *rights* of citizens. The implication of this statement is that the rights of citizens are being infringed because of the inherited system of denominational school patronage. A more accurate statement would have been to say that there is a mismatch between the inherited system of denominational provision and the *interests* of citizens in the much more culturally and religiously diverse society. This would frame the issue as a political discourse, not a legal or a rights discourse. It would place the main focus on a vision of society as more inclusive and responsive to interests.

To some extent, this reality was recognised in the Forum Report, although it was framed in terms of education expenditure rather than in terms of fundamental rights and freedoms: 'There is no absolute right to the education of one's choice. The State needs to act with prudence in the expenditure of taxpayers' money on schools.'[2] None of the Human Rights Covenants guarantee the context in which any of the freedoms they confer can be worked out. The case law of the European Court of Human Rights constantly points to the 'margin of appreciation' that exists in each State as part of the negotiated approach to the organisation of its society, based on historical, cultural, social and economic realities. This is true for both the freedom of religion and the freedom of parents to choose an education in conformity with their religious and philosophical convictions. What the conventions seek to establish is that individuals will be treated with the respect and dignity they deserve in making choices based on what is available.

The liberty expressed in any right is an ideal. However, having a liberty only becomes a reality when there are options to choose from. Establishing different options reflects individual interests, but does not mean that an enforceable claim will be made available. The liberty expressed in the right may give legitimacy to their specific interests but the interest is not, in itself, a right. The only clear claim that is established with regard to education is that primary education will be free. It is very difficult to conclude that rights are being infringed because a full range of options is not available to every individual. What can be asserted is that people do not enjoy the full freedom that they aspire to as equal citizens. To some extent this distinction is pedantic, as there was a general agreement on the need to change, yet it is important for the coherence of future policy. In that context, the interests of citizens, whether they arise from human rights, civil rights or some other basis, are powerful and legitimate subjects for political discourse. In fact, the Forum Report looked to the political dimension of the vision of the common good in promoting a broad consensus on the need to change:

> To achieve patronage change is a political and educational issue which requires good communication [and other virtues] so that people can understand the rationale for change and the values for the common good on which it is based, as well as the legal necessity for change.[3]

In promoting a change process, the Advisory Group dealt with the process of divesting denominational schools from their current Patrons to the State, so that the State could run these schools or assign them to different patrons, according to the demands of parents. It claimed:

- there is a moral obligation on all stakeholders to facilitate and encourage divestment, where appropriate, so that the conscientious concerns of citizens and neighbours for the form of primary education which they wish for their children can be accommodated, as far as is possible.
- the Advisory Group does not underestimate the complexity of the [consulting about divesting] processes involved here, but for progress to be made, it is incumbent on the patrons, as owners of schools, to promote this initiative. While parents' views are very important, expectations of a 'bottom up' initiative for change of patronage are unrealistic.[4]

There is no clear indication in the Forum Report of the basis for the language used here; it does not make explicit the moral norms underpinning the obligation to divest. The paragraphs are clearly directed at the Catholic Church, which is the main group that has schools to divest. It is an appeal to the common good, where a religious language (morality, conscientious concerns, neighbours) is mixed with a public language (interests, citizens, accommodation). Behind the appeal are unstated issues relating to power and established monopoly situations in school governance. The appeal is to a cultural norm, based on a vision of agreed values. There is no hint of a coercive approach. Neither is there a suggestion of a calculative approach, enticing patrons to cede some schools in return for other privileges. However, the existing patrons are expected to contribute to the process in a way that is 'cost neutral' to the State.

The patrons were also expected to be leaders in the negotiation, even promoting divesting their own schools. It remains to be seen how this works out in practice. All politics is said to be local: it is one thing to believe in divesting schools and promoting diversity in all schools; it is another to divest a particular school in a particular parish with particular parishioners. Commitment to diversity in a generic way works well until such commitment impinges on the resources available to my child in a particular class in a particular school. This will be the real challenge for politics.

2. DIVERSITY OF SCHOOL TYPES

One of the key strategies for creating greater diversity within the system is seen as the promotion of new patronage arrangements, particularly in areas of expanding population and also in some areas of stable population where schools could be divested from the Catholic Church and given to other patrons. There are three aspects to this strategy. The first is to focus on the barriers to becoming a patron and to facilitate different groups in setting up schools. The second, and perhaps the most surprising aspect, is the belief that different private patrons will solve the dilemmas with regard to pluralism on a national level. The third looks at the distribution of schools and the limited number of areas in which a choice of school types might be offered.

2.1. PROMOTING NEW PATRONS

It was readily agreed by all that the profile of Irish primary schools is unduly weighted towards faith schools. Historically, the criteria for establishing new schools, especially the contributions required of patrons in both setting up and maintaining schools had been a major disincentive to non-Church groups. Therefore, when groups such as Educate Together and Foras Pátrúnachta wanted to set up schools with an alternative ethos, the campaign was to create a more favourable climate for them to be able to act as patrons and to respond to those parents who wanted a different type of school. The campaign sought to level the playing field for new providers and to break the monopoly position of the Churches. It seems that there is little argument that parents with different educational interests should have equal opportunities to have the patron of their choice establish a school in their interests and that, if necessary, some affirmative action should be taken to facilitate these groups. The desirability of reasonably easy access to different school types had been established in the *O'Sheil* vs *Minister for Education* judgment, where Judge Laffoy ruled that if the Constitutional right to choice was not to be rendered meaningless, then the department's duty was not just about providing for school places (schooling) but had to consider the type of school (education) wanted by the parents.[5] The Forum Report reiterated this position.

2.2. SCHOOL CHOICE AND DIVERSITY

There is an assumption in the Forum Report that if parents can choose between schools run by a limited number of different patrons, the problem of providing for pluralism will be solved. This assumption endorses the situation whereby schools are managed by 'private groups' who acquire all the rights of a patron as outlined in the Education Act (1998). Each patron establishes a 'characteristic spirit' in the school, based on cultural, educational, moral, religious, social, linguistic and spiritual values and traditions. Adding to the stock of different patrons does indeed provide more choice within the system; however, it is not clear how this might satisfy the diverse needs of all parents. Swapping one patron for the other may simply change the distribution of issues that parents will debate with any particular patron. The concern is whether the patrons' promotion of their own 'characteristic spirit' will guarantee a fundamental change in how educational rights are envisaged, or if it will simply diffuse some of the conflict that exists in the system at the moment. Commenting on the Education Act, the Forum Report stated:

[T]he ethos of other patron bodies was to be protected and supported. Thus, the State facilitated the strengthening of the responsibility of boards of management to sustain the ethos of the existing patron bodies in the schools, but it did not take action to protect the rights of citizens who did not belong to a group which owned or managed schools.[6]

The Forum Report criticised the Education Act for not ensuring the rights of students in schools. In fact, the Education Act contains the same rights of citizens as are enshrined in the Constitution. It specified specific rights of admission to schools, especially for students with special needs. In terms of religious freedom, it actually extended the right of parents to withdraw their child from any subject, not just religious instruction, that was not in line with their philosophical and religious beliefs. The Forum Report itself did not turn to examine its own proposals in terms of the protection of rights of all students in multi-denominational or non-denominational schools. These proposals may well meet practical needs in the short term. A concern might be that the lack of theoretical coherence will bring even deeper divisions in the future.

The difficulties faced by some non-Catholic parents in Catholic schools were well documented in the Forum Report, the implication being that the rights of these non-Catholic parents are being infringed. It is not difficult to gather lists of difficulties, given the number and distribution of the schools. Yet the Forum Report made no effort to recount or anticipate difficulties in other types of schools. The idea of a 'secular' school, which is neutral to religious belief and caters for all denominations, all faiths or people of no faith as equals, was taken as an unproblematic solution to this scenario. However, this perspective does not deal with the complexity of the range of expectations a large number of diverse groups might bring to the 'secular' school. Áine Hyland's reflection on difficulties that had been experienced in setting up Educate Together schools can act as a case study:

Almost every school has encountered tension with some parents at some stage over the question of the timetabling of denominational instruction ... Deep-rooted resentments about 'the other side' sometimes emerge which can be disconcerting to parents and teachers who had no idea that their actions were being interpreted in this way ... The numerically smaller religious groups or parents who are not affiliated to any religious group are worried that their children might be marginalised or 'swamped' if the larger groups regularly come together within school hours for denominational instruction. They fear that their children will feel outsiders in a school where no child should be an outsider ... Catholic parents are familiar with the tradition of Catholic schools where arrangements for religious instruction are made on the assumption that all children are Catholics and often such parents have not fully faced the implications of sending their children to a multi-denominational school.[7]

The tensions that Hyland reports for Educate Together schools are just as real as for the tensions experienced in a denominational school. The same issues could arise when a parent feels they have no choice other than a multi-denominational school. Whatever the source of tension, the response of the school is to negotiate with the parents, aimed at finding a way to have parents re-evaluate their demands within the 'ethos' statement of the school. In Hyland's experience, this approach has been successful. The approach did not seek to accommodate the wishes of the parents.

It is entirely proper that the school should negotiate a solution in line with its stated ethos, as this is what it promises to the majority of parents. It may even be a good thing that parents are challenged about their assumptions and asked to rethink their needs in terms of a wider vision, taking the needs of other parents into consideration. However, what happens when the conflict situation is not easily resolved? What will be the response when the same claims are made against Educate Together as are currently made against the denominational school – the rights of a minority group within the school are not being fully met? The issue is that when difficulties arise in the denominational and the Educate Together school the focus is on the characteristic spirit defined by the respective patrons. Both are not-for-profit organisations with specific aims; this creates a very different context for a parent negotiating their interests than if the school was a State-run school. The authority of the State to determine the characteristic spirit of the school has its basis in the democratic role of the State in specifying the common good and protecting the rights of citizens. In the survey of different European countries, the role of the State is seen as promoting the integration of different minority groups in the 'common school'. In human rights legislation, the State has a 'margin of appreciation' to interpret the common good and to institutionalise it in laws and different protocols. The authority of the State determines a different type of relationship between parents and schools than that which exists between parents and patrons.

2.3. CHOICE AND GEOGRAPHY

In applying its analysis of the issues related to diversity of provision, the Forum Report recognised four different scenarios. One of these was specific to the provision of Irish-language schools. The report went on to propose different solutions to the diversity issues in each of the other three scenarios. In two of the areas, the aim was to promote diversity through choice of school types. In the third, the focus was on providing for diversity within the school:

- Diversity in relation to the demand for Irish-language schools, where the State is encouraged to support patrons with little regard for cost (pp. 69–70).
- Areas of smaller population, where diversity has to be sought within 'stand-alone' schools.
- Areas of major population growth, where parents want different types of schools. Here, patrons will be asked to bid in a competitive way for schools.
- Areas where there is sufficiency of schools for a stable or declining population, where the current diversity of school types is inadequate. Here, some patrons will be required to divest their patronage in favour of others.

Clearly, demographic contexts give rise to different possibilities for creative solutions to general difficulties. The solutions proposed in the Forum Report make practical sense, at least on the surface. Given that the problem was framed in terms of rights, however, when one casts the lens of rights over the solution, problems emerge. Broadly speaking, the proposal ends up in a situation where citizen's rights are framed by where they live. This determines the type of school they can choose.

For schools in a rural area, there is one vision of how life should be lived and how the common good might appear:

> There is an educational and social dividend to be gained from all the children in a rural setting, village or small town attending school together.
>
> The Stand Alone school should be an inclusive school open to children from differing religious or secular belief backgrounds, from a range of ability and special educational needs, from many cultural and linguistic backgrounds, from the Traveller and settled communities and from all socio-economic backgrounds.[8]

Yet, when it comes to large urban areas, what is valued is the free choice of individual parents, with elaborate schemes to gather and assess information about preferences. In this scenario, differences between groups are to be institutionalised; there is no vision for the urban area comparable with the vision for the rural community. Yet, a number of submissions to the Forum warned of the consequences of this policy. They pointed to the danger of a choice between different types of schools, where one school type was associated almost exclusively with the majority and the other school type was associated with 'others'. This can lead to the fragmentation of local communities based on ethnic or religious grounds, a process that is often exacerbated by town planning decisions on housing allocations, evidence of which can be found in the distribution of DEIS (Delivering Equality of Opportunity in Schools) schools at the moment. This scenario can create a challenge for denominational schools, especially when they cater for the majority group. In providing this service to parents, they are accused of contributing to social fragmentation. In disputes over schools admissions, terms such as social apartheid have been used. The issue of providing a choice of schools in an area can highlight tensions that arise from the unintended social consequences of parents and schools exercising legitimate rights. Giving choices often benefits those who are already privileged, because of their ability to navigate the system to their own advantage. The Forum Report referred to these tensions, but offered no solution to the problems that might arise:

> The Department of Education and Skills, with the education partners, is aware of the risk of social stratification and segregation inherent in increased diversity of school provision ... Greater choice should not lead to a hierarchy based on academic or social selectivity ... While recognising the inherent social divisiveness of many Irish town planning decisions, as illustrated by the clustering of DEIS schools in certain urban areas ...[9]

The vision for rural and urban areas works from two different approaches to diversity. The hope for rural areas is the integration of diverse groups within the school. In urban areas, the hope is that the accommodation of different interests in diverse schools will lead to integration in the wider society. There are major assumptions at work as to how established and marginalised groups interact and experience solidarity.

3. EQUALITY OF PATRONS

In the Forum Report, the demand for greater diversity in primary education was seen as a response to needs of pupils and parents:

> The whole aim of the change in the school patronage process is to provide the appropriate form of education for pupils and their parents in line with their beliefs and value systems. Hence, their needs are the priority concern.[10]

This is a clear statement of intent, and flows naturally and logically from reflection on the way the right to education is stated – that it will be in accordance with the religious and philosophical position of the parents. However, there are a number of problems with the internal logic of the statement. The basic response is that students should have an appropriate education in line with their beliefs and value systems. This is what is guaranteed by the Constitution and by human rights covenants. The context of such an appropriate education is not guaranteed and it is quite possible that an appropriate education could, and should, be negotiated with any patron. The proposed expansion of the patronage system aims to provide parents with choices of different types of schools; it does not guarantee them that they will not have to negotiate aspects of their child's education with the patron they choose.

The Forum Report statement declares that the needs of parents are a priority. This is true. However, separating the rights or needs of parents and the rights of patrons may not always be valid. The validity of the patron's right comes from their relationship with a group of parents. The patron ensures that the parents' rights are 'practical, not illusory'. Ensuring the right of the patron is also a way of ensuring the rights of those parents who depend on that patron for their rights. Patrons may also acquire rights as a result of the investment and commitment they make in setting up and managing the school. These rights are enshrined in the Education Act, and include the right to determine the 'characteristic spirit' of the school, consisting of cultural, educational, moral, religious, social, linguistic and spiritual values and traditions. This characteristic spirit is overseen by the patron; and the board of management is responsible to the patron in seeing that the school runs in conformity with the criteria agreed between the patron and the State which recognises the school and the characteristic spirit. The identity of the patron is therefore legally established in terms of the 'product' they offer. A political process that gives priority to parental rights must also deal with the rights that are not being prioritised and show how the different rights are balanced. One set of rights does not 'trump' another by making them inoperative or redundant. One of the surprising aspects of the Forum Report is the lack of treatment of the right of the patron.

The Forum Report endorsed the development of diversity by promoting different types of patrons. The report envisaged three groups of patrons: religious (denominational), secular (non-denominational or multi-denominational) and Irish language. There is an unexamined implication in the report that these patrons would be treated differently by the Department of Education and Skills. What follows are two scenarios which seem to imply differentiated treatment of both patron and parent rights.

3.1. DENOMINATIONAL AND IRISH LANGUAGE PATRONS
A case study can be used to illustrate the complex application of the problem of equality. The focus of this scenario is to explore the rights of the patron in setting the 'ethos' of the school. The scenario is built around two different patrons: the first runs a Catholic denominational school, the second an all-Irish school. Both patrons are interested in

promoting an immersion experience in a cultural value that is deeply embedded in Irish identity and enshrined in the Constitution as an important part of Irish culture. Both clearly state the characteristic spirit of the school and expect those families coming to the school to respect that spirit and cooperate with it. In theory, parents are free to choose to send their children to the schools or not to send them. Both patrons operate in situations where parents have a clear choice of school type (urban areas). They also operate in areas where they provide a unique service to the community (stand alone or Gaeltacht school). Those who run denominational schools have members with different levels of commitment to ideology. In all-Irish schools, all pupils are naturally bi-lingual. For many in urban areas, their home language is English and parents may have limited command of the Irish language.

The scenario develops by looking at a situation where a parent applies to the school and where there is an apparent conflict between the interests of the parent and those of the patron. Different levels of reaction have been present in Irish newspapers; often these have applied to one patron only, and in these cases we will consider a parallel argument for the other patron. The different situations pose the question as to whether the reaction is valid or appropriate. A second interest is whether there is a perception that a particular response is appropriate to one patron but not to the other.

The arguments used in these different scenarios reflect both appeals to the common good and to the rights of a 'minority' parent. The common good is the good promoted by religion and by language, their link to a valuable heritage and the contribution the preservation of these values make to the community as a whole. Rights are established by those who promote these values (the patrons) and by those who seek to pursue these values (parents who choose these schools). These same rights are challenged by others who feel excluded from the benefits of schools set up to promote these values, claiming that their own rights demand a different solution to educational provision in a local area or even nationally. The tone of debate in the media, and at times through the Forum Report, suggests that the two types of patrons should be treated differently. It is unlikely that an all-Irish school would be seen as promoting an immersion experience in Irish Studies or abandoning its language policy entirely to facilitate a minority group of students.

Denominational School An emigrant family arrives in the area and there is only one school. The family is very committed to its non-Catholic belief.	All-Irish School A foreign businessman comes to work on contract with a Gaeltacht company and decides to live in the area. The only school is an all-Irish school.
There is a public demand that the child be admitted otherwise there is an artificial division in society based on religion. The denominational school favours 'white, Irish non-migrant' children in its admissions priorities.	There is a public demand that the child be admitted otherwise there is an artificial division based on language. The all-Irish school provides for a 'white, Irish, non-migrant' environment because of its entry criteria.
There is a demand that the concept of denominational education be abandoned in the interests of a more cohesive society. In a multi-cultural society no privilege should be given to a particular religion. All students should be taught the same type of course in religion – in an objective, pluralist manner.	There is a demand that the concept of all-Irish education be abandoned in the interests of a more cohesive society. In a multi-cultural society the ethnic background of all should be equally respected. All students should be taught a course in Irish Studies in an objective, pluralist manner.
The school refuses to enrol the student on the basis that it is a Christian school and it would not be able to cater for the child's religious formation.	The school refuses to enrol the student because they have no command of the Irish language and it is not able to cater for the child's education through English.
The school agrees to admit the student on the understanding that the family respect the denominational ethos of the school. The school agrees to facilitate religious instruction for the child in their own religion.	The school agrees to admit the student on the understanding that the family respects the ethos of the school and undertakes that the child, with the help of the school, take classes in Irish to enable them to participate fully.
They agree the child will not have to study religion, or religious services, but will have to be in the classroom as they do not have the facilities to offer separate supervision.	The school cannot make any exemption to the Irish language requirement of the school.
Parents insist that the school adapt the religion curriculum to a more neutral approach so that their child can feel more comfortable.	Parents insist that the school teach most subjects through English so that their child can participate and be exempt from Irish.

Table 9.1. Case study illustrating the complex application of the problem of equality.

The point here is not to argue about promoting religion and the Irish language in the education system; it isn't even to dispute the government's right to prioritise one value over another. The issue at stake is, that if one agrees to promote the value by recognising patrons, on what basis then do you give different rights to the patrons in their capacity to respond to parental needs? It would appear that the way the rights of the patron and those of the parent are balanced is very different in the specific conflict situations mentioned.

3.2. RELIGIOUS AND SECULAR PATRONS

The expansion of choice of patron-run schools is seen as a better way to provide for the needs of a religiously diverse population. However, choosing between a limited number of schools does not guarantee that parents will not have to negotiate aspects of their child's education with the patron they choose. There is an assumption running through the Forum Report that a choice between a religious (denominational) school and a secular (non-denominational or multi-denominational) school will satisfy all parents.

Parents do not foresee all consequences of their schooling decisions. The implications only emerge in response to a problem in the area of discipline or special needs support or maybe religion. Section 2.2. above discussed Áine Hyland's account of some of the issues the Educate Together schools faced in their set-up phase. Hyland is positive and optimistic about the political resolution of these difficulties in local situations; she believes that, where values are clearly articulated, and where there is a spirit of community and the mentality of majority rule is not evident, real progress can be made. This optimism may not be rewarded in all cases and school patrons may have to make choices on how parental rights are accommodated. Conflict resolution of this type also requires that the mentality of 'minority rights' is also subjected to the common good. It would appear from the Forum Report that there would be a greater onus on parents to comply with the conditions set by a patron in a 'secular' school, whereas in a 'religious' school, the onus would be on the patron to accommodate the parent. If this is the case, then it amounts to different treatment of patrons on the basis of religious belief, and it shows a State preference for a particular philosophy. This problem was not dealt with in teasing out the recommendations of the Forum Report.

3.3. SUMMARY

The issue of the right of the patron can be framed as a set of questions. Does the patron establish a school, and then accommodate the State by supplying other services? Is the school a State school in which the patron has a limited autonomy? The Forum Report sidesteps this crucial issue. The first question would see the right of the patron to establish the characteristic spirit of the school and to take measures to protect that spirit. This protection would involve setting rules for admission and participation. The legitimacy of the position is based on the contribution of the 'product' to the common good. The second questions would see the right of the patron curtailed by the public funding they receive and the context of public policy. In the history of Irish education there have been tensions between *de jure* and *de facto* positions. This may be one other instance where different types of accommodation will be found on a practical level without immediate reference to the coherence of the system. In practice, the focus of many parents will not be on the diversity within the system, but on the quality of education for their child within whatever school they attend. Responding to the needs of parents within the school is more immediate than diversity issues within the system.

4. DIVERSITY WITHIN SCHOOLS

Different school types demonstrate institutional diversity within the system. The concern for most parents will be the experience their children have within whatever school they attend, and the ability of that school to manage the diverse needs – not just religious – of all students. Most States seek to go beyond a minimalist approach to human rights; they build on human rights to promote civil rights which aim to promote the rights of all citizens in a specific society. This is an important distinction in evaluating statements about rights. In Ireland, the human rights of the individual are protected in the exemption individuals have from attending instruction in religion, and indeed any other subject, against their beliefs. Irish citizens have acquired other rights which extend their basic human rights to having a particular positive support in the religious and moral, intellectual, physical and social education of their children. Until recently, the State has not been involved in providing religious education but has assisted others to provide it in schools. If citizens secured this right for themselves, it was because a provider other than the State was available. If the current debate is framed in rights terms, then three rights issues can be seen:

- The right of historic providers to continue to provide the service they have given and the right of those who used that service to avail of it in the future.
- The right of citizens to have access to providers of a different type of service, thereby increasing the diversity of provision with regard to religion.
- The right of the State to assume responsibility for teaching religion and ethics on the basis of developing knowledge about religion with a view to a more tolerant society.

4.1. PROVISION FOR DIVERSITY

In the Education Act (1998) schools are charged with a responsibility to the local community. There is specific reference to this responsibility in the day-to-day management of the school by the board of management, who are:

> to 'have regard to the principles and requirements of a democratic society and have respect and promote respect for the diversity of values, beliefs, traditions, languages and ways of life in society'.[11]

The board of management is appointed by the patron and is accountable to the patron for the running of the school in compliance with the requirements of the DES and also the characteristic spirit of the school. This relationship between the board of management and the patron is specified in the Roman Catholic Deed of Variation for Primary schools. The responsibilities of the board are to:

- Firstly, manage the school in accordance with the doctrines, practices and traditions of the Roman Catholic Church;
- Secondly, make and keep themselves familiar with the ethos of the Roman Catholic Church and the Roman Catholic faith insofar as the same relates to education and schools; and
- Thirdly, manage and cause the school to be managed in a manner which will uphold and foster such ethos ...[12]

The board of management also has clear responsibilities to the parent body. In effect, the board acts as a gatekeeper between the patron and the school community. The Education Act describes the responsibilities as follows:

> 15 2(d) publish [an admissions policy] and ensure that as regards that policy principles of equality and the right of parents to send their children to a school of the parents' choice are respected ... having regard to the characteristic spirit of the school and the constitutional rights of all persons concerned.
> 20. A board shall establish procedures for informing the parents of students in the school of matters relating to the operation and performance of the school and such procedures may include the publication and circulation to parents, teachers and other staff and a student council where one has been established of a report on the operation and performance of the school in any school year, with particular reference to the achievement of objectives as set out in the school plan provided for under Section 21.[13]

Where tensions exist between the 'status quo' of the current ethos and the demands of different groups within the school community, the resolution of conflict is a normal part of local politics. This is a core function of the board of management. The Forum Report seems to have an ambivalent view of local politics:

> The Advisory Group is not in favour of plebiscites or large town hall gatherings. They can be divisive and upsetting for communities. The solution, for the common good, needs to be sought in a calm, respectful and reasonable way.[14]

This is a worrying judgment about the quality of political debate in Ireland and the ability of citizens to engage with one another constructively. A key element of the pluralist society is the ability of different groups to engage with one another and reach mutually satisfactory solutions. This has been happening for years at local level on different Boards of Management and at national level in discussions between the DES and the patrons. It would be a strange result if diversity issues were to be dictated on a central level based on anonymous surveys which precluded different groups meeting with one another.

4.2. PROVISION FOR RELIGIOUS EDUCATION

The Education Act (1998) gives the minister power to give direction and make rules for schools, and constrains these powers in relation to the rights of the patron and of rights of parents and students:

> Without prejudice to the generality of subsection (1), the Minister –
> a. shall have regard to the desirability of assisting schools to exercise their powers as provided for under subsection (4),
> b. shall have regard to the characteristic spirit of a school or class of school in exercising his or her functions under this section,
> c. may give directions to schools, where he or she considers it appropriate, to ensure that the subjects and syllabuses pursued in those schools are appropriate and relevant to the educational and vocational needs of the students in those schools,
> d. shall ensure that the amount of instruction time to be allotted to subjects on the curriculum as determined by the Minister in each school day shall be such as to allow for such reasonable instruction time, as the board with the consent of the patron determines, for subjects relating to or arising from the characteristic spirit of the school, and
> e. shall not require any student to attend instruction in any subject which is contrary to the conscience of the parent of the student or in the case of a student who has reached the age of 18 years, the student.[15]

The focus of the recommendations in the Forum Report is on paragraphs (a), (c) and (e) of this article. The report passes over the problems that may arise with the provision in (b) and (d) of this subsection, and the rights that are conferred on patrons. In practice, these provisions may not be problematic for some patrons, although that is probably optimistic.

Different approaches to providing for religious education in schools across Europe were described in Chapter 6. States take different approaches to providing for denominational religious education in

State schools: some offer no support; others support denominational education, where it may be compulsory or elective, always with the safeguard of exemption. Where it is elective, the State may offer an alternative 'secular' course. A number of countries have developed an 'ecumenical' course, where there is a common core element and differentiated elements for each faith group. In a minority of countries, a religious studies programme is the only course available. In Ireland, the model of RE from the time of the Stanley Letter was for separate denominational education within the schools, provided for and overseen by the Churches, not the State. This is the purpose of the provision in section 30 2(d) of the Education Act, which guarantees that the minister will allow reasonable instruction time for subjects relating to the characteristic spirit of the school. At second-level in Ireland, State-owned schools in the vocational and community school sector are obliged to make provision for denominational education, although an 'ecumenical' course is offered in many schools. Students may use examination results in this subject as part of their school credentials.

The Forum Report saw the development of a new course, Education about Religion and Beliefs (ERB), as an answer to many of the difficulties that different groups had: 'The Advisory Group is of the view that all children have the right to receive education in ERB and Ethics and the State has the responsibility to ensure that this is provided.'[16]

In making this recommendation, the report indicated that its main concern was for those children who do not participate in religious programmes in denominational schools, who might go through their primary education with no exposure to this area. The proposed ERB course was not intended to supplant faith-formation education in denominational schools, but as an alternative. The recommendation was that this should be a compulsory offering within the school and that the school would have to satisfy the inspectorate as to the adequacy of provision. However, the recommendation that the curriculum design team should look to the current denominational courses on offer suggests that the Advisory Group were in fact looking for a single new course that could integrate denominational approaches rather than to design a course specifically directed to the needs of 'others' in a denominational context.

The report does not ground the Advisory Group's view that all children have a *right* to receive education in ERB and ethics. The actual *right* is that education will be in line with particular religious beliefs, not with some compromised approach to religious education. The appeal here cannot be to a right. There is a strong case to be made in terms of the common good, where knowledge about issues relating to religious history and culture are seen as contributing to the good of the individual. In a context where specific instruction in a belief system is not available, such a course might make a valuable contribution to the individual. However, as discussed in Chapter 6 when outlining different approaches to RE, not all parents will be satisfied with an approach that teaches 'about' religion. Although the Forum Report claimed general support for such a programme, the specific support base it relied on was from the Irish Humanist Society and Atheist Ireland. For some parents, this approach to teaching about values may be as disturbing as the worldview of any faith-based instruction is to a non-adherent. The problem was summed up by Fish:

> [Doctrine that assumes] the mind remains unaffected by the ideas and doctrines that pass before it and that its job is to weigh and assess those doctrines from a position distanced from and independent of any of them ... The chief danger is not of any particular doctrine to which the children might be exposed but the unannounced yet powerfully assumed doctrine of exposure as a first principle, as a virtual theology. This is where the doctrine comes in, not at the level of urging this or that belief, but at the more subliminal level at which what is urged is that encountering as many ideas as possible and giving each of them a run for their money is an absolutely good thing. What the children are being indoctrinated in is distrust of any belief that has not been arrived at by the exercise of their unaided reason as it surveys all the alternatives before choosing one freely with no guidance from any external authority.[17]

The point here is not to disagree with the intent of the recommendation in the Forum Report, but to point to the mixed use of language with regard to the common good and rights. The reliance on rights is often contentious. At a practical level, there may be more support for a positive and inclusive vision of the common good. Equally, the compromise position promoted here may be accepted by some as a 'good', but be rejected by others.

The Forum Report relies on the Toledo Guiding Principles as supporting the 'religious studies' approach to course design. It is worth pointing out again that these principles were drawn up by the Organisation for Security and Cooperation in Europe. The main focus of this group is security and producing tolerance between fundamentalist ethnic and religious groups that are in open conflict in different European countries. This is an order goal, not a culture goal as explored in Chapter 2. The aim is not religious education as normally understood, but citizen education. In Ireland, there is already a programme in place called Civic, Social and Political Education (CSPE), which is compulsory for all students. It aims to

> prepare students for active participatory citizenship. This is achieved through comprehensive exploration of the civic, social and political dimensions of their lives at a time when pupils are developing from dependent children into independent young adults. It should produce knowledgeable pupils who can explore, analyse and evaluate, who are skilled and practised in moral and critical appraisal, and capable of making decisions and judgments through a reflective citizenship, based on human rights and social responsibilities. Such pupils should be better prepared for living in a world where traditional structures and values are being challenged, and where pupils are being confronted with conflicting interests, impermanent structures and constant questioning.[18]

There are many different ways of designing and organising a RE course, both as stand-alone and in combination with other citizen courses. Depending on the design and delivery of such a course, it can promote different approaches to diversity. It can give rise to the 'melting-pot' model of assimilation, which seeks to reduce differences and make all religious experiences or traditions the same. Alternatively, it is possible to work from the 'salad-bowl' model, where there is an opportunity for each religious group to develop their own identity while contributing to the whole. It is important to realise that such a course, promoted by the State, works from assumptions in much the same way as a denominational course works from assumptions of their own.

4.3. EXEMPTION FROM RELIGIOUS EDUCATION

The right of parents to absent their child from any form of religious instruction is well established in both the Constitution and the Education Act. There are two aspects to parents invoking this right. The first is that the child might be deprived of all education in relation to religion because he or she was exempted from a particular approach to religious education. This gave rise to the proposal for an alternative course to be provided on a compulsory basis in denominational schools. The second area of concern is the way in which the exemption system works. Logistics might require the child to be in a particular classroom as an observer rather than a participant. In this context, the issue of exemptions can be examined from three perspectives – rights, community and logistics:

a. Rights perspective: In the Forum Report, the practice in one school was cited:

> The general practice for religion time is that the children of other faiths are present, sometimes engaging in an activity of their own and sometimes taking an active part in RE where conversation relates to non-religious elements. This seems to be a happy situation for teachers and also for the parents of the children of other faiths.[19]

In commenting on this as an opt-out provision, the Advisory Group made the damning judgment that '[t]his perspective does not illustrate sufficient understanding of the human rights issues involved'.[20] In the context of the wider discussion on opt-out provision, the school's approach can be classified as a partial exemption. It requires the pupils to be 'passive attenders' at some parts of the course, and allows them to be 'active participants' in others, depending on the topic. Clearly this would not satisfy all parents and could not be regarded as a universal solution. In line with the discussion on the Norwegian case in Chapter 5, this approach is likely to place a heavy burden on parents to anticipate what is taught on a particular course in order to exercise their right of exemption. It may also lead to informal pressure on parents to allow their children to attend classes with the majority. The focus on logistical problems may give rise to insensitive assumptions that the minority group should put up with a lower level of freedom in their own religious education, or the minority group might experience an oppressive culture where a request for different treatment might be difficult to make.

While there is no issue with the Advisory Group using school examples to illustrate human rights issues, there is a problem with the condemnatory tone used towards the school. The situation described here is not unlike that which might exist in many 'religious studies' classes – an element of learning 'about' a topic followed by differentiated exploration leading to learning 'into' the topic. When this is conducted by skilled teachers sensitive to student needs, then it can be a powerful learning environment. Unless there was other evidence that the Advisory Group considered, there is nothing to suggest that the school's assessment that this was satisfactory for teachers and for the parents of the children of other faiths, was inaccurate or naive *for their school*. Parents of other faiths may have been quite willing, as part of their understanding of freedom of religion, to allow the majority group to pursue their purposes. It may have been acceptable that the alternative activities were clearly defined and linked to the religion of the pupils and that they had opportunities to give input about their own tradition when that was being treated on the course. Specific solutions such as this one may be acceptable when other aspects of school life celebrate each child's tradition in some way.

In comparison with the statement critiqued by the Advisory Group and outlined above, a more articulate approach was presented by the Holy Rosary School (a Catholic school) in its submission to the Forum. However, the Forum Report failed to highlight examples of good practice in terms of diversity in denominational schools. The school describes itself as having a whole-school approach, not just with regard to religious education:

> ... we have sought ways to respect, acknowledge and celebrate the different ethnic and religious groups reflected in the school community. This has been done through a range of activities and programmes that have evolved over the years. Among these we can

highlight sports, games, music, choirs, family fun days, recipe books featuring meals from over forty countries, a festival of faiths, the annual arts week, meetings organised between parents and teachers to discuss curricular and educational concerns and the use of church rooms for instruction in other faiths. The net result of these activities is that the children do not see cultural or religious difference as a source of tension. Exploring difference offers an opportunity to grow in respect for traditions and cultures other than our own. The parents and teachers also acknowledged that the efforts to constantly promote a respectful dialogue have been a source of learning and greater understanding and have strengthened the sense of belonging in the local community. It should not be imagined that this work has proceeded without tensions and difficulties but when these have been addressed in the context of the school's ethos of respect, potentially divisive issues have been resolved.[21]

In reflecting on the RE provision in the school, the same submission noted the benefits to the Catholic community in the school, the practical arrangements that were made to accommodate and integrate others, and their response to these initiatives:

By and large the experience has been positive. The Catholic identity of the school and its close links with the parish has not been compromised by the religious diversity within the school population. On the contrary the situation has led to a growing culture of respect and understanding. The major feasts of the great religions are acknowledged while children of other faiths have shared in the celebrations surrounding the first Holy Communion and Confirmation classes. There has been an effort to cater for the RE needs of the other faith groups and this has included the use of church premises by the Muslim community for classes. The Muslim parents have expressed their appreciation for the efforts of the school and parish to assist them in providing for the religious formation of their children. A recent delegation of educators from Saudi Arabia who were sent to the school on a visit by the Department of Education expressed their amazement at the use of the Church for Muslim Instruction and the easy integration of the Muslim children in the school community.[22]

It is possible to cater for a diversity of religious needs in both multi-denominational and in denominational schools. If done sensitively and in the context of a whole-school approach to respect and inclusion, then parental needs to resort to exemption rights may be lessened. This will allow for some genuine inclusion of sharing information on faith. It will also allow for differentiated activities for different groups, helping them develop their own identity. In this, there is a need for exemplars of good practice as well as warnings against insensitive practices. However, schools must also be prepared to meet genuine needs for exemption.

b. Community perspective: One of the issues that is raised in a discussion on exemptions is that of building community. The problem posed is that separating children for religious education makes them feel different, especially if they are a minority, promoting a sense of exclusion. A proposed solution is to keep all students together for a 'one-size-fits-all' course. The solution is criticised as creating a tension between two perspectives: 'let's pretend we're all the same, and there are no real differences between us' and 'let us acknowledge differences and find ways of celebrating these differences so that being different is part of a positive identity rather than a sense of exclusion'. For others, it is a question of timing; they argue that the notion of difference is more acceptable as a child develops, but in the early primary school years, the concept of diversity is more difficult. Different religious groups have different approaches to the links between information and formation and between doctrine and devotion. Parents also have different approaches to how they want their children to be raised. The policy issue at stake is whether the State should be involved in imposing a solution within the school system.

The social argument is very powerful, especially when young children are involved. However, it needs to be examined critically. Imagine taking a similar approach in a parallel subject – music. A course is designed to develop musical appreciation and to help pupils develop their musical skills through singing or playing an instrument. However, imagine that some parents object to rock and roll and want any reference removed from the curriculum.[23] Then other parents object to another part of the course, and so on. Another possible scenario is that some parents do not want their child to be different from the others and therefore all pupils must learn the same instrument, together. In response, the school develops an orchestra of, say, tin whistle players. A final scenario might be a child who is tone deaf and feels embarrassed in music class because they cannot participate with any degree of success or confidence. To avoid this, the school decides to teach about music in 'an objective and pluralist way' without any engagement in playing it. Obviously music education is not a human right and religious belief is a different genre, but this scenario demonstrates how the social argument, pushed to an extreme, can lead to ludicrous situations that destroy the integrity of a particular subject and invoke solutions to the issue of difference that undermine the very concept of diversity itself.

c. Logistic perspective: In this context, the focus is on the distribution of majority and minority groups in a school and State involvement in deciding on approaches to religious education. It will also focus on the resourcing issues in providing appropriate courses to all.

Providing for diversity can be resource intensive. It is one thing to provide a class in their own religion to a group of 15–20 students; however, in rural communities, diverse needs may be thinly dispersed. This makes for logistical problems in providing equal access to their own programmes. It might be impossible to offer any alternative programme, or even adequate supervision in an opt-out situation. In such a scenario, the provision of a single course for all students looks like an attractive solution, although the course itself may not meet the needs of any student. Providing for exemptions can often be very difficult, as there is a duty of care to the child who opts out and the preferred solution is to have some positive learning experience for the child. There are other situations in which parents may seek an exemption from a compulsory part of the school programme. A comparison of these different contexts can raise challenging issues about a different approach to the common good and to rights when talking about religion and other areas of the programme.

Study of Irish is compulsory for all pupils, except in exceptional circumstances.[24] The question arises as to how schools handle this exemption and deal with opt-out pupils. Do they become 'spectators' or 'occasional participants' in a classroom where there is no provision for alternatives? How does the school manage the sense those students might encounter of 'being different' from the mainstream? In some cases, native pupils may experience resentment that they are compelled to study a subject they do not like. In others, the differences can give rise to creative approaches to affirming cultural identity for all. This parallel is not unlike the challenges that exist in teaching religion.

4.4. General Religious 'Ethos'

There is a recommendation that sacramental preparation should be confined to a half-hour period for religion. This is directed mainly at Catholic schools and cites an internal document of the Catholic Church promoting greater parish involvement in sacramental preparation in support of its position. However, the Forum Report seems insensitive to the current position of such events in the school and their connection with the characteristic spirit of the school which is guaranteed in the Education Act. The events highlighted are not just events for the individual – the Catholic child in a Catholic school – they are also school events, where the school celebrates what it is and presents itself to parents and others. The sacramental preparation is multi-disciplinary in its approach; it involves children singing in choir and reading in front of adults. These activities build skills and self-confidence – all of which are curricular outcomes. The preparation close to an event is often intense – just as it is for a Christmas or end-of-year concert, Feis Ceol or a football competition. The context of a public performance gives extra motivation to pupils and new opportunities for learning. Schools often invest time and energy in these events, with very positive results in the classroom. Good teachers are flexible with their scheduling and seek to build on such opportunities, finding a way to balance the time for other core activities linked with the basic skills of literacy and numeracy.

This is not to deny that there can be problems, and some of these are well rehearsed in the Forum Report. However, as one of the student voices pointed out, in a school play there are many different types of activities that allow for participation without having to compromise belief – stage management, lights, costumes, etc. Admittedly, this level of participation runs the risk of an insensitive assumption about the neutrality of the religious content of the event. However, as discussed above in relation to comments from the Advisory Group and in the example of Holy Rosary School in Tallaght, local dialogue may allow for a healthy, respectful participation of the whole community, which is reciprocated in celebrations involving other faiths and philosophies.

In the Forum Report, the dissatisfaction of some minorities who attend denominational schools were taken as an indication of 'human rights' infractions. The report recommended a number of new activities aimed at redressing the 'rights' issues. In doing so, it rarely referred to the rights of the majority group, or the need to balance the rights of different groups. The report is admirable in its concern for the minority group and the desire that this group should pursue their own religious beliefs with the same freedom as the majority group do. This is a compelling appeal to the common good. However, the very fact that a minority group seeks to do this in a denominational context leads to a tension in rights. Debating on a rights level, with a view to one set of rights 'trumping' the others, is not helpful. Assuming that minority rights are trumps is even less helpful. Clearly, when a minority group are in a school run by the majority, they do not lose or forgo these rights. However, the context of the denominational school is a factor. No one can take away the 'negative' right any group has not to be coerced or proselytised, or put at a disadvantage in other aspects of their education in the school. However, their 'positive' claim is less clear in this context. In a State-run school, all such claims would be equal.

Posing the issue this way, it becomes clear that using rights language in this context runs into a complexity, and this complexity needs to be named and dealt with. The suggestion is not that a majority group would stand on its rights, or indeed that the rights are necessarily mutually exclusive and that a practical accommodation cannot be found to benefit all parties. One would hope that majority groups would freely support a minority group as part of their contribution to the common good. The recommendations of the Forum Report reflect some of these practical accommodations. The concern is that ambiguous use of language confuses issues and does not facilitate a coherent solution.

5. THE POLITICAL RESPONSE
Government provision for education faces a number of significant challenges. The first is to provide for education on an adequate basis

for every citizen: 'The first objective of the DES must be that a school place is available to every child.'[25] The problems that arise in this provision have been outlined in great detail in the Forum Report and are very evident in the problems faced in the four areas outlined in the Report and discussed above – the stand-alone school, areas of stable population numbers but changing demographics, areas of expanding population and responding to the demand for all-Irish language education.

The issue of promoting parental choice in a shrinking system is an interesting challenge. We have a growing population, and the budgetary demand seems to be for a smaller number of bigger schools. It is difficult to see how the two match up. The focus of choice has been almost entirely on the religious identity of the patron (denominational or non-denominational); there has been little focus on the complexity of an ethos that encompasses cultural, educational, moral, religious, social, linguistic and spiritual values and traditions.

In his response to the Forum Document in June 2012, the Minister for Education and Skills outlined the issue with regard to diversity:

> There is a need to balance making real and substantial progress on ensuring diversity of choice of primary schools for parents, with the longer term need to ensure buy-in by the education partners to agreed arrangements for more diversity and inclusiveness, particularly in schools where choice of patronage is not available.[26]

The long-term project would seem to move to a more universal 'one-size fits all' type of education, underpinned by greater State involvement and legislation. Heralding the approach to divesting schools in some areas and by implication, the new approach to patronage in expanding areas, the Minister went on to claim: 'For many parents this will be the first time they will have a real say in the type of primary school they want their children to go to, whether it is denominational, multi-denominational, all-Irish or other.'[27]

This is an interesting political spin. In the first place, it seems to assert that parents in the past did not have a say. This glosses over the positive relationship that has existed between most parents and the providers of education in the past. It is certainly true that parents in the past operated from a limited menu of choices, but it does not mean that they were hard done by. There is a tendency in the education debate to judge the lack of choice in the past as an aberration rather than a reflection of the society at the time. It applies criteria related to the early twenty-first century to the nineteenth and early twentieth centuries. A close look at the system shows that many parents exercised a definite choice. Some, especially Protestant parents at primary and post-primary level, invested very heavily in making a real choice for their children. Parents have always had a say in the type of school their child will attend, although that choice was constrained by distance, expense and convenience.

NOTES

1. Forum Report, p. 1.
2. Ibid., p. 55.
3. Ibid., p. 3.
4. The first three points are taken from page 55 of the Forum Report, although the order of the points has been changed. The fourth point is from page 62.
5. This case was discussed in more detail in Chapter 7; it involved the setting up of a Steiner school. *O'Shiel* vs *Minister for Education* (1999), 2 IR 321, (1999), 2 ILRM 241.
6. Forum Report, p.19.
7. Áine Hyland, 'Educate Together Schools in the Republic of Ireland: The First Stage 1975–1994' (Belfast: Fortnight Educational Trust, 1993), http://www.educatetogether.ie/reference_articles/Ref_Art_001.html
8. Forum Report, p. 73.
9. Ibid., pp. 56ff.
10. Ibid., p. 93.
11. Education Act (1998), section 15 2(e).
12. Deed of Variation, Primary Schools. See Forum Report, p. 19. A similar phrase exists in the deed of variation of the Protestant schools.
13. Education Act (1998), section 15 2(d) and section 20.
14. Forum Report, p. 56.
15. Education Act (1998), section 30(2).
16. Forum Report, p. 92.
17. Stanley Fish, 'Mission Impossible: Setting the Just Bounds Between Church and State', *Columbia Law Review* 97 (1997), pp. 2255, 2289–90.
18. Primary School Curriculum Handbook (1997), Civic, Social and Political Education 1.1.1.
19. Forum Report, p. 82.
20. Ibid.

21. http://www.education.ie/en/Press-Events/Conferences/Patronage-and-Pluralism-in-the-Primary-Sector/Patronage-Forum-Submissions-June-2011/Organisations-June-2011/?pageNumber=3
22. Ibid.
23. This was a scenario proposed in the film *Mr Holland's Opus* (1995).
24. Revision of Circular 18/79 on exemption from the study of Irish (2005).
25. Commission on School Accommodation, Revised Criteria and Procedures for Establishment of New Primary Schools (February 2011).
26. Government Press Release (20 June 2012).
27. Ibid.

10

CONTEMPORARY ISSUES: REGULATING PROVISION

This chapter considers three practical issues pertaining to the regulation of provision of schooling. The focus is on the practical – the way in which more theoretical perspectives are institutionalised. These practical decisions can have indirect, but very serious, consequences on the continued existence of denominational schools. These decisions can also indicate subtle changes in approaches to provision that are not debated at a policy level.

1. CAPITAL PROVISION

Traditionally, the site for schools was provided locally. As a result, the land on which primary schools and voluntary secondary schools are built is mostly owned by dioceses and religious congregations. The patron has also made a contribution to the capital cost of building, creating a complex relationship between the patron and the Department of Education and Skills with regard to the ownership of the building. The complexities of the legal issues in this arrangement have become apparent in the recent negotiations on divesting primary schools. Four scenarios suggest themselves:

Scenario 1. *The Catholic Church has traditionally been the major provider in an area and is patron to a number of different schools. It recognises that the demand for Catholic schooling has changed, and that it has spare capacity in all its schools. One option is for the patron to consolidate the provision by amalgamating some schools and freeing up the property.*

In this scenario, the property is closed as a school and there is no question of it being needed to provide school places. The action contributes to the general efficiency of the system. In general, it has been accepted that such properties belong to the patron who is free to dispose of them. There may be some obligations on the patron to refund grant money to the DES if the patron realises the assets of the property through a sale. This has a moral basis, as the DES had not intended to contribute to the capital assets of the patron, but to help them in providing a service. If assets were gained, then some portion of these assets could be returned to the State. This may have been stipulated in the vesting leases of the properties. In general, at post-primary level, when voluntary secondary schools have been amalgamated, there has been no demand on the patron of a closed school to contribute to the establishment of the new school. Around Ireland there are quite a number of such 'closed' schools. They have been abandoned or converted to community use.

Scenario 2. *As in scenario 1, the Catholic Church has traditionally been the major provider in an area and is patron to a number of different schools. It recognises that the demand for Catholic schooling has changed and that a number of parents do not want to send their children to these schools. It has been calculated that the patron could consolidate the provision by amalgamating some schools and this would meet the demand for Catholic schooling. There is a demand that the closed school be handed over to another patron in order to meet the need for alternative schooling.*

The issue in this scenario focuses on the freedom the patron has to dispose of the property, particularly in view of the department's investment in the building on the land. At a practical level, one response might be that the patron sell the property or lease the building to the department or to the new patron. In this solution, there is no interference in ownership issues with regard to the site, and the intention of the capital funding for the building is honoured. In a sale, the terms of the deal could take into account the history of funding. In a lease, a clear relationship would be established between the owner of the property and the tenant. If the department were the tenant, then it could assign the enterprise of the school to a different patron.

In the Forum Report, this issue was touched on briefly, although no solutions or definitive guidelines were presented:

> While the ownership of most primary schools lies primarily with the bishops or religious congregations, submissions to the Forum emphasised that the resources for such schools came from the parish, school communities and patrons. This is in addition to the considerable exchequer funding for the common good purpose of public education ... If the divested primary schools were to continue to supply public primary education under new patronage arrangements, monetary compensation to the divesting patrons should not be a significant issue.[1]

The suggestion here, seemingly endorsed by the report, is that since the funds for the purchase of the property and the local contribution came from 'parish, school communities and patrons' then there is some moral obligation on the part of patrons to divest the property with little or no cost to the State. This statement makes a number of assumptions about the relationship between the Church and the funds it collects. It also expects the Church to behave in a different way than might be expected of any other property owner in comparable circumstances. For instance, would the same expectation exist if the government wished to change the terms of a public-private partnership arrangement on a toll road or bridge? These statements raise moral and legal issues about Church ownership of school property. The rhetoric is couched in terms of the common good, with a demand that Church groups forgo their rights to property.

The Church may not always be in a position to sell or lease the land to another body. This depends on how the property, or the funds for the local contribution, was obtained. For instance, a number of school sites have been donated or bequeathed to the Church for the benefit of the Church and its activities. At times there are stipulations on such bequests that the property be used in a particular way – for education, for Catholic education or for the education of Catholic children. In other donations, the terms may not be very specific and may simply indicate that the property should be used for activities related to the Church. This type of bequest is protected by both civil and Church law and limits the ability of the property holder to change the use of the property.

A similar issue arises with donations to the Church. Some of these donations may be collected as general membership dues, where the expectation is that the money be used for Church activities. The members accept that the provision of Catholic education is one of these functions. However, if the demand for Catholic education were to diminish, they would expect such assets to be applied to other areas of Church activity – social work, care of the poor and sick. Such funds may be regarded as general funds, and are not linked to specific parishes or communities. There are ethical issues associated with the use of these funds similar to the issues arising from legally protected bequests.

Other funds were collected for specific purposes, such as the building of a school. The patron may have appealed to the local community for support in funding the local contribution. These contributions may have been given with the expectation of having a distinctly Catholic school. For other donors, it was for the provision of a school, any school. It is sometimes difficult to decipher such intentions, especially when the bulk of such donations may have been made twenty to twenty-five years previously by a different generation of parents than are now attached to the school. The issue for Church groups is to discern their obligations to the wishes of the donors.

Within these complexities of the relationship between Church patrons and the property they hold, creative and generous solutions have been found. Many Church bodies believe that they hold property for 'public benefit' and have taken ethical positions on the use of their assets. For instance, in disposing of some properties, congregations have stipulated that a portion of a development should be given to affordable social housing. This has been written into agreements with developers, although the conditions have not always been honoured. As a result, some congregations feel that advantage has been taken of them, and they are more wary of this type of donation. In the field of education, quite a number of congregations have either donated or licensed property to new Trust bodies. This designates the land for a particular educational use; it is an investment in securing the public good of Catholic education into the future. By designating property in this way, the congregations commit the property to the 'common good', making a clear statement that the property is not for their own benefit. To date, no similar process has been undertaken with parish or diocesan property.

Scenario 3. *The Catholic Church runs one large primary school in the area which has capacity to serve all the needs in the area. It is claimed that there is a change in demand for different types of school, and the suggestion is made that the school building be divided and that a second non-Catholic school be established in one part.*

In this scenario, the issue focuses on control of the use of the building. The issues that emerge relate to ownership and the rights and responsibilities of being in receipt of public funding. Since the State gives a major part of the funding for the building, the question is the level of control it has over the use of the building. In primary schools, the relationship between the patron and the State is worked out in a vesting lease which ensures the property is used for educational purposes. In post-primary schools, this relationship has been conducted mainly on the basis of mutual trust, with few formal agreements in place. Clearly, the State would have a claim on the value of its investment should the patron decide to close the school. It is not so clear what claim the State might have should the State itself initiated the changed conditions. The question might be posed as follows: Is the building a State-owned building, and the contribution of the patron simply to acquire certain privileges in the running of the school? Or, is the building owned by the patron and the money paid by the State a grant, with no entitlement to ownership? The first option would make for a complicated situation, in that the building is on privately owned land. The second would be similar to many situations where different organisations have received government or lottery funding for buildings – there are conditions of use attached to these funds, but no expectation of ownership arises on the part of the government.

The ownership issue creates a problem for the proposed solution of a shared building. It is one thing to suggest that schools share a campus or a building when the DES is the owner of the property and manages the lease. However, it would be a different issue to have two schools in the one building and one patron having a different 'right' to the building. There is an old saying that an empty house is better than a bad tenant. It is easy to see a practical arrangement working in the short term, with each school working to agreed quotas of students. It is also easy to imagine a situation arising with changing demographics where one school might want to expand and encroach more on the other school. This would not make for an easy legal situation. In human terms it might also be exacerbated by the historic contribution one patron made to the site, and the freer arrangements made for the second patron.

Scenario 4. *The State owns the land and the building and leases it for a fixed term to a particular patron.*

This allows a level of flexibility for the DES in deciding on the provision for schooling in an area, and also gives them control over the property. This is likely to be the format used in the future and it seems a tidier solution to the complexity that exists at present. However, it is the historic situation that has to be dealt with in the process of changing the profile of patronage in the primary sector.

The aim of the section is to demonstrate the complexity of the issues. It places in context the sometimes naive claims that are made as to what the Church should do. In the context of the approaches to politics outlined in earlier chapters, the appeal to the common good is often used as moral persuasion. In contrast with outlining the 'rights' of minority groups, the moral persuasion pays little attention to the 'rights' that the Church might have because of its historic contributions to the establishment and maintenance of the schools. It seems that different behaviours are expected of the Church with regard to the use of property than might be expected of any other group.

The regulation of patronage is not simply a question of providing for new schools or negotiating new arrangements over land and buildings. Capital funding for schools can be used as a political tool in managing schools. This occurs in the way that schools are granted funds for refurbishment and extensions, such as halls and gymnasia. Decisions on the distribution of such funds can have a major bearing on how parents might prefer one school to another in an area. The story of one parent illustrates the point:

Last week I attended a school fête at a multi-denominational primary school set up by parents coming together as a private company. It was a series of rundown shacks made of corrugated iron and wood. Plans for a new building were pinned on the wall. Only when a school has been up and running for a number of years will the State invest in it. How brave of those parents, I thought, to submit their children to substandard school accommodation in the meantime. I doubted whether I would be so pioneering, especially if my children would have moved on by the time the new building was completed.

My local primary school is bright and sparkling. I am a coward and will stick with the mainstream, something I would be less likely to do were I not a parent. Thus are societies bent into submission and questionable authorities and practices maintained. Thus are things set in stone.[2]

This parent had been very much in favour of a values-based education in a liberal tradition, and wanted her children integrated into the local community. Although happy enough with the education her child received, her first choice would have been something else. The story illustrates that parental choice is strongly influenced by the tangible. The school is 'set in stone'; it is defined by such things as place on a bus-route, facilities, number of computers, etc. Parents may be confident that all schools will provide a guaranteed basic level of care for children. They will then seek any extra advantage they can for their child. There are many hearsay stories of the differential treatment of requests for capital funding and the profound effect this has on school numbers. It has been suggested in some cases that the DES has actively conspired to change the profile of schools in particular areas by supporting some schools more than others and allowing some schools to expand their intake with no concern for the effect on other schools.

2. OPERATIONAL FUNDING

The allocation of teachers to schools follows a per capita system. Teachers are allocated to schools based on the number of students in the school. The basic formula is the total number of students in the school divided by a fixed student–teacher ratio set by the DES: so for every X students in the school, you get a teacher. There are special concessions made for small schools which allow for extra teachers to be appointed and there are also extra posts allocated in large schools for administrative purposes. The idea is that the funding of teachers follows the student, not the school. The effect of this system can be seen by looking at the effect of this funding mechanism in two secondary schools, each with the same number of students but with different profiles.

	Number of Students		Class Groups of 24 students each	
School	A	B	A	B
1st	96	115	4	5
2nd	96	115	4	5
3rd	96	115	4	5
TY	95	n.a.	4	n.a.
5th	96	115	4	5
6th	96	115	4	5
Total	**575**	**575**	**24**	**25**

Table 10.1. A possible profile of students in two different schools and the resulting needs for teachers.

School A offers the Transition Year, and School B does not. Both schools try to keep class size to twenty-four. The two schools end up with different provision needs – school B has one extra class group to teach, a total of forty class periods each week. Yet, the formula for teacher allocation assigns the same number of teachers to the school.

A second area where a per capita basis for funding is evident is in the payment of grants to schools for running costs. School C may be a new school, working to full capacity, with the latest of energy-saving features. School D may be an older building, with spare space owing to changing demographics and very hard to heat. The energy bills of these two schools are very different, yet the resourcing mechanism does not take that into account. Differences can also exist in terms of insurance premiums and a series of other services, including maintenance and refurbishment costs. Large schools may also benefit from economies of scale in acquiring supplies.

A third example of this funding approach is the support given to students with special educational needs. This support is organised through the National Council for Special Education. Schools apply for resources following a professional assessment of a child. A decision is made in the light of that assessment and the DES resource parameters. The allocation works on a personal basis, not a school basis. It may include resource teacher hours (an extra-quota allocation of teachers). Each student is assigned an amount of time, and the total time is aggregated for students in a school. A school may be allocated an equivalent of say 1.5 teachers for resource work, and this can be managed by the school. Special needs assistants (SNA) are recruited for individual students who require special care arising from a disability. The allocation of an SNA is related to named students for a particular amount of time each. In this way the school may coordinate the work of a single SNA around a number of pupils. However, the contract of the SNA is determined by their relationship to the student, not to the school.

Funding for interventions with students who were deemed to be disadvantaged has seen an evolution that moved from a school base to an individual base. In the early days of such schemes, designated schools were allocated an ex-quota concessionary teaching post and also qualified for special supplementary capitation funding. Over time, the mechanisms for allocating funding became more sophisticated. At first, it was related to the size of the school and later to the percentage of students in the school who are considered disadvantaged. Schools were encouraged to prioritise their interventions to the students who attracted the funding.

In operating a recent national budget cut, the Minister for Education and Skills proposed cutting some of the grants associated with disadvantaged students at primary level. On appeal, he later reversed that decision but cut the capitation grant in primary schools to fund it. This gave rise to cries of 'robbing Peter to pay Paul', yet it reflects the reality of budgeting in times of constraint. The lesson we learn is that the funding mechanism for education is a mixture of the politics of the common good and responding to individual rights. The common good is seen in the general allocation of finances worked out in competition with other needs such as health, social welfare and other government departments. Once the total is determined at that level, it is then distributed within the education system. This too reveals different concepts of the common good. The bulk of the finances seem to be distributed according to a general formula dictated by historical funding procedures and levels. It is based on percentage rises and cuts rather than on specific needs of schools and there is very little flexibility for discretionary spending. This has a knock-on effect in schools, and frequently schools depend on voluntary contributions from parents and on fundraising activities.

When payment to schools is based on a per capita scheme (consumption) rather than a school-based scheme, there is a strong argument for saying that the government does not support the school directly, but supports the individual student in receiving their education. The support can be seen as an entitlement for each student. Rather than paying the grant directly to the student, it is paid to the school as a collection agency for all students in the school. This has the added benefit of easier supervision that the grant is used for its intended purpose. This perception is strengthened by looking at the history of post-primary funding. Originally, all secondary schools were fee paying. When free secondary education was introduced, schools were enticed into the scheme by the promise of an extra 'grant-in-lieu of fees'. In other words, the schools would receive a payment from the government replacing the fees that would normally have been paid by the students.

While a strict system of per capita payments applies to primary schools and voluntary secondary schools, the running costs of VEC, community and comprehensive schools are met on a different basis. The historic anomalies in the way that funding has been calculated have led to major differences in terms of the real funding given to schools in the different sectors. On average, students in voluntary secondary schools are State funded by €80 less than their counterparts in community schools and €212 less than those in VEC schools. In schools of six hundred students each, this means a vocational school would have a budget allocation of €125,000 more than a secondary school, whereas a community school would have €48,000 more. As this money is controlled at local VEC level, rather than at individual school level, this allows the VEC group to target particular projects with their extra-funding. In some places, this has included strong public relations campaigns to showcase their schools and attract students away from other schools. The funding also makes a major difference in what schools can offer students and places an expectation on the voluntary secondary sector to enhance their budget through the voluntary contribution of parents. There is a stated policy to equalise such funding between schools, but delays in doing this can be seen as a mechanism in controlling patronage and parental preferences for schools.

2.1. The Debate on Fee-Paying Schools

A particular application of the rhetoric on funding schools is the debate on fee-paying schools. In January 2012, the Minister for Education and Skills announced an audit of fee-paying schools, with special reference to the €100 million paid to teachers in these schools. The media commented that the 'new investigation is designed to identify which schools are most in need and which no longer deserve the same level of State support' and also reported that unidentified education sources say 'it is difficult to justify State support for well-heeled schools'.[3]

This raises important questions about the basis of educational funding. There is a suggestion that schools should be means-tested, and that State support should be based on the wealth of these schools. This would be a radically new approach to State funding for schools. In general, there are two different issues raised in the debate. The first focuses on the legitimacy of the fee-paying sector and their right to receive any State funding; the second on social policy and the way these schools contribute or contradict that policy.

When the free education scheme was introduced, schools were offered a grant-in-lieu-of-fees if they agreed not to charge fees to parents. Most schools accepted this proposal, but some did not; they stayed outside the scheme and still received capitation grants and support for teachers as they had previously. Fee-paying schools are all in the voluntary sector. There is bias of those schools in the Dublin area and they cater more for boys than for girls.

	Nationally		Dublin Area	
	Boys	Girls	Boys	Girls
All Schools	176196	181276	47130	47850
All voluntary	87322	99316	24319	27849
All Fee paying	14969	11250	10223	8665
Catholic Fee	9753	6120	7553	5634

Table 10.2. Distribution of pupils in post-primary schools in 2011 nationally and in the Dublin area. (For the purpose of this exercise, Newbridge, Clongowes and Bray were included in Dublin Area for Fee-Paying schools).

When the debate focuses on the financial issues involved, the argument goes as follows: education funding is mainly student-based; the capitation grant and the payment of teacher salaries can be seen as a form of social welfare that all families benefit from in much the same way as welfare payments of children's allowances are paid to all families and are not means tested. This is the historic understanding of the grant-in-lieu of fees arrangement. The argument continues that parents then have a choice as to how to invest their post-tax assets. Some people may choose to supplement their children's education by sending them to grind schools or other enrichment experiences; others may choose to send their children to fee-paying schools. Another strand of the argument focuses on the cost benefit to the State. Given the fact that fee-paying schools work with a lower teacher-student ratio in the allocation of teachers, and that they do not get any capitation support, it is claimed that these schools save the State approximately €22 million a year – the amount it would cost the State if all these students were in voluntary secondary schools in the free education scheme.[4]

The debate on these schools also embraces social issues. From this perspective, it is claimed that government support for fee-paying schools supports privilege, thus contributing to divisions in society. The fees charged by these schools help parents to create artificial social barriers between those who can and those who can't pay.[5] It is contended that support for these schools is incongruent with policies of social cohesion. This discussion is not limited to the political sphere; it is also alive within Church circles, where religious congregations involved in running such schools are regularly challenged as to how their commitment to this type of education contributes to stated Church policy of a 'preferential option for the poor'.

The social argument is not simple. In Ireland, the same system of fee-paying schools that may contribute to an undesirable form of diversity (unequal class divisions) is also a major contributor to promoting a positive form of diversity (the denominational identity of Protestant families). In particular, fee-paying Protestant schools in rural areas are seen as a necessary contribution to preserving the cultural identity of a Protestant minority. These schools resent the notion that all fee-paying schools enjoy huge reservoirs of disposable income. In fact, many Protestant schools are struggling to survive.

The purpose of this section is to point to the complexity of the arguments, and how the debate often takes place at different levels. Speakers come from different perspectives, and in the end are not really talking about the same issues. The common good from the perspective of the financial argument is seen in terms of the accumulated personal goods that arise from individuals using their post-tax wealth to pursue their own interests. Part of this good is the financial savings to the State for the benefit of others. From the social perspective, the common good is postulated as a form of social cohesion and shared experience. The arguments point to different views of the common good. Within these perspectives there are also different views on balancing individual rights and the right of the State to set social policy.

3. ADMISSIONS POLICIES

In June 2011, Minister Quinn published a government discussion paper on a regulatory framework for school enrolment. The document sought a possible basis for legislation based on twin concerns:

- An application of the principle of 'subsidiarity' whereby decision making is with the board and patron as far as possible.
- To build confidence among parents about the fairness of enrolment policies and processes operated by schools.[6]

The issue of admission and enrolment in schools embraces issues about the common good and affects patrons' right of selection, parental rights to choose a school and the State's right to determine policies supporting social cohesion and fairness. The intensity of the debate depends on where one lives and the general provision for education in the area. It is important to distinguish different sources of tension in school provision, and how these tensions arise in different contexts.

3.1. THE DYNAMICS OF SCHOOL CHOICE

Parents balance a number of different issues when choosing a school for their children. This chapter has already outlined how capital and operational investment in schools has an impact on how a school is seen in the local area. Decisions on such investment often reflect political and ideological perspectives on the common good. The dynamic of school choice can also be considered from the perspective of the individual.

As stated in the Education Act, the characteristic spirit of a school includes the cultural, educational, moral, religious, social, linguistic and spiritual values and traditions of the school. All of these factors, together and separately, can act as 'positive' or 'negative' issues in parents' perception of a school, leading them to prefer one school over another.

These factors can be classified in three general areas:

Physical: these will include issues such as proximity to home; the state of the buildings; school transport to the school; the curricular and extra-curricular facilities of the school.

Social: the ethos of the school; the fact that the child's friends go there; easy progress from primary to post-primary; family tradition of sending a child to a particular school.

Quality: one school may be seen as producing a better quality education than another.

A set of powerful assumptions underpin judgments about the suitability and effectiveness of schools in each of these three factors. These assumptions, though usually tacit, have considerable influence on the decision-making of parents and school managers. Some common assumptions on a social level include the belief that children do better at school if they are with children who are just like them. This can work with social class, ethnic or gender issues. For instance, some parents have a strong belief about the advantages of single-sex education rather than co-education, especially at post-primary level. Preferences may also reflect the social composition associated with the local postcode, as people tend to stay in their local communities. Minority groups may develop a preference for one school where they will have a sense of support by going together. Other parents may seek out particular schools because of the facilities they have to offer in support of their child and the reputation of the school in giving special support when needed. For other parents, this same reputation can be a disincentive, for they believe that the additional support provided for some children will mean less support for their child. As a result, they prefer schools where there is a lower profile of students with special needs or who are in need of other supports; they feel that their child will get more attention if teachers are not 'distracted' dealing with other students. Schools respond to such parental concerns. Frequently, discussions about different schools demonstrate a belief that for every inclusive school there is an exclusive one that benefits from that inclusion. This results in the perception that some schools play an unequal role in promoting pluralism. In that scenario, the psychological inclusion within one school institutionalises the sociological experience of exclusion at a system level.

The reputation of quality in a school may be based on ideological perceptions of the patron. Parents sometimes assume that certain school types or certain congregations have higher standards than others. This may be related to the ethos associated with the patron. For instance, parents may reflect positively on their own school, and want to replicate that for their children. They opt to send their children to a school like the one they attended. Of course, if the parent was not happy with their own experience of schooling, they might opt to avoid a particular type of patron.

Quality can also be associated with social issues. The choice of a Catholic primary school, for example, may be linked to easy access to 'rites of passage' in sacramental preparation. At another level, minority parents may reject a Catholic school assuming that it is only for children of Catholic families or that it will be less inclusive. The parents' own religious beliefs and political ideology may also give rise to a strong preference for a particular kind of school. Sometimes this can be articulated proactively with expectations articulated in positive statements. Other times it is more reactive and intuitive, articulated as 'not that type of school anyway'. Quality will also be association with academic performance, either in general or in terms of particular subjects (science, maths, art, practical subjects). These perceptions may be based on the reputation of teachers, on the reported results of the school or on the known destination of students in third level. There is a growing media industry in publishing league tables of schools based on these criteria.

The way parents make judgments may be based on objective data, well understood, or it may be based on hearsay evidence. It is possible to debate the validity of many of the criteria outlined above and the quality of the evidence that supports them. The reality is that they exist and they are supported by enough parents and schools to make the process complex and often fraught with tensions. The intensity of this experience often depends on the context in which the decision on schooling is made.

3.2. THE CONTEXT OF SELECTION POLICIES

The issue of a school making a selection of students only arises in particular circumstances. Three possible scenarios suggest themselves:

Scenario 1. *The total number of school places is greater than the number of applications.*

Each school in the area has a flexible capacity and is able to satisfy all applicants. In this scenario all students are guaranteed a place in a school. The parent may not be able to choose a school of their particular liking, but when they come to a school, they have an entitlement to be there, and the school has an obligation to take them. The only source of conflict in such a situation is the lack of choice that may be available to the parent in choosing the school, and this may lead to conflict about the internal organisation of the school and its ability to cater for the students it enrols. This situation is similar to that which prevails in the 'stand-alone' school outlined in the Forum Report and discussed in Chapter 9. From the DES perspective, provision has been made for the child as a place is available. From the parent's perspective, none of the schools in the area provide the education they want for their child. From the school's perspective, there is a challenge of trying to accommodate the legitimate interests of individual parents, especially if a number of diverse interests emerge. The conflict here is over school provision, not over admissions.

Scenario 2. *The total number of school places in an area is lower that the number of applicants for these places.*

This can happen if an area experiences rapid growth or for some reason, a school building programme does not proceed in line with population growth. In this scenario, schools will make a selection of students to fill the places available in the school. All selection processes, no matter how fair, will result in some children being excluded, simply because the capacity to accept all children does not exist. Although parents may feel aggrieved with a particular school or schools when their child is not enrolled, the real problem is with the State which has not provided for sufficient places. The school is the immediate focus of the parents' disappointment because the process of application is concrete – this school – rather than the more generic focus of the State's provision.

The scenario outlined above has been the source of public controversy in recent years. For instance, in 2008 a Catholic primary school in Diswellstown in Dublin was over-subscribed. The school applied a selection procedure that determined priority groups on a faith basis. This meant that those who were refused a place were non-Catholic and also happened to be non-white immigrant children. This led to headlines claiming that denominational schools created apartheid, focusing on the selection made by the school rather than the lack of places available in the area. The necessary selection process, in line with the school's stated aim of providing a service to a particular faith group, had the unintended consequences of highlighting different religious and ethnic groups in the community. Due to the lack of alternative school places, these groups experienced exclusion. The rhetoric in the media blamed the Church and the school for the outcome and questioned the legitimacy of faith schools.

At post-primary level, the education editor of the *Irish Times*, Seán Flynn, commenting on a DES audit of admissions policies, claimed that a subtle type of apartheid permeates the system. He wrote that the two-tier nature of Irish education at second level was exposed in the audit.[7] In many areas, provisions for the children of immigrants, those with special educational needs and Travellers was largely confined to vocational and community schools. Although the discussion section of the Audit of School Enrolment Policies (2008) discussed a range of policy questions, it found no evidence of any system-wide enrolment practices that, in themselves, gave rise to concern, although some practices may give rise to unintended social consequences.

The argumentation in the Diswellstown scene and in the commentary on admissions policy confuses issues of legitimacy with issues of distribution and consequences. In another context, had the Catholic school been bigger and the students had been welcomed into it, the debate in Diswellstown might well have been on the provision of different types of schools for the community so that non-Catholics would not be forced to attend a Catholic school. However, the provision of an alternative school type would also institutional ethnic and religious differences. The creation of any choice within the education system runs the risk of institutionalising differences along the lines of majority and minority groupings. The risk is that diversity issues follow a dynamic of accommodation rather than of integration. The alternative seems to be to remove choice in favour of a 'common school'. The risk here is of creating a dynamic of assimilation rather than integration.

Scenario 3. *The total number of school places exceeds the number of applicants, but the level of application to some of the schools exceeds the number of places in these schools.*

The result in this scenario is that all children can be offered a school place, but not the place of their first choice. All schools are obliged by the Education Act to have an admissions policy and to publish the criteria to ensure that it operates in a transparent way. These criteria may not be arbitrarily chosen, as there are guidelines related to discrimination, especially with regard to special needs. The schools have some autonomy in relation to promoting their ethos, and there is an obligation on any publicly funded body to contribute to the common good. When a choice is made not to admit a particular student to a particular school, there is understandably a sense of disappointment, frustration and anger on the part of families. It is worth exploring some of the factors that contribute to the intensity of parental responses.

The parents' evaluation of the school will influence their reaction if their child is refused a place in a particular school. Some parents may make a choice between schools that are equal or near-equal; it is simply a choice between two goods, and not getting a first preference creates no great difficulty. In other situations, the choice between schools is not seen as benign. Being offered an available place in a 'less-desirable' school certainly gives rise to distress for parents and is seen as damaging the life-chances of their children. Faced with this situation, parents frequently appeal school decisions, but over 60 per cent of such appeals turn out to be futile.

Where parental concerns about the quality of a school are based on facts about physical, social or quality issues within a school, then some system intervention is necessary. It would be difficult to defend any system where parents are forced to accept a 'no-good' school. However, the choice is not usually that stark; it is often a choice between a 'preferred' school and an 'adequate' school. Having the right to choose does not imply that the choice made can be realised in all cases. No selection system can take away the disappointment that exists on not obtaining something desired. However, in making choices, schools are bound by principles of justice and fairness in their criteria and in their procedures. This is overseen by the board and the patron, and parents rightly have a path of appeal, either through section 29 in the Education Act, or, if necessary, the courts.

3.3. SELECTION CRITERIA

The Education Act (1998) underpins the right of the school to manage its affairs, subject to the common good. In general, the criteria adopted by schools include:

> **Compliance** – related to legislation on equality and discrimination, particularly with regard to the special needs provisions contained in the various Acts.
>
> **Ethos** – related to its own characteristic spirit, with regard to cultural, educational, moral, religious, social, linguistic and spiritual values and traditions.
>
> **Traditional** – responding in loyalty to particular groups who have supported the school's development, particular in terms of the voluntary contributes (time, money, expertise) given to the school.

These criteria can have different effects and consequences in different communities and in different contexts. A number of common criteria in published admissions policies reveal functional and dysfunctional aspects of the criteria.

Catchment areas are developed based on distance from the school, or in the case of post-primary schools of assigning particular primary schools as feeder schools with priority right of entry. Geographic catchment areas give a clear pathway of access in that it indicates particular schools within easy reach. For schools, it gives access to data that allows for future planning. However, defining catchment areas on a narrow geographical basis has a dysfunctional side to it, given the stratification that can exist because of factors such as local government housing schemes.

Similarly, the existence of **feeder primary schools** offers a sense of comfort to parents as to progress from primary to post-primary without having to worry too much about application processes on transition. This approach can be dysfunctional if the number of places assigned to particular feeder schools is disproportionate, making the school exclusive to those in other schools. Both the geographic and the feeder school approach could have the effect of diminishing parental choice if a particular pathway was made compulsory.

Some schools organise their admissions on the basis of date of application: **first come, first served**. This approach gives rise to schools collecting early expressions of interest, rather than working on 'current-year applications only'. Schools may have the promise of full enrolment for a number of years, with other children on waiting lists. With a dearth of places in schools, newcomers to an area will be at a disadvantage in trying to secure a place in a school operating from this criterion.

Other schools give priority to applications from **siblings of current pupils, children of past pupils and teachers**. This criterion helps to simplify logistics for families. It recognises that families have a deep sense of loyalty and commitment to a school and that this contributes to the continuance of the school's service to the community. This community may be the local area or it may range wider in terms of heritage and tradition. The effect of this criterion was highlighted recently in Clonmel. In 2009, John, the eldest son of a Traveller family, did not secure a place in the secondary school of his choice, as the number of applicants exceeded the number of places available. Applicants were prioritised according to three criteria, the third being 'having a brother or father who attended the school'. John qualified under the first two criteria. However, as the eldest son of a Traveller family, he could not have a brother who attended, and as the first male in his family to progress to secondary school, he did not have a father who attended the school. The family contented that this criterion was a form of indirect discrimination against Travellers, although the school had taken other Traveller families in previous years when places were available. The family's position was upheld by the Equality Tribunal in 2010 but rejected on appeal to the High Court.

In denominational schools, **the faith affiliation** of the applicant may influence selection in the case of over-subscription. Some schools operate this giving absolute priority to a particular affiliation. Others have voluntarily undertaken to make places available to applicants not of their faith. They have also made places available to applicants with no faith. One of the suggestions of the consultation paper was to make such a provision mandatory. This creates a real tension with the role of the patron as providing a particular service to a particular group of people.

In the current debate, this criterion generates heated debate. This can lead to inaccurate use of terminology, heighten a sense of grievance and promote a different outcome. For instance, critics of this measure use the term 'discrimination' when equality legislation clearly defines this practice, in certain circumstances, as non-discriminatory and within the rights of the organisation to protect its objectives:

An educational establishment <u>does not discriminate</u> under *subsection* (2) by reason only that —

a. where the establishment is not a third-level institution and admits students of one gender only, it refuses to admit as a student a person who is not of that gender,

b. where the establishment is a school providing primary or post-primary education to students and the objective of the school is to provide education in an environment which promotes certain religious values, it admits persons of a particular religious denomination in preference to others or it refuses to admit as a student a person who is not of that denomination and, in the case of a refusal, it is proved that the refusal is essential to maintain the ethos of the school.[8] [my emphasis]

Assigning catchment areas and feeder schools is a way of regulating school provision. Population patterns give clear indications to planners on what the needs will be in a particular area. In many communities in Ireland, there is little conflict over admissions – the conflict is over school choice. Where conflict over admissions does exist, the most intense conflict is in communities where there is a choice of schools.

In this scenario, the assignment of catchment areas and feeder schools is unlikely to provide a solution. Some schools will not have the capacity to take all its applicants. Trying to regulate admissions policies in this case, beyond the general anti-discriminatory laws that apply to all organisations, would appear to be an undue interference with the rights of patrons to determine and protect their own ethos. In particular, this has major implications for denominational schools.

4. THE TASK OF POLITICS

This chapter has discussed three areas where there is a practical politics in how schools are controlled. These areas reflect decisions where the demands of a local situation intersect with national policies. The dynamics of providing new schools or extensions, allowing capital refurbishments and giving differential operational funding to schools impacts on how well individual schools can serve their students. In a competitive environment, where different schools seek to attract students, this can give advantages to one school over the others. Such decisions can be used to manipulate uptake in favour of a particular school or school type. More frequently, there are unintended consequences that arise from the timing of such decisions in a local area. For instance, a much-needed refurbishment in one school can change the perception of that school in a local area. This gives rise to a local response.

The political issue here is that local decisions are often seen as just that – a response to a complex local situation. It is only over time that patterns can be detected in a series of local decisions. These patterns can reveal policy preferences at government level, which are debated or affirmed as policy issues. The patterns also reveal changing values within a local community over time. These values may reflect ideological changes, or they may simply reflect more cosmetic preferences related to local personalities rather than any deep-seated ideology. The task for government is to ensure a transparent approach to decision making at a local level, ensuring that decisions respond to an inclusive approach to the common good rather than responding to sectional interests who happen to be well-versed in political lobbying. For community groups, the task is to understand the dynamics of public discourse and to learn to have their voices heard in terms of a public language that commands respect.

Conflict over admissions policies generally reflect a local politics which includes the availability of places and the perceptions among parents of different schools. The sources of these problems are often complex. Some of the proposals to regulate school response seem to aim at promoting the rights of individual parents over the rights of school patrons. The effect here is to treat the school as if it were a State school, which has a different responsibility to citizens than a private patron may have. Negotiating the contract of service and support between the State and patrons requires a cooperative approach to the common good of the local community, as well as an appreciation of the respective rights of all involved.

There are other issues in the education debate that impact on denominational education, particularly the issue of teacher education and employment. The restructuring of third-level provision has serious consequences for the denominational teacher training colleges, which in turn has an indirect effect on the ability of patrons to preserve and promote their ethos. The issue of teacher employment in denominational schools was mentioned briefly in Chapter 6 (section 2.4). The current profile of denominational schools in Ireland impacts on the way individual teachers experience freedom of religion, when the only employment open to them is in Catholic schools. There is also the issue of the Teaching Council's failure to acknowledge any rights of teacher employers and the responsibility of the teacher to that employer. These points are noted here, but the exploration of the complex issues behind them is for another day.

NOTES

1. Forum Report, p. 63.
2. Quoted in Áine Hyland, 'Multi-Denominational Schools in the Republic of Ireland 1975–1995', paper delivered at Education and Religion Conference, organised by CRELA (University of Nice, 21–22 June 1996).
3. Seán Flynn, Education Editor, *Irish Times* (3 January 2012).
4. This figure is calculated as the capitation grant plus the amount the effect of reducing hiring extra teachers to cater for the students at a lower teacher–student ratio. It assumes that the school places would be available and there would be no need for capital expenditure in relation to the change.
5. Some members of the TUI are reported to have termed this 'educational apartheid' and called for the abolition of support for these schools; Journal.ie (23 April 23 2011).

6.   DES, discussion paper on a regulatory framework for school enrolment (June 2011), p. 20.

7.   Seán Flynn, 'Subtle form of apartheid permeates school system', *Irish Times* (5 April 2008).

8.   Equal Status Act (2000), #7(3).

CONCLUSION:
REFLECTIONS ON A JOURNEY

This book started as an exploration of a topic – politics and denominational education. The journey started by looking at what is meant by denominational education with particular reference to Catholic education, which led to an exploration of the political context in which denominational education exists. Chapter 2 explored how diverse interests arise and are managed in the political context, exploring different types of conflict over the legitimacy, distribution and consequences of individual interests, and the different political responses of assimilation, accommodation and integration. Chapter 3 considered the way the language of the common good and of rights has developed over time. The exploration of the chapters that followed was in part a search for how these two concepts are used in the current debate on education, both in Europe and in Ireland.

Part II looked at a general application of the concepts of the common good and rights to religion and education. The exploration was partly philosophical and partly legal. In particular, it looked at the way the European Court of Human Rights interpreted individual rights and linked them to the common good of the State – the 'margin of appreciation'. This was followed by a survey of how denominational education was provided for in different European countries. Some countries provide for denominational instruction within the State-run system; others allow denominational schools to develop as part of an alternative provision for schooling.

The journey then returned to Ireland in Part III. Chapters 7 and 8 reviewed the historical developments of the primary and post-primary sector. This history revealed a high level of philanthropy in the provision of Irish education, with the Churches trying to establish rights and contribute to the common good. The story of Church involvement in the process showed diverse perspectives – those of the dioceses and those of the religious congregations. One aspect of the story shows a major commitment to philanthropy and to ensuring that schooling was widely available; another shows paternalism. The story of the State demonstrates a mixed commitment to central control of the core curriculum, seen in setting a cultural agenda, and a commitment to the principle of subsidiarity in giving some local autonomy in the governance of schools. It was only in the 1930s that the State became involved in providing schools rather than providing *for* them. It took until the late 1960s before it became involved in providing for secondary education, driven by systemic changes in economic policy. A particular feature of this development was a new model of governance based on participative democracy. This was seen in the new community schools where there is collaboration between religious and VEC patrons. It is also seen in the Boards of Management of all schools, where the voice of patrons, parents and teachers work together to develop the school.

Chapters 9 and 10 explored contemporary issues in education in Ireland against the background of the issues raised in other European countries and in our own history. The recent Forum on Patronage and Pluralism in the Primary Sector and three specific issues related to the regulation of patronage provided a particular focus. While some of the issues received more detailed attention than others, the hope has been that the information gathered inspires others to a deeper analysis of the issues and provide a resource as they map out that analysis. Four main themes that stood out in looking at this topic – philanthropy, the role of the State, the comparison with other European countries and, finally, the way that the current debate on pluralism fits into the pattern of policy development in Ireland – will form the basis of this closing chapter, concluding with some personal impressions of the leadership challenges that exist in the development of the Irish education system.

1. PHILANTHROPY

One striking feature about educational provision in Ireland has been the role of philanthropy and the idealism of 'patrons' to serve a local community. At primary level, most schools have been built on privately supplied grounds and patrons have made a substantial local contribution towards buildings. Historically, a contribution has also been made to the running costs of the schools, and in some places, fundraising and voluntary contributions by parents are still an important part of school finances. At post-primary level, the country is also in debt to the philanthropy of Church groups for the infrastructure of the current system. From the days of the hedge schools, individuals took it on themselves to provide for the needs of a local area, their service being linked to an entrepreneurial approach. The involvement of churches in the provision of primary education was also driven by a sense of service and philanthropy, with pastors seeking what was best for a local community. That this involvement later developed a strong sense of paternalism and became caught up in power and identity issues should not distract from the dynamic that was, and still is, involved. In particular, service and philanthropy were strongly evident in the setting up of indigenous religious congregations, where large numbers of a newly prosperous merchant class dedicated themselves to providing social services for poorer members of society. A major focus of these congregations was on education, a skill and dedication many of them brought to other countries as they followed the Irish diaspora in the years following the famine. In more recent times, the development of *Foras Pátrúnachta*, Educate Together and to a large extent the reconfiguration of education to children with special needs, are also results of 'bottom up' initiatives. In each of these cases, interested and committed groups have had to promote the legitimacy of their interests against an established 'status quo'. Their political campaigns involved, first of all, establishing the 'good' of the position. In the case of the Irish language, the good was posed in terms of a cultural value linked to national identity and enshrined as a value within the Constitution. In the case of Educate Together, the good was established as an interest in a particular type of education. Initially, this education focused on rights related to freedom of religion and the desire to have a different approach than that offered by the majority Churches. In more recent years, this vision is taken to incorporate ideals of an integrated society where the Educate Together schools make a symbolic and real contribution to helping diverse groups live and work together. The struggles of parents with children who have special educational needs looked more to a politics of distribution than of legitimacy. That said, the focus on the special needs student has helped clarify the notion of the right to 'education' rather than a generic right to 'schooling'. It has linked education to the real needs of the child rather than some abstract process. Here too the driving force for change has been a small number of parents taking a lead role in pursuing a vision.

At post-primary level, a similar pattern of local initiative was evident. Religious congregations set up networks of secondary schools alongside the minor seminaries run by dioceses. After independence, the origin of the vocational sector is also an example of local initiative responding to the needs of local employers and their potential employees. To some extent, the secondary and vocational sectors complemented one another, giving real choices to parents and different career pathways to the students. However, in a mainly agrarian economy, the academic education provided by the secondary schools tended to be selective. It provided for a relatively small elite who sought occupations with high status and privilege. It was not until the 1960s when there was a shift in economic policy to a more industrial or service base that a universal, comprehensive education became viable. The result has been a more flexible involvement of the religious congregations in partnership with the State. This can be seen in the number of amalgamations of small secondary and vocational schools and the establishment of the community school model. No similar creativity in provision has been seen at primary level.

A second perspective on the role of philanthropy in education is the amount of voluntary service given in the governance of schools on boards of management. The board of management ensures that different voices are heard in the governance of education. The establishment of the boards of management, their training and support remains the responsibility of the patron. It is up to the patron to ensure that boards are not only representative of the community, but also have the necessary legal, financial and educational expertise to run the schools in a complex environment. This role of the patron remains a major philanthropic contribution to the system, and the extent of it is overlooked in the debate on property and ownership. It would be an interesting exercise to cost this involvement, and to speculate how this level of voluntarism might be handled in a State-run system.

2. THE ROLE OF THE STATE

State involvement in the early stages of the Irish education system is often portrayed simply as a support role, with the main issues fought out on a governance level with Churches gaining power and control. There is no doubt that that is part of the story of Irish education, but it is by no means the full story. The involvement of government funding for the Board of Commissioners in 1831 was not simply a paternalistic welfare payment to poor Irish peasants; there were cultural and economic ideologies at work as well. By focusing on the disputes that arose over teaching religion, it is easy to overlook the rest of the curriculum that began to forge a more anglicised culture, at least as far as language was concerned. The State decided on textbooks, inspected the schools and graded the teachers. The inspectors had the power to remove teachers who were not up to standard. There were pockets of resistance to this cultural programme, particularly in the refusal of the Christian Brothers to entrust their schools to the board.

From a political perspective, the task of the education system was to assimilate an alienated Catholic majority into a mainstream culture. It is likely that the driving vision for this policy was a view of the common good linked to the spread of a British worldview throughout the 'colonies'. The strategy of giving preferential treatment to the Churches in setting up schools, clearly enunciated in the Stanley Letter, was based in part on a principle of subsidiarity that recognised local rights. It was also linked to the moral authority of the Churches in bringing about cooperation and compliance from their members and this contributed to the desired social outcomes for the State. In return for their cooperation, the Churches sought areas of autonomy in the management of the schools. Control focused mainly on religious education. This was partly inspired by a concept of rights. It also took the view that the common good of the majority group was best served by ensuring the religious aspect of education.

After independence was achieved in 1922, the State continued the same relationship with the Churches. The Constitution of that year stated that 'all citizens of the Irish Free State (Saorstát Éireann) have the right to free elementary education'.[1] However the State did not take on the full extent of that provision; what it did was change the funding system from a 'payment-by-results' system to a capitation system and still demanded a sizeable local contribution to be collected by the Churches. The Church was seen as having access to alternative funding and this relieved the State of some of the burden of the Constitutional aspiration for free elementary education. During this period, we see the same reluctance of the State to be involved in the setting up and day-to-day management of the provision of schools. Yet it retained control over the curriculum and the inspection of teachers. The State saw a definite benefit in having the Church involved in the management of the schools. By providing capitation grants and teacher salaries, the State also developed a strong position of influence in determining procedures in schools, as it could always change, or threaten to change, the funding base in real terms. During that period, if the Church developed an influence in education, it is important to recall that the State also had a powerful influence on overall policy. The common good was stated clearly in terms of a vision of a Gaelic Ireland. This was a political rather than a religious vision. The Church became a willing partner in the promotion of that policy, giving rise to a greater entanglement of Irish cultural identity and religion.

The contrast between provision in the primary and post-primary sectors is quite revealing. There was greater experimentation of State involvement in post-primary education. Primary education had been seen as an entitlement for all children, and the State made every effort to ensure ready access by helping with provision. However, there was no help available in providing for post-primary education. Any funding had been given as a reward for achievement at examinations rather than as a means of promoting the uptake of education. At post-primary level, education was seen as a liberty that individuals could undertake for themselves if they had the resources. It therefore catered for a minority elite. The Churches, particularly through the religious congregations, were the main providers and the lack of money available often meant a very spartan experience of schooling. Alongside that aspect of the story is also the influence of the curriculum, which was not particularly a Church curriculum but an academic Renaissance curriculum accepted and endorsed by the Church. After independence, as in the primary sector, there was a shift in emphasis. Operational grants were paid as part of a capitation system, which changed the perspective from the 'product' of education to the 'individual being educated'. This was a reframing of an understanding of the common good, placing the individual at the centre, rather than their economic value judged by achievement. On this, the State imposed its own interpretation of the common good by promoting the Irish language. The approach was to offer extra grants and rewards to those who cooperated with this policy. The State maintained control of the secondary curriculum through the examination system.

The State was also involved in the development of technical and vocational education through local authorities. This was the first instance of public money being used in the provision of post-primary education. The focus here was a response to an economic aspect of the common good, in that it was linked with promoting the local economy and employment. The initiatives for such developments were very much centred in the local community observing a principle of subsidiarity.

In the 1960s, the State became involved in a major 'top-down' initiative with the development of a more economy-friendly curriculum and the provision of free education, with a strong emphasis on social issues and equality of access to the rewards of education. From this initiative arose the idea of the community school. This school type is based on a multi-denominational philosophy and managed locally by a board of management where different voices are represented – local government (VEC), denominational interests, parents and teachers. Given the current debate at primary level, the lack of controversy that accompanied the setting up of these schools is remarkable. In hindsight, it might be said that the religious congregations involved in these schools were more concerned with education than with schooling. Once they were guaranteed a voice in the decision-making process, they were happy to forgo ownership of buildings and infrastructure and cooperate in the enterprise of education. The community school model was the preferred model in cases of amalgamations. In the case of new schools, however, there has been a preference for VEC patronage. This may reflect the lack of capacity among religious congregations to provide for new schools during this period. It may also reflect a new confidence and energy in the VEC sector and their political skill at rebranding their image. No similar model has been tried in the primary sector.

The involvement of the State in educational provision gives rise to a tension between a centralised universal system and a system responsive to local needs. In the time of the hedge schools, the emphasis was entirely on the local. Education was seen as a personal good, and market forces of supply and demand dictated provision and consumption. Early attempts at a national system of education built on the local and made it more systematic. At primary level, the State linked with the corporate governance structure of the Church rather than local government. Within the framework of local dioceses there was a means to drive provision at parish level thus ensuring that schools were established for poorer communities as well as for those who could afford them. The approach involved here was a principle of subsidiarity, where decision-making was delegated to the local level. However, the main control of the enterprise of education – control of the curriculum – was kept at the centre. The choice of the Church as the focus of local devolvement was strategic. It created a very different dynamic around education as a social welfare entitlement than say the reaction to the boards of guardians that were responsible for implementing the Poor Relief Act 1838. After independence, the government opted to manage the tension between the centre and the local in the same way as it had been managed in the nineteenth century. Although a local government system had been organised, it was to have responsibility for technical and vocational education only, with primary and secondary education coordinated at the centre and managed by 'private' patrons.

The tension between central and local functions has also been an issue in recent proposals for organising education. Regional education authorities have been proposed in various White Papers on education. A version of this proposal made its way into the Education Bill (1998) but was never implemented. A new version of this level of organisation is currently being developed in the Further Education and Training Authority (SOLAS) Bill, which aims to cut the number of VECs and to develop their role in the coordination of State provision in education and training. The system itself creates a possible conflict of interest, in that the VEC may well be in a position of coordinating provision of primary and post-primary education where it is one of the providers. How this system will interact with the many different 'centres' in Irish education remains to be seen. For instance, the Church diocesan structures do not correspond to the proposed VEC boundaries, which may have issues in the organisation of primary education and the working of redeployment panels. However, a number of dioceses cross jurisdictional boundaries and have schools in Northern Ireland as well, so diversity of administration is possible. Similarly, the 'centre' for many secondary schools is an 'ethos' boundary rather than a geographical boundary. We see an increasing tendency from the government to treat all these different groups as a 'single voice' for negotiation purposes, although they may have very different approaches to education.

The principle of subsidiarity can also be seen at school level. The board of management is an example of participative democracy and gives some degree of local autonomy. It becomes the gatekeeper between the demands of a central government or patron and the local school community. The functional aspect of this subsidiarity is the empowerment of people to be involved in decisions that affect their lives. There can be a dysfunctional side in that local power can be so circumscribed that it is merely a device to ensure compliance to central dictates. It can also focus attention on and give legitimacy to local turf wars, which typically block progress in the development of national policies.

3. IRELAND IN A EUROPEAN CONTEXT

The Irish education system, especially at primary level, has been described as a 'State-aided' rather than a 'State-owned' system. In reviewing State involvement in the provision of schooling in other European countries, what is surprising about the Irish system is not so much the partnership between the State and various private patrons, but the extent of that partnership. The closest to the Irish situation is the Netherlands where 75 per cent of schools are in the hands of private patrons, and these are fully supported by the State.

The education system in most European countries developed from the base of Church or monastery schools. These had been founded to provide training in literacy mainly for would-be clerics. This literacy was also a functional pathway to administrative positions in civil society. With the Industrial Revolution, governments became more involved in educational provision, seeking a more literate population. Most decreed that children should go to school and prescribed a curriculum of reading, writing, arithmetic and religion. The schools pursued cultural, national, social and ideological goals. They taught vernacular literature and national history introducing students to their own cultural heritage. Most countries taught one version of the national language, even though most children spoke regional dialects. The moral dimension of education was to encourage honest, hardworking and useful citizens, devoted to family and country; citizens who would not seek to rise above their station in life. This was aligned with Church anthropology of the time and made for an easy partnership. Governments took over the running of schools and developed a universal provision of education for all citizens. In building on the inherited infrastructure, religion became a core subject in the curriculum and most countries accommodated minority groups in having their own religious instruction.

The partnerships that were forged between the Churches and the State reflected the history of these States, and this historical context is a key element of the 'margin of appreciation' recognised by the European Court of Human Rights. Across Europe, three broad dynamics can be seen in how partnerships develop. The first reflects a context were there was a pluralism of beliefs and different groups sought to establish and maintain distinct identities. In these countries religious groups established their rights either in separate schools or by ensuring that denominational religious education was available within the State system. The political approach was to accommodate the different groups in order to maintain peace. This approach is still operative in countries like Germany, Austria, Switzerland and the Netherlands, and the issue now is the recognition of new groups seeking a role in education. In Southern Europe, countries like Spain, Portugal, Italy and Greece had little experience of religious pluralism. They had a strong Catholic or Orthodox majority. In these countries the dynamic emerged from an antipathy to State involvement in many welfare issues, including education. This antipathy was based on a strong commitment to the family as the centre of values, and the subsidiary role of the State. From that philosophy, the State is seen as helping families to provide for the welfare of their children and every effort is made to distance it from direct decision-making on welfare issues. In these countries the Church sought a strong influence in the governance of education or in the teaching of religion to a majority group. In a more pluralist society, the political dynamic focuses on rebalancing the role of the State in education with the Church playing a support role to its own members rather than as a main player. In France, the response was to become totally secular and not to engage with religion within the education system. In Spain and Italy, there was a greater emphasis on appeasement and special concordats were signed with the Vatican, ensuring a role for Catholic religious education in the schools. The changed political approaches are informed by reframing the concept of the common good in economic rather than moral terms. The third dynamic can be seen in those States under Communist rule until the 1990s, where the focus had been on the State education that excluded all forms of religious education. Here we see the Churches negotiating a place in the State education system.

Ireland is immersed in the second dynamic. The Church has been very heavily involved in the provision and governance of education. This has worked from a curious promotion of State involvement through tax-based funding and an antipathy to State involvement which can be read as a paternalistic protection of the rights of parents from State interference in their lives. There has been little reflection on the disempowerment that accompanies this type of paternalism and the internal Church rhetoric is often nostalgia for the past rather than facing the challenges of a changed context. Over the past thirty years or so, there has been a growing demand to disentangle the Church from the provision of education yet there seems to have been little political will to do this. The State has continued to expect the Church to become patron in many new primary schools and has actively pursued this partnership. It is only in the last ten years that serious efforts have been made to facilitate new patrons in setting up schools thus providing some diversity and choice within the system. However, there is still a lack of willingness on the part of the State itself to set up and run schools as part of its responsibility to the common good. In this, Ireland is very different from other countries in Europe.

4. DIRECTIONS IN EDUCATION POLICY

4.1. LENSES ON POLICY

O'Sullivan analysed three different paradigms that have driven Irish educational developments since 1922.[2] The first of these he named a **theocentric** paradigm, and this paradigm can also be traced to the setting up of the system in 1831. The aims of education were determined by unchanging, and largely undisputed, Christian principles. Policies on how these principles were applied were decided by authority, based on expertise. Education was carried out by trustworthy professionals, and there was a paternalistic relationship between the giver and the receiver. The role of the State was subsidiary to that of the providers. In the period after 1922 this paradigm developed a strong cultural and linguistic basis that arose from a political rather than a theological ideology. The dynamic was similar. The approach sought to reproduce an enduring and unchanging image of a Gaelic Ireland.

The second paradigm O'Sullivan named **mercantile**. This approach developed in the late 1960s with the Investment in Education Report. Greater emphasis was placed on the role of the 'client' or 'consumer'. Policy making was seen as more broadly based and democratic. Parents and teachers were given more choice within education and were given a role in its governance. There was a greater emphasis on the managerial and coordinating role of the State and on the accountability of the provider to the client. This approach to education reflected a new economic appreciation of the common good and reframed the education system in terms of supporting new directions in national economic policies.

The **social** paradigm describes a third approach to policy. This paradigm has two axes. The first of these is a human capital approach, which charts the interaction between market thinking and government response. The focus is on the way the product of education is valued rather than the process focus of the mercantile approach. The second axis is linked to the modernist discourse and the understanding of equality, difference, virtue, control and power.

These three paradigms provide a useful lens through which to view approaches to provision. In many ways, all three are present at any time, although there are patterns where one approach has dominated the others in different periods of Irish history. Currently, the dominant paradigm is a social one built around a postmodernist discourse on identity. This paradigm has helped to accelerate acceptance of diversity as a value in itself, and has driven policies to focus on issues of quality within education, with a greater focus on equality of consumption and achievement rather than equality of opportunity.

The theocentric, mercantile and social paradigms also help us to chart a changing understanding of the common good in Irish society. The theocentric approach tends to focus on particular virtues and capacities. The product of education was seen in terms of personal moral characteristics; education was seen as socialising or assimilating individuals into this 'moral' vision. The mercantile approach had a greater focus on individuals and their needs. The aim of education was seen as catering to different capacities and interests. The common good was being reframed in terms of the interests of individuals, but in the context of them making a contribution to society through the skills they developed. One aspect of the social paradigm focuses on increasing individual autonomy by developing the capacity of the individual to enjoy the freedoms they have. This gives rise to greater diversity. As in the mercantile paradigm, the individual's interest is accommodated in society and the focus is to attract or persuade individuals to use their skills for the common good. A second aspect of the social paradigm is to promote social cohesiveness. It focuses on promoting tolerance and acceptance. This gives rise to a genuine pluralism.

4.2. DIVERSITY AND PLURALISM AS A POLICY FOCUS
Chapter 2 outlined Etzioni's classification of goals as order, economic and cultural. Etzioni contended that the pursuit of different goals is successful when there is a match between the goals and the methods used to promote them. The moral dimension of the theocentric paradigm outlined above is a cultural goal. It appeals to the inherent value of the virtues it proposes. Ideally this creates a symbolic power that elicits the commitment of individuals. These virtues are reinforced through practice – living a virtuous life brings rewards of meaning and personal satisfaction. When morality is interpreted as an order goal rather than a cultural goal, the transmission of values usually involves coercion. This gives rise to a mismatch between the goals and the lived experience of those being taught. Coercion is seen in an insistence on compliance, and this dynamic has been evident in

religion and with the Irish language. The typical reaction to coercion is alienation.

Diversity and pluralism are cultural goals. Behind these concepts is a vision of a society that both caters for different individual interests and at the same time promotes a high level of social cohesion. Chapter 2 also outlined different approaches to policies on diversity. The assimilation approach works on the basis of the symbolic power of a single national vision, but frequently uses coercive means to bring that about. The process of accommodation is based on an economic framework that supports the interests of individuals and groups in return for their cooperation in a common good. The integration approach is based on a vision of equal citizens working together and able to benefit from the common vision; it has a strong symbolic element to it. However, the methods used to promote this vision are often based on coercion or remunerative benefits. An example of this can be seen in the Toledo Guiding Principles for teaching about religion, which were developed by the Organisation for Security and Cooperation in Europe (OSCE). The rationale for the guidelines includes concerns over interfaith conflicts around Europe. This might be interpreted as seeing religious education as instrumental in achieving order goals rather than as promoting cultural goals. At another level, the approach to differences in society is often conceptualised as an attempt to 'normalise' those on the fringe to fit into the mainstream. The 'deficit modelling' approach is criticised as being the dominant concept in many of the approaches to disadvantaged groups. The approach is partially coercive, as it defines success by reference to the norms of a majority group. The methods used may also be remunerative, giving rewards of extra grants for cooperation and compliance.

The current debate on pluralism in education focuses on religious diversity – the picture presented is of a cultural goal. Its cornerstone is the moral symbolism of the dignity of each person, free to pursue their own religious or philosophical truths. This vision of the common good is certainly part of the discourse. Unfortunately, the way this vision is presented is often not very inclusive. In seeking to establish a place for minority or alternative groups, there is sometimes a sense of exclusion of the established group. Developing a more pluralist society is seen as a conflict between competing groups in which there must be winners and losers. This approach to the debate fails to promote a 'win-win' approach to pluralism. Another reflection on pluralism looks at groups with different religious interests working together, but it fails to recognise the dynamics of the religious worldview. Religion is presented in anaemic terms. Where it is recognised in the public forum, it is allowed only in very restricted conditions, determined by 'outsiders'. For some advocates, the vision of the common good has no place for religion. In practice, this approach to the common good fails to be inclusive of all groups, and also fails to be inclusive of all aspects of a religious worldview.

Other aspects of the debate also fail to capture the symbolic persuasion of the vision of a positive pluralism and undermine commitment to this cultural goal. For instance, the use of rights language is often ambivalent. A positive focus on rights situates the individual's interest in religious freedom in a perspective that is wider than local politics. This helps others understand the legitimacy and seriousness of the individual interests. It also demands some positive response. A by-product of this focus helps a majority group to understand the privilege it enjoys in having its interests met. A negative focus on rights sets up a confrontational situation, which can lead to fragmentation. In particular, the terms 'interests' and 'rights' are often used interchangeably. This can have a negative effect as it moves the argument from the political to the moral sphere where people can be more defensive.

The demand for a more pluralist approach to education is based on particular interests not being met. Such a deficit has serious consequences for citizenship and is, in itself, justification for response. To frame the demand for a response as redressing an infringement of rights escalates the conflict. Frequently, there is no infringement of rights in the way that rights are actually framed. Freedom of religion is a liberty that is guaranteed to everyone. However, the context in which that liberty is exercised is not guaranteed. Similarly, citizens do not have an absolute claim against the State to provide for a particular type of education. What they do have is a claim that the education will be in conformity with the religious and philosophical beliefs. At the very least, they are entitled to a negative freedom *from* 'indoctrination' by any education provided. This is exercised by the power of exemption. The positive aspect of the right, the claim for an alternative form of schooling is dependent on other factors related to the 'margin of appreciation' afforded each State in negotiating its approach to the common good. There is a distinction between a situation in which there is an actual infringement of one person's rights by another and a situation in which an individual finds it difficult to pursue legitimate interests that are linked to their rights. An example might help to clarify the distinction: we have a right to live where we like. We see a house we would like to buy but cannot afford it. This does not mean that our rights are being infringed. In particular, it does not mean that our employer infringes our rights to live where we want by not paying us a higher salary. These distinctions are important in the use of rights language. The argument on infringement of rights moves to a moral level, and people are likely to be defensive about their moral positions. An accusation of this sort is often seen as a form of coercion and leads to alienation and resistance.

The distinction between rights and the context in which these rights are exercised is important for the majority group as well. The context in which they enjoy the freedom they currently have is not guaranteed as a right. The freedom is enjoyed because, in the past, they had the resources and the support to realise that right. Some of that support came from the State. In a context where there are other demands on the State in terms of the common good, some of that support might be diverted. The fact that they have enjoyed a certain liberty and support may well raise expectations that this level of support will continue. Often groups acquire new rights as a result of custom and practice. The negotiation about such established rights is different from the negotiation about establishment. Ireland is no stranger to the dynamic of interventions aimed at affirmation action being seen as entitlements, even when the original purpose of the intervention has been achieved.

An important perspective on diversity is that it should not focus on just one characteristic of individuals – religious affiliation. There are many different ways of being a person. One other perspective is that of language. In Ireland, the comparison between approaches to the religion and to the Irish language can be very instructive. Both religion and language are cultural values with a central place in Irish identity. However, our approach to rights and interests often change chameleon-like when talking about these areas. In education provision, this lack of consistency and coherence can lead to anomalies in provision and funding. It can also lead to situations where patrons are treated in different ways, although performing the same role in relation to the State. If such differences were based on religious issues, there could be major issues with regard to religious freedom.

The current focus on pluralism in Irish education seems to be limited to the idea of religious diversity and language. However, schools operate with a much wider range of diversity. The characteristic spirit of the school is defined in terms of 'educational, moral, religious, social, cultural, linguistic and spiritual values and traditions of the school'. Many educational projects aim at a better integration of diverse groups in society. The integration of Travellers takes place in mainstream schools with a special support structure. DEIS projects are aimed at tackling disadvantage. Schools provide differentiated language services to students newly arrived to the country from different ethnic backgrounds. New curricula in these languages have been developed to allow different ethnic groups maintain contact with their home language and culture. An example of the diversity that has developed can be seen in the number of languages that are facilitated at Leaving Certificate – Arabic, Bulgarian, Czech, Chinese, Danish, Dutch, Estonian, Finnish, French, German, Greek, Hebrew, Hungarian, Italian, Japanese, Latvian, Lithuanian, Polish, Portuguese, Romanian, Russian, Slovakian, Slovenian, Spanish and Swedish. A key issue is how this level of diversity in schools can be sustained, and how the balance that exists between integration and assimilation can be managed.

5. LEADERSHIP CHALLENGES FOR THE FUTURE

The general literature on educational leadership distinguishes four perspectives on leadership:

> **Moral leadership** involves a clear analysis of the systemic causes of social issues. It promotes an educational vision based on ethical responses rooted in the dignity of each person and the equality rights of citizens.
>
> **Instructional leadership** addresses differentiated approaches to education based on the needs of individual students. It sees approaches to successful learning within the community context and seeks a multi-faceted approach.

Organisational leadership promotes system-thinking whereby provision and support are coordinated.

Collaborative leadership promotes a sense of teamwork between all stakeholders, including giving voice to students and parents as well as the professional service providers.

These different perspectives can be helpful in outlining some of the challenges facing Irish education. They incorporate a focus on the future, as there is a need to develop a vision of what we want to be like in that future. The development of that vision must also generate commitment, so that it becomes a vision we are prepared to work at. The perspectives also focus on the past and the present. Setting out for the future is a process of transition, and it must recognise where we are at the moment. Leading change is leading the transition. This requires a respectful analysis of where we are now and the values and people who helped shape this reality. We do not sit around waiting for the future to come to us; we shape that future by developing a sustainable system in the present.

5.1. Challenges for the State

Arising from its role as a 'moral leader' there seems to be two main challenges for the DES. The first challenge relates to the analysis of social issues as they affect Irish education. The key challenge here is to honour the complexity of these issues and not to simplify them in terms of popular slogans. History is often told as a 'single story'; a unilateral reframing of the past in the light of current knowledge and needs. In reality, the history of any institution, including education, involves many different stories, co-existing often in contradictory ways. One example of this has been the Church's involvement in education. It involves positive contributions in terms of philanthropy and service to the common good, yet it involves a history of power-struggle with governments. It has provided educational opportunity and social mobility to many people, and the approach to teaching and learning in the past might now be seen as a censorship of the imagination. It has also embraced new approaches within the curriculum and in co-curricular and extra-curricular activities, given a focused service to the majority Catholic population and welcomed others into its schools. There are stories of success worthy of celebration, but there are also stories of failure and shame. All of these diverse contributions make up the full story. Attempts to isolate part of that story, either to the advantage or disadvantage or a particular advocacy position about the future, is problematic.

A similar issue arises in the analysis of issues using 'rights' language. The distinction between 'rights' and 'interests arising from rights' has been considered. The analysis of issues needs to be clear about these distinctions. This helps those who have the opportunity to enjoy their liberties to appreciate the privileges they have and to understand the interests that other groups may have in finding similar opportunities for themselves. The distinctions give rise to different realms of action. If rights are infringed, then the issue is a moral one; it needs immediate legal remedy. If a right gives rise to legitimate interests, then the issue is political; the solution is found through negotiation. Setting the agenda for negotiating the legitimate interests of minority groups as equal citizens becomes the challenge.

A second element of the moral leadership perspective is developing a vision for the future. At the time of writing, we are awaiting the publication of a White Paper on diversity in education. The key concern that has arisen in the course of this book is how inclusive such a vision will be. Inclusivity can fail in two ways. It can fail to include certain groups in the vision, or it can institutionalise their existence as second-class citizens. There is a clear focus on the need to respond positively to minority belief groups in Irish education. There is also a need to talk about balancing the rights of majority groups. Finding a win-win understanding in vision is important. Cultural values are essentially immaterial goods; their distribution is not a 'zero-sum' commodity – more for some does not necessarily mean less for another. Treating cultural values as material goods in limited supply is a distortion of the picture.

An inclusive picture also has to embrace values in a holistic way. The focus in this book has been on how religion is valued. A number of contributors to the current debate in Ireland and in Europe want to exclude religion from the sphere of public education and, if it is not excluded, they want to harness its manifestation. This is a political ideology and is based on legitimate personal interests. This ideology has the same status as one that seeks accommodation for denominational education, either in separate schools or in religious education. The issue here is how the respect that is given to the person who holds a particular value will be realised. Valuing the notion of religious freedom from the perspective of the believer, the 'insider' is an important aspect of genuine pluralism. The imposition of 'outsider' standards on what that belief should be, or how it should be supported, is problematic.

Linked to the inclusive approach to different values is the role of instructional leadership. A key challenge here is to distinguish between order, economic and cultural goals. This discussion has wide implications for the organisation of the national curriculum. No approach to education is without an underlying anthropology; a chosen curriculum will promote an approach to science, languages, technology, the humanities and culture. It will also involve a vision of the school's role in the moral formation of citizens. In an inclusive approach that values religion from the perspective of the believer, religious education will be a cultural goal. If it is only valued in instrumental terms as promoting social cohesion, then it becomes an order goal. This undermines the values and interests of the believer and seeks to assimilate different religious beliefs into a form of 'religious studies'. Instructional leadership is complex, given that order, economic and culture goals overlap and impact on one another. For instance, the RE course in post-primary schools combines elements of a culture and an order goal. The culture goals are to be seen in the content of the curriculum and the instructional methodologies employed. The fact that the subject can be included in school credentials gives it a status comparable to other subjects and motivates student participation. This is an order goal within the school. Negotiating the different goals of the curriculum requires clarity on what parents can expect from the experience of schooling, and where they have to develop further benefits from their own resources.

Organisational leadership develops coherent structures and institutionalises 'joined-up thinking'. The starting point for a number of people discussing Irish education is to project particular interests in education and to claim that, if we were starting from new to address these interests, we would not design the current educational system. That is true. However, we are not starting from scratch. We are a country with a history. Some people may not like where that history has brought us, but that is where we are. Dealing with the reality of current structures, and making a transition to new structures, is likely to be time consuming. In setting up the Forum on Patronage and Pluralism, the Minister for Education and Skills said that he hoped than 50 per cent of primary schools would be divested from the Catholic Church. The rhetoric of his approach focused more on the notion of divesting from a monopoly group rather than on what would happen to these schools once divested. In particular, Ruairí Quinn offered no vision on what the role of the State should be in those schools. If the vision had been stated that Ireland might move to a situation whereby half the primary schools were State-run schools and the rest were run by private patrons, then there would be a definite shape to the debate. As it is, the debate is focused on which private patron should run which school, and there is no clear thinking on what the benefits of this structure will be to the State and to the Patron who takes on the role. Chapter 9 discussed the tensions that can arise when depending on private patrons to take full responsibility for State policy, rather than cooperating with it. This runs the danger of either undermining the role of the patron or treating patrons with different philosophies differently, with some philosophies having State preference. There is already some evidence of such problems in the support for all-Irish schools in the present system. Extending this to a choice between religious-based patrons would give rise to constitutional issues.

In his response to the Forum Report, Quinn indicated that the State would look for an expanded role in determining the way patron-run schools were managed:

I am very conscious of the need to balance making real progress in divesting patronage in the short-term and the longer term aim of ensuring commitment by all concerned to more inclusiveness and diversity in schools.[3]

The challenge focuses on providing real choice for parents, and guaranteeing them quality within that choice. Providing greater choice, while at the same time decreasing the number of schools in the interests of efficiency, will demand real creativity. There is also the challenge of negotiating the transfer of schools from the 'monopoly' group to the State. This process must be based on justice to the ownership rights of the Church and also to the historic investment the Church has made in the system.

A feature of the Forum on Patronage and Pluralism has been the level of engagement of the different stakeholders in education. There has been a ready recognition of what the issues are, although the analysis of their cause and impact may have differed. There is a willingness to do something, and that is currently being negotiated. This links with the role of politics outlined in Chapter 2 and focuses on the collaborative leadership role of the DES. Maintaining this level of collaboration and the trust of the different stakeholders is a key role in the politics of developing the education system.

5.2. Challenges for the Church

The future development of the education system in Ireland is not just a matter for government policy. The different stakeholders are also challenged to develop their vision of education in the changing political, social, economic, cultural and demographic picture. This book began by exploring what denominational education is, looking at the Catholic approach to education; it is fitting then to finish by looking at some of the challenges facing the Church if it is to continue to make a valuable contribution to the education system.

Religious groups are very conscious of the powerful formative influence of education and seek to ensure that religious sensibility is developed in the school context alongside learning about other aspects of life. In their involvement in education, and particularly in setting up their own schools, the aims of faith groups will encompass three outcomes:

- **Witness:** The group wishes to manifest its own religion in the public space. The motivation arises from the personal commitment of individuals and their corporate sense of identity. They simply wish to be known and recognised, that their presence may inspire others to reflection and questioning. This may also be a way of attracting others to join the group, but this is not its primary object.
- **Teaching:** Arising from the meaning they derive from belonging to a religious tradition, the group wants to teach others about that tradition. It wants to teach in a way that demonstrates the positive aspects of belief. The teaching is typically directed at 'outsiders', and the aim is to inform them and to invite them to a deeper exploration of the issues.

• **Initiation/support:** This approach to education is directed to 'insiders'. It seeks to support parents who are committed to a particular religious viewpoint and want their children to have an immersion experience in it. It seeks to deepen the understanding a child has of the faith they experience in the home, and support them in their development in that faith.

Faith schools typically work from all three dimensions at the same time. The balance between these areas is worked out in particular circumstances. It aims to be respectful of the freedom that each individual has in how they respond to the religious dimension of their lives.

In the debate on Irish education, different perspectives and assumptions about the involvement of religious groups in education are clear. This occurs in statements from the religious groups themselves as well as from commentators. Catholic bishops have spoken about some schools being 'surplus to requirements'. Senator Ronan Mullen has advised Catholic schools to 'divest rather than dilute'.[4] These positions promote the image of the Catholic school as being weighted in terms of initiation and support for Catholics. Those who propose that Catholic schools divest to other patrons point to advantages for the Catholic school in becoming 'more Catholic'. This also assumes that a teaching or initiation/support model is the preferred model within the Church. In more strident terms, opponents of Catholic schools refer to the teaching and initiation roles of religious groups as indoctrination and proselytising. As a result, they reject the right of the Church to witness to its own beliefs. The debate is not helped by the historical reality of religious groups being closed to outside influences. Thus the Church faces a major problem promoting the current positive reality of their schools when negatives images from the past dominate the public discourse. The Church also faces internal tensions among its own members, often characterised as a liberal/conservative divide. Some want to develop a 'fortress' Church; others are comfortable with dialogue and see contact with diverse views as enriching.

In the changing demographics of Ireland, the 'witness' role of the Catholic patron has taken on new dimensions. In being hospitable to different religious groups, the Church has been challenged to provide an education for all students without making uninvited religious approaches to them. Some have found that the 'teaching' project in this new context is also an opportunity to learn. The teaching-learning dynamic is a two-way process; schools have found richness in the diversity of their students and have learnt to celebrate this diversity as a positive learning experience for all. Spreading such good practice is still in its infancy.

Internally, the Church must also face the question about whether a 'hot-house' approach is the best way of forming religious belief in a pluralist society. This challenge exists at two levels. The first applies to the timing of when young people are exposed to the diversity of religious beliefs and their consequences. The second applies to the formation of 'cultural Catholics' – those who have an experience of Church while in school but have little contact with it in their homes or local parish. The positive anthropology of Catholic education, outlined in Chapter 1, is attractive to many parents. In other countries, it is very attractive to people from other Christian denominations and from other religions, making Catholic schools a preferred choice for them. Whereas the ethos of the Catholic school may continue to offer strong benefits to the psychological development of their students, there is also a danger that the value dimension of the schools will be colonised by other 'market concerns' where their main impact is to create social capital for those who reject the religious dimension of the school. The sociological impact of the school may have a damaging effect on the social cohesion of the local community. In some countries, Catholic schools have become elitist and there is a danger that this might happen in a different way in Ireland, causing even greater inequality than currently exists. The anthropology of Catholic education has always been very strong on the personal 'good' of education and this is the way that the Church has seen its contribution to the common good. In a more pluralist society, the sociological assumptions behind this approach are challenged.

The main focus of the Church is on Catholic education – not necessarily Catholic schooling. Catholic schools have a place to play in supporting the tasks of witnessing, teaching and forming. There is no one approach to Catholic education and schooling. There is a danger that the Irish Church might be trapped by the experience of the Irish Catholicism responding to its own context over time. Looking creatively at how the Church forges a relationship with the State in different countries and integrates religious education with education in other subject areas can be a resource for new creative responses to the changing situation in Ireland. Around the world, many Catholics attend schools that do not have a specific Catholic ethos. These students are not deprived of opportunities to grow in knowledge and practice of their faith. In Ireland, approximately 45 per cent of Catholics at post-primary level are not in Catholic schools. The model of the community school or a multi-denominational structure that guarantees denominational religious education may be realistic alternatives that have to be considered for the primary as well as the post-primary sector.

For the Church, Catholic schools are not an end in themselves. They are a means of fulfilling the basic mission of the Church – to announce the good news of the gospel. It is from this mission that the three perspectives of witness, teaching and support emerge as specific initiatives. How the Church in any country organises around these three functions reveals (a) how the Church thinks about itself and (b) how it sees the needs of the community. In the past, the energy of the Irish Church was very much engaged in supporting its own members. However, times have changed; there is a greater need to focus energy into teaching and witnessing – both to 'insiders' and 'outsiders'. Mission is no longer defined by institutional maintenance with a commitment to spreading the faith across geographical boundaries by going to foreign countries. It is defined by intellectual and ideological boundaries where God is excluded from any understanding of creation and human existence, and the ability of faith to coexist with reason, modern science and the demands of a just society are questioned. Catholic education is one response to that mission and Catholic schools are part of that response. The challenge for the Church is to show that it can find a creative response to these different needs and that it can manage the three functions of witness, teaching and support, simultaneously in service of its own mission and respectful of those with whom it works.

NOTES

1.	Irish Constitution (1922), article 10.
2.	Denis O'Sullivan, *Cultural Politics and Irish Education Since the 1950s: Policy Paradigms and Power* (Dublin: IPA, 2006).

3. Ruairí Quinn, speaking at the launch of the Forum on Patronage and Pluralism in the Primary Sector report (April, 2012).

4. Ronan Mullen, 'Better Divest than Dilute: Why We Should Protect Denominational Schools', *Catholic Schools: Faith in our Future*, Maedhbh Uí Chiagáin, ed. (Milltown: AMCSS, 2012), pp. 103–26.

BIBLIOGRAPHY

Printed Sources

Alberts, W., *Integrative Religious Education in Europe: A Study-of-Religions Approach*, Germany: De Gruyter, 2007.

Aldous, R. and N. Puirseil, *We Declare: Landmark Documents in Ireland's History*, London: Quercus, 2008.

Arthur, J., L. Gearon and A. Sears, *Education, Politics and Religion: Reconciling the Civil and the Scared in Education*, London: Routledge and Francis, 2010.

Ball, S. J., 'Privatising Education, Privatising Education Policy, Privatising Educational Research: Network Governance and the "Competition State"', *Journal of Education Policy* 24.1 (2009): pp. 83–99.

Barker, E., *Church, State and Education*, Ann Arbor: University of Michigan Press, 1957.

Beiter, K. D., *The Protection of the Right to Education by International Law*, The Hague: Martinus Nijhoff, 2005, p. 19.

Bray, M., 'Privatization of Secondary Education: Issues and Policy Implications', *Education for the Twenty-First Century: Issues and Prospects*, J. Delors, ed., Paris: UNESCO, 1998, pp. 109–33.

Bryk, A., V. Lee and P. Holland, *Catholic Schools and the Common Good*, Cambridge, MA: Harvard University Press, 1993.

Burton, W. and M. Weninger, eds, *Legal Aspects of the Relation Between the European Union of the Future and the Communities of Faith and Conviction*, Symposium Report, Brussels: Group of Policy Advisers European Commission, 2002.

Byrne, G., *Religious Education Renewed: An Overview of Developments in Post-primary Religious Education*, Dublin: Veritas, 2004.

Callahan, D., *Taming the Beloved Beast: How Medical Technology Costs Are Destroying Our Health Care System*, Princeton, NJ: Princeton University Press, 2009.

Cassidy, E., ed., *Measuring Ireland: Discerning Values and Beliefs*, Dublin: Veritas, 2002.

Catholic Schools Partnership, Catholic Schools in the Republic of Ireland: A Position Paper, Maynooth, 2011.

CEEC, Information on Catholic Schools in Europe, Brussels, 2008.

Clear, C., *Nuns in Ireland*, Washington DC: Catholic University of America Press, 1987.

Conaty, C., *Including All: Home, School and Community United in Education*, Dublin: Veritas, 2002.

Coolahan, J., *Irish Education: Its History and Structure*, Dublin: IPA, 1981.

Corish, P., *The Irish Catholic Experience: A Historical Survey*, Dublin: Gill and Macmillan, 1985.

Covey, S., *The 8th Habit: From Effectiveness to Greatness*, New York: Free Press, 2004.

Cranston, M., 'Human Rights, Real and Supposed', *Political Theory and the Rights of Man*, Bloomington, IN: Indiana University Press, 1967, pp. 43–53.

Dale, R., 'Globalization and Education: Demonstrating a "common world educational culture" or locating a "globally structures educational agenda"?', *Educational Theory* 50.4 (2000), pp. 427–48.

Davie, G., 'The Significance of the Religious Factor in the Construction of a Humane and Democratic Europe', *Legal Aspects of the Relation Between the European Union of the Future and the Communities of Faith and Conviction*, W. Burton and M. Weninger, eds, Symposium Report, Brussels: Group of Policy Advisers European Commission, 2002, pp. 11–14.

De Bono, E., *I Am Right, You Are Wrong: From This to the New Renaissance, From Rock Logic to Water Logic*, London: Penguin, 1991.

De Botton, Alain, *Religion for Atheists: A Non Believer's Guide to the Uses of Religion,* London: Penguin, 2012.

Delors, J., ed., *Education for the Twenty-First Century: Issues and Prospects*, Paris: UNESCO, 1998.

Delors, J. et al., *Learning: The Treasure Within: Report to UNESCO of the International Commission on Education for the Twenty-First Century*, Paris: UNESCO, 1996.

Doyle, E., *Leading the Way: Managing Voluntary Secondary Schools*, Dublin: Secretariat of Secondary Schools, 2000.

Duffy, E. ed., *Catholic Primary Education: Facing New Challenges*, Dublin: Columba Press, 2012.

Dworkin, R., 'Rights as Trumps', *Theories of Rights*, Waldron, J., ed., Oxford: Oxford University Press, 1984, pp. 153–67.

Dworkin, R., *Taking Rights Seriously*, London: Duckworth, 1978.

Emerson, M., *Ethno-Religious Conflict in Europe: Typologies of Radicalisation in Europe's Muslim Communities*, Brussels: Centre for European Policy Studies, 2009.

Erikson, Erik, *Identity, Youth and Crisis,* New York: W. W. Norton, 1968.

Etzioni, A., *Modern Organizations*, Englewood Cliffs, NJ: Prentice-Hall, 1964.

Feldman, N., *Divided by God*, New York: Farrar, Straus and Giroux, 2005.

Finnis, J., *Natural Law and Natural Rights*, Oxford: Clarendon Press, 1980.

Fish, S., 'Mission Impossible: Setting the Just Bounds between Church and State', *Columbia Law Review* 97 (1997): pp. 2255, 2289–90.

Friel, B., *Translations*, London: Faber and Faber, 1981.

Gleeson, J., 'Sectoral Interest Versus the Common Good?: Legitimation, Fragmentation and Contestation in Irish Post-Primary Curriculum Policy and Practice', *Irish Education Studies* 19 (2000): pp. 16–34.

Glendenning, D., *Education and the Law: Irish Law–Education Law*, London: Bloomsbury, 2012.

Government of Ireland, Legislation Prior to 1922 and Reports and Circulars 1922–85, Irish Educational Documents, Hyland, A. and Milne, K., CICE, 1987.

Grace, G. and J. O'Keefe, eds, *International Handbook on Catholic Education: Challenges for School Systems in the Twenty-First Century*, Dordrecht: Springer, 2007.

Haught, J. F., *Christianity and Science: Towards a Theology of Nature*, Maryknoll, NY: Orbis Books, 2007.

Healey, J. F., *The Sociology of Group Conflict and Change*, sixth edition, Thousand Oaks, CA: SAGE Publications, 2012.

Hersey, P. and K. H. Blanchard, *The Essentials of Situational Leadership: Theories, Concepts, Applications*, Escondido, CA: Leadership Studies Productions, 1980.

Hogan, P. and K. Williams, eds, *The Future of Religion in Irish Education*, Dublin: Veritas, 1997.

Honohan, I., *Civic Republicanism*, London: Routledge, 2002.

Hutton, W. and A. Giddens, eds, *On the Edge: Living with Global Capitalism*, London: Jonathan Cape, 2000.

Hyland, A. and K. Milne, *Irish Education Documents*, Church of Ireland College of Education, 1987.

Hyland, A., 'Multi-Denominational Schools in the Republic of Ireland 1975–1995', Paper delivered a Conference on Education and Religion organised by CRELA, University of Nice, 21–22 June, 1996.

Hyland, A., 'The Curriculum of Vocational Education 1930–1966', *Teachers Union: The TUI and its Forerunners 1899–1994*, John Logan, ed., Dublin: A. & A. Farmar, 1999.

Hyland, A., 'The Multi-Denominational Experience', *Irish Education Studies* 8.1 (1989): pp. 89–114.

Irish Episcopal Conference, Primary Education in the Future, Maynooth, 2007.

Jackson, R., 'European Institutions and the Contribution of Studies of Religious Diversity to Education for Democratic Citizenship', *Religion and Education in Europe: Developments, Contexts and Debates*, R. Jackson et al., eds, Münster: Waxmann, 2007, pp. 27–56.

Jackson, R., *Teaching about Religions in the Public Sphere: European Policy Initiatives and the Interpretive Approach* 55 (2008): pp. 151–82.

Jackson, R., et al., eds, *Religion and Education in Europe: Developments, Contexts and Debates*, Münster: Waxmann, 2007.

Janis, I. L., *Victims of Groupthink: A Psychological Study of Foreign-Policy Decisions and Fiascoes*, Boston: Houghton Mifflin, 1972.

Lane, D., ed., *New Century, New Society: Christian Perspectives*, Dublin: Columba, 1999.

Layard, R., *Happiness: Lessons From a New Science*, London: Penguin, 2005.

Lee, J. J., *Ireland 1912–1985: Politics and Society*, Cambridge: Cambridge University Press, 1989.

Logan, J., ed., *Teachers Union: The TUI and its Forerunners 1899–1994*, Dublin: A. & A. Farmar, 1999.

Lundskow, G., *The Sociology of Religion: A Substantive and Trans-Disciplinary Approach*, Thousand Oaks, CA: SAGE Publications, 2008.

Lynch, K. and A. Lodge, eds, *Diversity at School*, Dublin: IPA, 2004.

Lynch, K. and A. Lodge, *Equality and Power in Schools: Redistribution, Recognition and Representation*, London: Routledge-Falmer, 2002.

Lynch, K., *Equality in Education*, Dublin: Gill and Macmillan, 1999.

Lynch, K., B. Grummell and D. Devine, *New Managerialism in Education: Commercialization, Carelessness and Gender*, London: Palgrave Macmillan, 2012.

MacManus, S., *The Story of the Irish Race*, New York: Devin-Adair Publishing Co., 1921.

MacMullen, I., *Faith in Schools?: Autonomy, Citizenship and Religious Education in the Liberal State*, NJ: Princeton University Press, 2007.

Mahoney, J., *The Challenge of Human Rights: Origin, Development and Significance*, London: Blackwell, 2007.

Maygray, M., *The Transforming Power of the Nuns: Women, Religion and Cultural Change in Ireland 1750–1900*, Oxford: Oxford University Press, 1998.

McGrady, A., 'The Religious Dimension of Education', *From Present to Future*, Woulfe, E., and J. Cassin, eds, Dublin: Veritas, 2006, pp. 139–89.

McKinney, S. J., ed., *Faith Schools in the Twenty-First Century: Policy and Practice in Education*, Edinburgh: Dunedin, 2006.

McLaughlin, T. J. O'Keefe and B. O'Keeffe, eds, *The Contemporary Catholic School: Context, Identity and Diversity*, London: Falmer Press, 1996.

Mullen, R., 'Better Divest that Dilute: Why We Should Protect Denominational Schools', *Catholic Schools: Faith in our Future*, M. Uí Chiagáin, ed., Milltown: AMCSS, 2012, pp. 103–26.

Murray, D., 'The Catholic Church's Current Thinking on Educational Provision', *Catholic Primary Education: Facing New Challenges*, Duffy, E., ed., Columba Press, 2012, pp. 52–72.

Nickel, J., *Making Sense of Human Rights*, second edition, London: Blackwell, 2007.

O'Sullivan, D., *Cultural Politics and Irish Education Since the 1950s: Policy Paradigms and Power*, Dublin: IPA, 2006.

O'Toole, F., *Enough is Enough: How to Build a New Republic,* London: Faber and Faber, 2010.

Raphael, D. D., ed., *Political Theory and the Rights of Man,* Bloomington, IN: Indiana University Press, 1967.

Riordan, P., *A Grammar of the Common Good,* London: Continuum, 2008.

Riordan, P., *A Politics of the Common Good*, Dublin: Institute of Public Administration, 1996.

Rosenbaum, A. S., ed., *The Philosophy of Human Rights: International Perspectives*, London: Aldwych Press, 1980.

Rossiter, G. M., 'Catholic Education and Values: A Review of the Role of Catholic Schools in Promoting the Spiritual and Moral Development of Pupils', *Journal of Religion in Education* 4 (2003): pp. 105–36.

Schreiner, P., ed., *Religious Education in Europe,* Münster: ICCS and Comenius Institute, 2000.

Seligman, Martin E. P., *Flourish: A Visionary New Understanding of Happiness and Well-being*, New York: Free Press, 2011.

Sullivan, J., *Catholic Schools in Contention*, Dublin: Veritas, 2000.

Tuohy, D., 'Celebrating the Past, Claiming the Future: Challenges for Catholic Education in Ireland', *International Handbook on Catholic Education: Challenges for School Systems in the Twenty-First Century*, Grace, G. and J. O'Keefe, eds, Dordrecht: Springer, 2007, pp. 269–90.

Tuohy, D., *Our Faith Community*, research sponsored by Church of Ireland College of Education, Church of Ireland, The Board of Education and Church of Ireland Primary Schools Management Association, 2011.

Tuohy, D. and P. Cairns, *Youth 2K: Threat or Promise to a Religious Culture?*, Dublin: Marino Institute of Education, 2000.

Uí Chiagáin, M., ed., *Catholic Schools: Faith in our Future*, Milltown: AMCSS, 2012.

Waldron, J., ed., *Theories of Rights*, Oxford: Oxford University Press, 1984.

Waters, J., *Was It For This?: Why Ireland Lost the Plot*, Dublin: Transworld Ireland, 2012.

Whyte, J. H., *Church and State in Modern Ireland: 1923–1979*, Dublin: Gill and Macmillan, 1980.

World Council of Churches, 'Concepts on Teaching and Learning in Religions', EEF-Net 6 (2000): pp. 10–11.

Woulfe, E. and J. Cassin, eds, *From Present to Future: Catholic Education in Ireland for the New Century*, Dublin: Veritas, 2006.

Online Sources

Aristotle, *Nicomachean Ethics*, downloaded from http://classics.mit.edu/Aristotle/nicomachaen.html

Augustine, *Confessions*, downloaded from http://www.ccel.org/ccel/augustine/confess

Commission of Bishops' Conferences of the European Union, The Evolution of the European Union and the Responsibility of Catholics, 2005, http://www.comece.org/site/en/publications/pubcomece

European Court of Human Rights, Case Law Judgments, http://www.echr.coe.int/ECHR/EN/Header/Case-Law/Decisions+and+judgments/HUDOC+database/

European Court of Human Rights, Cultural Rights in the Case Law of the European Court of Human Rights, 2011, http://www.echr.coe.int/ECHR/EN/Header/Case-Law/Case-law+analysis/Research+reports/

European Union Publications, http://publications.europa.eu/index_en.htm and *Handbook on European Non-Discrimination Law*, http://www.echr.coe.int/ECHR/EN/Header/Case-Law/Case-law+analysis/Handbook+on+non-discrimination/

Government of Ireland, Department of Education Circulars, http://education.ie/en/Publications/

Government of Ireland, Education Curriculum Information, http://www.ncca.ie/

Government of Ireland, Legislation 1922–Present, http://www.irishstatutebook.ie/home.html

Government of Ireland, Our Children, Their Lives: National Children's Strategy, http://www.dohc.ie/publications/national_childrens_strategy.html

Government of Ireland, Programme for Government, 2011–16, http://www.socialjustice.ie/content/programme-government-2011-2016-full-text

Government of Ireland, Strategy for the Irish Language 2010–30, http://www.ahg.gov.ie/en/20YearStrategyfortheIrishLanguage/index.html

Hyland, A., Educate Together Schools in the Republic of Ireland: The First Stage 1975–1994, 1993: http://www.educatetogether.ie/reference_articles/Ref_Art_001.html

Irish Human Rights Commission, Religion and Education: A Human Rights Perspective, 2011, http://www.ihrc.ie/publications/list/religion-and-education-a-human-rights-perspective/

Legal Judgments for the High Court and Supreme Court in Ireland, http://www.bailii.org/ie/cases/IEHC/toc-O.html

Motilla, A., 'Thematic Overview: The Right to Discriminate, Exceptions to the General Prohibition', *Religion and Discrimination Law in the European Union*, M. Hill, ed., European Consortium for Church and State Research, 2012, http://www.churchstate.eu/

National Council for Curriculum and Assessment, Primary School Curriculum, 1999, http://www.curriculumonline.ie/en/Primary_School_Curriculum/Introduction/

Smyth, E. et al., Religious Education in a Multicultural Society: School and Home in Comparative Context, 2011, http://www.esri.ie/research/research_areas/education/Remc/

United Nations Publications, http://www.un.org/en/documents/index.shtml and http://www.unesco.org/new/en/unesco/resources/online-materials/publications/unesdoc-database/

Vatican, Congregation for Catholic Education publications, http://www.vatican.va/roman_curia/congregations/ccatheduc/index.htm

Vatican, Documents of Second Vatican Council, http://www.vatican.va/archive/hist_councils/ii_vatican_council/ Vatican II

Vatican, Papal Encyclicals, http://www.vatican.va/holy_father/index.htm or http://www.papalencyclicals.net/